Hispanic Presence
In the United States:
Hi

Commission

National Hispanic Quincentennial Commission

Washington, D.C. 20002-4205 • (202)289-1661 (202) 289-8173 Fax

Hispanic Presence In the United States: Historical Beginnings

Frank de Varona

Editor

The National Hispanic Quincentennial Commission

MNEMOSYNE PUBLISHING COMPANY

MIAMI

1993

93 488

SUSAN E. WILLS, SENIOR STAFF EDITOR

Manufactured in the United States of America.

Typesetting by Jeffrey Young & Associates.
Typeset in Monotype Columbus.

Library of Congress Cataloging-in-Publication Data
Hispanic Presence in the United States: historical beginnings
Frank de Varona, editor.
p. 272 cm. 5.5" x 8.5"
Includes bibliographical references.
ISBN 1-56675-029-6
1. Hispanic Americans–History. I. De Varona, Frank.
II. National Hispanic Quincentennial Commission.
E184.S75H5834   1993   93-5327
973'.0468—dc20   CIP

This book has been made possible through a grant from Philip Morris Companies Inc. to the National Hispanic
Quincentennial Commission. The NHQC and the Editor gratefully acknowledge their steadfast support of this project and their commitment to greater understanding of the role of Hispanics in the forging of our nation.

Prefatory Remarks

As Hispanics, we are fond of saying that five hundred years ago half of our ancestors came to this land and were met, though not necessarily welcomed, by the other half of our forebears who had been here for over ten thousand years. The historical truth, of course, is far more complicated, but the essence of that statement is as compellingly powerful as it is largely unappreciated.

Latinos in the Americas are a *mestizo* people, a melding of many cultures and of all the "races" in the world. Our Spanish heritage that began as a synthesis of Celtic, Phoenician, Germanic, Greek, Roman, and Arabic cultures and bloods, became further enriched by the bloods and cultures of Africans and indigenous Americans.

Hispanics and other American sub-groups, especially indigenous Americans, have been systematically denied access to their own history. This is not a call for drastic revisionism; it merely states a well-established fact. In the final analysis, only the factually supportable presentation of our past will endure.

The work presented here is but one small effort to pique the American awareness of our heritage. Hispanics are particularly interested in this body of knowledge, but it would be tragic and misguided if it were viewed as only for Latinos. We must all — Hispanics and non-Hispanics — understand our true American past, with all its foibles and warts, as well as its glories.

This presentation is not advanced as a definitive history of Hispanics in the U.S., but rather as a sketch of the early endeavors of our forefathers. Our hope is that it will stimulate further research on the intertwinings of the various cultures toward an expanded understanding of what really happened.

We must also acknowledge one important circumstance: Every scholar works with the available tools, and this work is no exception. The available historical records represent the view of the conquerors, our Spanish forefathers. The basic materials from our Anglo and African roots are left out of our focus or not developed.

The Board of Directors of the National Hispanic Quincentennial Commission is grateful to Philip Morris Companies Inc. for underwriting this project.

Raul Yzaguirre
Chairman of the Board
National Hispanic
Quincentennial Commission

Acknowledgements

No man is an island, especially when he is exploring a field that has been neglected by historians and publishing houses for many years. As Editor of this volume, I wish to express my deep gratitude to all the contributors and organizations that supported this effort.

I am most grateful to the Superintendent of Schools and the School Board of Dade County, Florida for endorsing the publication of this volume and the effort to provide teachers in the Greater Miami area with new information about Hispanics that is absent from most textbooks and supplementary materials.

My thanks go also to Raul Yzaguirre, chairman of the National Hispanic Quincentennial Commission, its president, Pablo Sedillo, and the entire Board of Directors for their support in their effort to publicize the Hispanic contributions to the nation.

This project began several years ago as a joint undertaking of Dade County Public School students, teachers, and administrators with scholars from various universities to research the contributions of Hispanics to the nation. Due to space limitations, this volume includes only a small portion of the more than fifty articles written. Perhaps a future book can include these unpublished articles. I want to recognize the following individuals and thank them for their work: Carol Cortes, Margarita M. Alemany, Dr. Aurora Villar, Margarita and Héctor Castro, Sergio A. Rivera and Mercedes Toural, Charlotte C. Christensen, Dr. José Fernández, Rolando Vásquez, María M. Rodríguez, Hector Hirigoyen, Dr. Joaquín Roy, Clea Sucoff, J. Manuel Fernández, Dr. Caroline Hospital, Luis Mario, Dr. Arnhilda Badía, Les Todd, Joseph Torres, Anh Do, Dawn Domínguez, Ana Gancedo, David Kuritz, Kathy Lamas, Christine Marambio, Andrew Zahis, Kathy Bunce, Phyllis Chin, Arthur Lavade, Mary Pinder, Christian Labbie, Monica Taylor, María S. Takkas, Roberto de Varona, Jeordan Legon, and Elizabeth Padrón.

Many thanks to the Florida Humanities Council for permission to use the articles on Hernando de Soto, Pedro Menéndez de Aviles, and Blacks in Spanish Florida.

My appreciation to Margarita Castro and Dr. Judith Margulies for proofreading the manuscript. Eddie S. Rivas, Toni Kirkwood, Celia Ramírez, Paul Hanson, Esther Sobrino, and the late Elba Machín helped to publicize this project in the community.

Many individuals assisted in the typing of the various drafts and related work over the years. My competent secretary, Sonia Stevens, has worked very hard. My deepest gratitude to Sonia and the following Dade County Public Schools employees: Marisa del Rio, Rebeca Selesky, Angeles Toraño, Sharon Holley, Alicia Núñez, Silvia González, Alicia González, Christina Pérez-Ibañez, Lillian Delgado, Joan Maloly, Alina Viera, Esmeralda Fajardo, José Castellanos, Ricky Iglesias, Jaime Machado, and Danny Lavandeira.

The editor gratefully acknowledges the financial support and generosity of the following corporations, organizations, and individuals to the initial stages of this project:

Abraham Construction Corp.	Aurea V. Fleites
Alameda Homes	Gilberto Flores
Norma Alfaras	Josefina A. Flores
American Hispanic Educators	Florida Power & Light Co.
of Dade, Inc. (AHEAD)	Manuel Garmizo
Anheuser-Busch, Inc.	Globe Book Co.
Yvette Armand	Carolyn Gray
Burt Arnold	Alicia C. Green
Dr. Eduardo Arteaga	Hispanic Heritage Council, Inc.
Asociación de Dentistas	Kensington Park Elementary PTA
Cubanos en el Exilio	Kinloch Park Junior High
Bacardi Imports, Inc.	Kiwanis Club of Little Havana
Bahamas Line, S.A.	Lavin Baby Center
Isabel Barbosa	Julia O. León
Dolores A. Barsa	Victor López
Miguel A. Cano, M.D.	Elba Machín
Graciela Castrex	Meadowlane Elementary PTA
Magdalena Cerri	Carlos Medina
Citrus Grove Elementary PTA	Miami Edison Senior High
Citrus Grove Middle School PTA	Nelson & Sunatha Pérez
Citrus Grove Middle School	Jorge L. Quadreny
Police Club	Celia Ramírez
María A. Crespí	José & Gloria Ramos
Norma L. Delgado	Thomas Reilley
Isabel L. de Moya	Eddie Rivas
Gladys de Salto	Daniel Rodríguez
Servando Diego	Seminole Elementary PTA
El Camagüeyano, Inc.	Esther Sobrino
Rolando Espinosa	Joline Steinfeld
Fairlawn Elementary PTA	Frederick Craig Sturgeon
Lillian M. Farnet	United Schools of America
Silvia R. Fernández	George Valladares
Wilfredo Fernández	Mireya Valls
Faustino Fernández	Leopold & Susan Van Bergen
H.M. Flagler Elementary	Wayne C. Becker & Associates

It should be obvious that this book is a team effort and a labor of love.

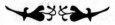

TABLE OF CONTENTS

EIGHTEENTH CENTURY

NINETEENTH CENTURY

PREFACE

Hispanic Presence in the United States: Historical Beginnings is not intended to be a comprehensive treatment of Hispanic contributions to the history of North America. Such an endeavor would require many volumes. The articles included here address some of the significant events in U.S. history in which Hispanics played an important role. The size of this book dictated excluding many noteworthy persons and events, as well as the entire 20th century. To partially remedy these omissions, a fairly extensive chronology is added, touching upon individuals and events not featured in the articles, from 1492 to the present. Later volumes are planned to fill more of the gaps in the standard social studies textbooks. It is hoped, as is stated in the chapter on the Quincentenary, that "each omission [will] . . . be a challenge to others to read, to research. . . [and] to spread the word, to complete the history of the Hispanic presence in the United States."

The inspiration for this book was a September 1983 Proclamation in which former President Ronald Reagan stated:

> Through the years, Hispanic American citizens have risen to the call of duty in defense of liberty and freedom. Their bravery is well-known and has been demonstrated time and again, dating back to the aid rendered by General Bernardo de Gálvez during the American Revolution.

Few Americans are aware that Bernardo de Gálvez was the Spanish governor of the Louisiana Territory during the American Revolution, a territory that encompassed thirteen of our present states, or that long before any formal declaration of war, General Gálvez sent gunpowder, rifles, bullets, blankets, medicine, and other supplies to the armies of General George Washington and General George Rogers Clark. Once Spain entered the war against Great Britain in 1779, this dashing young officer raised an army in New Orleans and drove the British out of the Mississippi Valley and, later, out of the Gulf of Mexico. General Gálvez captured five British forts in the Lower Mississippi Valley and took over 1,000 British prisoners. His lieutenants later fought in the Upper Mississippi Valley. They repulsed a British and Indian attack in St. Louis, Missouri and captured the British fort of St. Joseph in present-day Niles, Michigan. With reinforcements from Cuba, Mexico, and Puerto Rico, General Gálvez captured Mobile and then Pensacola, the capital of the British colony of West Florida. At Pensacola, Gálvez commanded a multinational army of over 7,000 Black and white soldiers. The men were born in Spain, Cuba, Mexico, Puerto Rico, Hispaniola, and other colonies of Spain, such as Venezuela. The city was defended by a British and Indian army of 2,500 soldiers and British warships.

The siege of Pensacola has been called by an American historian "a decisive factor in the outcome of the Revolution and one of the most brilliantly executed battles of the war." Another historian stated that General Gálvez's campaign broke the British Army's will to fight. This battle ended in May, 1781, just five months before the last battle of the war at Yorktown.

Other Spanish naval and military campaigns in Central America and in Europe, the capture of the Bahamas by Cuban-born General Juan Manuel de Cagigal, and the tremendous financial assistance given by Spain, Mexico, and Cuba to the thirteen colonies contributed to the final victory against Great Britain. It is doubtful that without the strong support of Spain, France, and, to a lesser extent, the Netherlands, the thirteen colonies could have defeated Great Britain, then the strongest power in Europe.

United States history textbooks seldom mention the important contributions by our "forgotten allies," Spain and Hispanic America, during the American Revolution, nor do they mention that thousands of Hispanics fought and died in the many battles during the American Revolution or that they helped in the establishment and growth of the first democracy in the modern world.

On July 13, 1990, Senator Orrin Hatch spoke in the U.S. Senate on the 500 years of Hispanic contributions to the nation. At that time, the National Hispanic Quincentennial Commission was holding its first conference in Washington, D.C. These two events highlighted the fact that Hispanic men and women have fought in all of America's wars, from the Revolutionary War to Vietnam, to our most recent invasions of Grenada and Panama. There were thousands of Hispanic soldiers who fought bravely in the six-week war against Iraq in the Persian Gulf area. Thirty-seven Hispanic soldiers have been awarded the highest decoration our nation can bestow: the Congressional Medal of Honor.

The neglect in reporting Hispanic contributions extends to all periods of American history. People for the American Way, a non-profit organization in the social studies, published a report in 1986 called *Looking at History: A Review of Major U.S. History Textbooks.* Thirty-one current history textbooks were analyzed in great detail by historians, who concluded:

> Overall the treatment of Hispanics. . .perpetuates their invisible roles in building this nation. Hispanics, whose ancestors were the first European settlers within the nation's current boundaries, have long been ignored or casually mentioned in conventional U.S. history textbooks. . .By the end of this century, Hispanics will constitute the largest minority group in the nation and their valuable contributions to our country's history must be included in school textbooks.[1]

Entire generations of American historians have excluded Hispanics from the nation's history. Perhaps our earliest historians inherited the traditional British dislike for Spaniards. After all, both nations fought each other for centuries. It is as if the Black Legend propagated by Great Britain to discredit Spain at the peak of her glory in the sixteenth century persists to the present. The fact that there was such a strong anti-Catholic sentiment in the nation during the 19th century and the early part of the 20th century may also be a reason for the neglect. Spain, after all, was identified as the strongest defender of the Catholic faith.

Also contributing to the neglect of Hispanics was the 1893 "frontier hypothesis" developed by Frederick Jackson Turner and accepted by many historians. According to them, the Anglo-American pioneers settled along the Atlantic Coast and then moved westward over the Appalachian Mountains, across the Great Plains to California and Oregon. The Anglo-British were joined by other Europeans, such as the Germans. However, the British civilization remained, except as it was modified by the American frontier. Turner invented the frontier explanation, observing the situation in his native Wisconsin. By emphasizing this east to west historical viewpoint and excluding all others, the truth was distorted.

It is true that the most important population stream was Anglo, and that it laid the foundation of the nation, but there were other migrations important to the nation. One came from Canada. French Canadians moved southward along the Mississippi River to Louisiana and started fur-trading operations. Later, Spaniards controlled the Louisiana Territory for a period of almost forty years.

A second population stream originated in the Caribbean Islands. Spaniards, Cubans, Puerto Ricans, and Dominicans moved north into Florida, Georgia, the Carolinas, and Virginia. The third migration came from Mexico. Spaniards and Mexicans moved north into Texas, New Mexico, Arizona, Utah, Colorado, and California. Enslaved Africans were brought into the nation against their will and their labor contributed much to this society.

Eventually, the westward-moving Anglo-Americans clashed with the Spanish frontier, as they had earlier with the French. Anglos, with a handful of Mexican allies from Texas, fought the Mexican Republic, and later the entire nation went to war against Mexico. The Anglo victory in the Southwest, as well as the earlier victory in the Southeast against Hispanics, accounts for the exclusion of Hispanics from the textbooks.

It is a truism that the victors write the history and in the case of the Hispanics, they lost the contest for the North American continent. The fact that the nation fought four times during the nineteenth century against Hispanic countries explains why the strong Spanish heritage from our nation's beginnings was kept silent.

It also explains why few people know our first "Founding Father," Pedro Menéndez de Avilés. He was one of the best admirals in Europe. He had taken Prince Philip on his ship to London to marry Queen Mary Tudor. He had participated in many European wars and had commanded the Fleet of the Indies, the convoy of Spanish galleons that brought the gold and silver to Spain for many years. Later, King Philip II of Spain sent Menéndez to drive out the French, who had built a fort in Florida and posed a threat to the Fleet of the Indies. Menéndez quickly drove the French out and later established a permanent Hispanic presence in Florida. More than a great seaman and military leader, Menéndez was a builder and a missionary. As Governor of *La Florida*, he founded St. Augustine in 1565 — the first permanent European settlement in North America. He also founded six other settlements in Florida and South Carolina, and founded the first missions in Florida, Georgia, the Carolinas, and Virginia. Pedro Menéndez de Avilés also celebrated the first Thanksgiving in the United States when he founded St. Augustine. Father Francisco López de Mendoza Grajales celebrated the first Mass in the nation. The Spaniards invited the Indians to pray and share their food. They ate salted pork, garbanzo beans, and biscuits, and drank red wine. The Spaniards gave thanks to God for being alive after their dangerous ocean voyage and earlier encounters with the French. How could it be that a man who ruled the Southeastern part of our nation for almost a decade is virtually unknown?

Most history textbooks mention David Glasgow Farragut, the Union hero of the Civil War who split the Confederacy in two with his naval victories along the Mississippi River and the Gulf of Mexico, and successfully blockaded the South. Farragut became the first American awarded the rank of Admiral of the Navy and was recognized worldwide as a hero. Yet, almost none of these textbooks mention the fact that he was of Hispanic origin. Textbooks also fail to mention the role of 10,000 Hispanic soldiers who fought on both sides of the Civil War.

The lack of information about minority group achievements contributes to the development of stereotypes and myths. It also erodes the image of the minority in the eyes of the public. Only when all ethnic groups can be respected for what they have contributed to the nation will the American dream come true.

Frank de Varona
July 1993
Miami, Florida

INTRODUCTORY REMARKS

Multicultural education is a current reform movement that is at the forefront of curriculum change throughout the United States. Dade County's pluralistic society demands that multicultural education be an integral part of our instructional program. To this end, I am pleased that all of the district's schools will have copies of *Hispanic Presence in the United States: Historical Beginnings* for their media centers and that copies of this book will be available to all secondary social studies teachers and selected administrators.

Hispanic Presence in the United States: Historical Beginnings is a compendium of articles that fills a void in the history of the United States from the sixteenth century through the nineteeth century. American history textbooks used in the classrooms all too often focus on some of the Spanish explorers of the fifteenth and sixteenth centuries as the only interaction Hispanics have had with our nation's history. Few Hispanic names appear in the textbooks in spite of the fact that, with the exception of Native Americans, Hispanics are the nation's oldest immigrants. Fortunately, *Hispanic Presence in the United States: Historical Beginnings* will rectify the omission of the many important contributions made by Hispanics to our nation.

The essence of multicultural education is to help students to understand that the American culture is a mosaic comprised of people representing racial, ethnic, and religious groups, and both genders. Both Hispanic and non-Hispanic students will benefit by learning that the fabric of America's development was woven together by the contributions of many cultures. This book is not only an excellent work of historical perspective, but it is also a tribute to the greatness of the United States and the pluralistic society that makes our nation unique among nations throughout the world.

Octavio J. Visiedo
Superintendent
Dade County Public Schools

FOREWORD

Hispanics comprise the fastest growing minority in the United States. It is estimated that more than ten percent of the nation's population will be Hispanic by the year 2000. Recognition of Hispanic contributions to the founding, growth, and development of the United States is long overdue. In 1986, to begin the process of rectifying this pressing need, the National Council for the Social Studies approved a resolution that called attention to the flagrant absence of Hispanic contributions in history textbooks used in our nation's schools. This splendid volume, *Hispanic Presence in the United States: Historical Beginnings*, conceived and directed by Frank de Varona, is a major step toward filling this void.

Hispanic Presence is the product of an extensive collaboration among many people, representing and cutting across a wide variety of ages, occupations, and cultures. This cooperative process is itself as important to understanding our future as the book is significant to understanding our past. Participation and communication across the boundaries that separate us is a key factor in creating the innovative solution needed to chart our survival as a species.

The book is richer by far as a direct consequence of its participatory and collaborative development. The purposeful activity that gave life to the final product required dialogue, communication, reciprocity, empathy, singly and in combination, the positive approach needed to learn and to teach in our increasingly complex and interdependent world.

Hispanic Presence in the United States: Historical Beginnings helps us to better understand our pluralistic past, and it points us to a more enlightened future.

Dr. Jan L. Tucker
Professor of Education
Director of Global Awareness Program
Florida International University
Past President, National Council For The Social Studies

National Hispanic
Quincentennial
Commission

THE QUINCENTENARY:
ITS SIGNIFICANCE FOR HISPANIC AMERICA

On a small, grassy divider near the Department of State in Washington, D.C., stands a modest statue of a young man in uniform astride a horse. In a city of monuments, it commands little notice. The man's name: General Bernardo de Gálvez.

How that statue got there and why Gálvez is so little known are sufficient reasons in themselves to explain the great interest of Hispanic Americans in the Quincentenary. Gálvez, whose exploits are recounted elsewhere in this volume, was the governor of Spain's territories in what is today Louisiana, Texas, and other states. Spain declared war on England and became an ally of the American revolutionaries, and Gálvez scored numerous victories against the British along the Mississippi and the Gulf Coast.

Those actions denied supplies, weapons, and reinforcements to British forces in the upper Ohio River Valley, thereby helping to assure an American victory in the Revolutionary War. In addition to Gálvez's decisive military engagements, the Government of Spain proved a vital ally and significant factor in the securing of American independence.

The monument to General Bernardo de Gálvez was a gift from the Spanish government to the American people in 1976 during the American Bicentennial. In a year of great celebration across the land, it attracted little attention. But if nothing else, it demonstrated the gaps in Americans' knowledge about a pivotal ally in the struggle for our independence. Spain's gift proved visionary, for twelve years later, during the Quincentenary, the Iberian presence in the Americas would become the focus of much long-deserved scholarly inquiry.

In September, 1980, a group of Hispanic Americans organized a wreath-laying ceremony at the monument to Gálvez, their way of commemorating Hispanic Heritage Week. Officiating were the Spanish Ambassador and the Secretary of the United States Navy at that time, Edward Hidalgo. Also present was Raul Yzaguirre, President of the National Council of La Raza.

Three years later, recalling that no Hispanic American was chosen to serve on the U.S. Bicentennial Commission, and that Hispanics were overlooked in 1976, Yzaguirre and a handful of other Hispanic leaders in the nation's capital founded the National Hispanic Quincentennial Commission (NHQC). They vowed that Hispanic America, excluded from the Bicentennial, would be present for the Quincentenary. Created in 1983, the NHQC pre-dated the official "Christopher Columbus Jubilee Commission of the Discovery of America" by one year. And the official body counted only four Hispanics among its more than two dozen members.

With few resources but with unbridled determination, the NHQC began mapping plans for conferences, research, tracking projects and providing services to organizations around the country. Much of its fine work is now a matter of record, and as this book goes to print, NHQC is moving forward with a plan to create a permanent, Washington-based Hispanic culture foundation.

Hispanics and the Quincentennial

It is significant that two hundred years after having fought for American independence, Gálvez has helped to raise the consciousness of Hispanic and non-Hispanic Americans alike.

That he and so many others of Hispanic origin who helped shape our country are absent from or minimized in our history books explains the origin of this book. It explains, furthermore, why Hispanic Americans have embraced the Quincentenary as an opportunity to "explore" their own origins and "discover" pride in their contributions.

The notion of "celebrating" a half millennium of history and the birth of lands and peoples more diverse than any that had preceded them was fraught with controversy from the outset. For one thing, the United States Congress provided the Jubilee Commission with a budget which scarcely allowed for an office and a small staff in Washington. Funds for projects would have to be raised from the private sector and foundations. This proved a daunting task.

As the anniversary approached, controversy swirled. For many Americans the anniversary focussed on Christopher Columbus and his exploits. The "Admiral of the Ocean Seas" occupies a prominent place in our folklore and our spirit of nationalism. The nation's capital, patriotic songs, broad avenues, majestic monuments and, of course, history books honor him.

Armed with new insights and the sensitivities of growing multiculturalism, however, critics have held that we should not "celebrate" the impact of misdeeds committed long ago, nor extol the virtues of the malefactors. Many American Indians justly claimed that rather than celebration this would be a period of mourning. Some Chicanos in the Southwest, proud of the Native American blood coursing through their veins, objected to commemorations by a dominant culture that in their eyes denigrated their own. And environmentalists lamented the destruction of natural resources set in motion by the arrival of the Europeans.

The controversy, charges of past mismanagement at the Jubilee Commission and a weakened economy precisely when funds would be needed most, combined to dull the lustre of what some envisioned as a period rivaling the Bicentennial in activities and excitement. The controversy notwithstanding, much talent, enterprise, energy, and money went into projects the impact of which will endure for decades. Official commissions were created in scores of nations; and in our own country each state had a commission, and in cities across the land people came together to help mark the anniversary as they saw fit.

Besides the Jubilee Commission, national organizations that played major roles were those of Portugal, Italy, France, England, Canada, the Dominican Republic, Puerto Rico, and The Bahamas. The *Sociedad Estatal del Quinto Centenario* (State Quincentenary Society) of Spain was among the most visible, having organized, with others, the construction and commemorative voyage of replicas of Cristóbal Colón's three ships. Spain also created the "Spain '92

Foundation" to help raise monies and coordinate projects in the United States.

Italy opened its libraries, museums, and archives to scholars from around the world who wished to explore documents, paintings, sculpture, and other sources for clues to improved understanding of the period of discovery and its aftermath. Some works were made available to researchers for the first time, while others were examined with a new focus of inquiry, a Quincentenary focus.

Perhaps one of the least heralded but most fascinating projects during the Quincentenary period was a major exhibit at Yeshiva University in New York City. Entitled "A Sephardic Journey," it portrayed the consequences of the expulsion of Jews from Spain in 1492. The Sephardic "diaspora," it was shown, had immeasurable impact on much of the world, beginning with Spain herself and including the United States. Despite the tragic origins of the expulsion, the introspection and objective analysis of history spurred by the 500th anniversary have had a salutary, healing effect. King Juan Carlos of Spain, for example, publicly apologized for the misdeeds, and commissioned a gold sculpture by Joan Miró to symbolize that sentiment.

Similar to the Yeshiva University project is "Al Andalus," an unprecedented exhibition of the Metropolitan Museum of New York, "La Alhambra" in Granada, and various institutions in Spain, Europe, and North Africa. Gathered for the first time were objects that reveal as never before the powerful cultural, religious, linguistic, and economic hold that Islam had on Iberia for eight centuries. Many of the works have never before been displayed in public.

The Sephardic experience, the impact of Arab culture and Islam, and countless other examples during this period of "discovery" have illustrated the great diversity of Spain — Iberian, Celtic, Phoenician, Greek, Roman, Visigoth, Arab, Jew, and others. Never before has that earlier "melting pot" been studied with such great interest as a possible explanation for Spanish acceptance of varied cultural influences, particularly in the Americas where new "razas" (races) arose. It is interesting to note that in Latin America, Columbus Day is commemorated as "El Día de la Raza," proud recognition of the new societies forged in this hemisphere from European, Indian, and African peoples.

One of the most striking examples of the fecundity of the Quincentenary period is "Seeds of Change," the largest exhibition in the history of the Smithsonian Institution. Housed in the National Museum of Natural History in Washington, it documents how five factors propelled by the "interaction" of Europe, the Americas, and Africa altered world history. The five "seeds" are corn, sugar, the potato, the horse, and disease. Scheduled through the fall of 1993, the display will have been seen by some 16 million people, and millions more will view smaller travelling versions throughout the country.

It candidly presents evidence of the impact of trade in new and old agricultural commodities on Europe, Africa, and the Americas. It describes the enslavement, torture, and killing of Indians and the diseases that reduced their numbers. It explains the introduction of African slaves to replace Indians in the harvesting of sugar in the Caribbean and South America, and cotton in the United States. Warts and all, "Seeds" sheds new light on forces that shaped world history.

Public Broadcasting Service, with the support of Xerox Corporation, produced a much acclaimed television series "Columbus and the Age of Discovery." The Interior Department created a Center for Spanish Colonial Research at the University of New Mexico in Albuquerque. Headed by Dr. Joseph Sánchez, this institution has been in the forefront of efforts to explore and make known little known aspects of the impact of the clash of the Spanish and the Indians in the Southwest.

Hispanics and the Quincentenary

The foregoing are but a few examples of the countless projects which illustrate that, rather than a celebration of deeds, the Quincentenary was an opportunity to explore and discover unknown, little understood, and distorted aspects of world history and American history. More importantly, for Hispanic Americans it was an opportunity to learn what textbooks never taught us, an opportunity to nourish not only our minds, but our hearts and souls as well.

As some have pointed out in speeches and articles, "we Hispanics were there at the creation." Many Spaniards and Americans of Hispanic ancestry helped secure American independence, of course. One of these, Jorge Ferragut, was the father of our nation's first Admiral and a courageous Civil War hero: David G. Farragut. Their stories are recounted in this volume.

Jorge Ferragut, Bernardo de Gálvez, and other Spanish names are not easily found in American history books, particularly in secondary school texts. And the period of exploration, conquest, and settlement by the Spanish and their descendants is treated all too briefly and in folkloric terms (e.g., the dreamer Juan Ponce de León and his quest for the fountain of youth).

Historians and scholars have come to accept the term "The Black Legend" to explain history's treatment of the Hispanic presence in America. In large measure, the recording of history was the province of the English, those who for centuries had been bitter rivals of the Spanish in Europe and in the "New World." And historians in the colonies and the United States were, for the most part, descendants of English colonists who acquired values and attitudes toward the Spanish that had prevailed in Europe.

Thus, when it came time to record the history of the United States, events relating to the Spanish — enemies of the British — were minimized, distorted, or simply left out. Events since the early period have helped to burnish a negative stereotype in the minds of many. Our own war with Spain, war and conflicts with Mexico, much publicized immigration from Mexico, and other factors have fueled the notion that Hispanics in the United States are interlopers, foreigners who "do not belong here."

A recent national survey on attitudes toward ethnic and racial groups found that Hispanics rated near the bottom, just above gypsies. In fact, they were rated lower than a fictitious group that researchers had invented for the questionnaire. In another recent study, respondents were asked to list terms that best describe their perception of various ethnic groups. The terms most often used for Hispanics: lazy, ignorant, foreign.

The consequences of the recording of history and the negative stereotypes may not be tragic, but they are unfortunate indeed. Youngsters already denied so many opportunities are also denied role models from their own community. And role models are often the prime ingredient for dreams and aspirations. Young people's self worth, their place in American society are brought into question. And the ravages of abuse and discrimination, too numerous to mention here, weaken the spirit.

It should surprise no one, therefore, that Hispanic Americans should wish to avail themselves of opportunities to set the record straight, to demonstrate their contributions to their fatherland by birth or their fatherland by choice. (More than half of the nation's 25 million Hispanics were born in the United States.) Hispanic Americans want to have textbooks, museums, and art galleries that include them, that can provide possible role models for their children, for the explorers of tomorrow.

Each sub-group within the mosaic that is Hispanic America claims significant achievements. Puerto Ricans, Cubans, and Dominicans whose lands of origin were home to the first European settlements in the Americas are today being elected in unprecedented numbers to public office. Although concentrated along the Atlantic coast, these Hispanic Americans are dispersed throughout the United States. Their contributions are many. And where they constitute a minority within the Hispanic minority, they join hands with their fellow Hispanics to seek a better tomorrow.

Most Mexican Americans, more than sixty percent of Hispanic America, trace their ancestry to pre-Columbian times, proudly celebrating a unique culture and a unique history going back centuries. They, too, embrace their fellow Hispanics of other backgrounds, helping to open doors and create opportunity. Their resilience over centuries of exploitation and misfortune is a quality that speaks to a brighter future. Volumes have yet to be written on the richness of their experience.

Airplane travel, high mobility, television, growing interaction, and other factors have combined to help Hispanic Americans of diverse backgrounds understand one another. A Hispanic can be of any race or of any combination of races. And his or her origin may be in the United States of America or a score of other countries. But whatever the origin, and despite their cultural differences, Hispanics are united by two factors: Spanish heritage and an appreciation for the Spanish language.

It is a mistake to think that Hispanics do not want to assimilate and become "as American as apple pie." Quite the opposite is the case. Hispanics have fought and died in defense of liberty; and they shed a tear when they hear the National Anthem. Those who do not speak English sacrifice greatly to learn to do so, recognizing that it is the key to higher education, to employment, to increased opportunity. Hispanics, although often rejected, strive to be part of the American mainstream, able to compete on an equal footing with the rest of society. But unlike earlier generations of Americans, they do not believe they must surrender cultural and linguistic attributes they hold dear in order to do so. For assimilation is not an "either-or" proposition. One can be both American **and** Hispanic.

The Quincentenary, in conclusion, has opened the door to the discovery of realities old and new. It has fostered introspection, analysis, research, writing, interaction, and, above all, pride. It has also uncovered truths about many other aspects of American society, from the enslavement of Indians and Africans to contributions of Asians and others. In the process, we have all gained.

So much more needs to be done, however. This book is a "*grano de arena*," a grain of sand. But many grains can make a mountain. Compiling data on historical truths that have been overlooked has been a daunting challenge. And trying to meet a deadline has meant much sacrifice and less than full satisfaction with the final product. There are omissions — many of them. But let each omission be a challenge to others to read, to research, to write and to publish, to spread the word, to complete the history of the Hispanic presence in the United States.

In his Quincentenary book, Mexican author Carlos Fuentes observed:

> People and their cultures perish in isolation, but they are born or reborn in contact with other men and women, with men and women of another culture, another creed, another race. If we do not recognize our humanity in others, we shall not recognize it in ourselves.

HERNANDO DE SOTO
AND THE EXPEDITION INTO *LA FLORIDA*

A half-century before Sir Walter Raleigh's ill-fated Roanoke colony was established on the coast of North Carolina, the Spanish conquistador Hernando de Soto had organized a major overland expedition to conquer, fortify, and settle *La Florida* (the Southeast United States). De Soto landed 600 men, camp followers, livestock, and supplies at Tampa Bay in May 1539. Aided at times by hundreds of Indian bearers, the expedition traveled northward through Georgia and the Carolinas before crossing the Appalachian Mountains into Tennessee. De Soto and his army then turned southwest and traveled through northwest Georgia, Alabama, and across Mississippi. They crossed the Mississippi River, which they called the *Río Grande*, and into Arkansas before returning to the Mississippi. Finally, the army tried to traverse Texas on foot, in order to reach the Spanish settlements in New Spain (Mexico). After failing in this objective, the army returned to the Mississippi River a third time. They built boats which they floated down river and into the Gulf of Mexico, eventually reaching a Spanish settlement near Tampico, Mexico.

This incredible journey was not an isolated expedition by Spain into *La Florida*. It was only one of a number of such attempts occurring over the half-century from 1513 to the 1560's, beginning with Juan Ponce de León's first voyage along the Florida coasts and continuing after the founding of St. Augustine in 1565. Spain's New World empire was fueled by the fabulous wealth found in Mesoamerica, Central America, and South America. It was hoped that *La Florida*, which had been explored along the Gulf and Atlantic coasts by 1520, might similarly contain wealth in its interior.

Spain wished to explore those interior lands and establish a protected overland route from the Atlantic coast westward to the Gulf of Mexico and on to New Spain (Mexico). Control of the coasts was also sought as protection for the treasure-laden Spanish ships carrying New World wealth back to Spain.

Hernando de Soto, Conquistador

The most ambitious of the Spanish attempts to explore the interior of *La Florida* was financed and led by Hernando de Soto. De Soto was born about 1500 in Jerez de los Caballeros in the area of Spain called *Extremadura*. This region produced many of the New World conquistadors, including Vasco Núñez de Balboa, Hernán Cortés, and Francisco Pizarro. Like many of the Spanish aristocracy, de Soto's family had distinguished itself fighting the Moors during the *reconquista*. Military successes had embellished the family's coat-of-arms and resulted in many family members being knighted.

Little is known about de Soto's early years in Spain, and it is uncertain exactly when he came to the New World. The best evidence suggests that he sailed in 1514 in the entourage of the newly-named governor of the Castilla del Oro (modern Panama). Also accompanying the governor was Francisco Vásquez de Coronado, who would later explore the Southwest United States.

By 1520 de Soto was already a captain and had participated in military actions against the Panamanian Indians. As a portion of his share of booty, he received the right to use a number of Indians as laborers. This arrangement provided him a source of revenue. His partner in many ventures was Hernán Ponce de León. Another associate was Francisco Pizarro.

Throughout the 1520's, de Soto participated in a number of military exploits in Panama and Nicaragua, some against rival Spaniards. By late 1531 when he left Panama, de Soto had amassed great wealth from slave trading and from gold taken from the Indians. With this wealth he was able to build ships and maintain a cadre of military aides, infantry, and cavalry.

De Soto was to garner even greater wealth. From 1531 through 1535, he accompanied Pizarro and other Spaniards in the conquest and looting of the Inca civilization in Peru. De Soto played an important part in the military engagements, experience that would later serve him well in *La Florida*. Following the execution of the Inca leader Atahualpa by the Spanish and their occupation of Cuzco, de Soto helped to distribute the stolen wealth to the conquistadors. He left Peru in late 1535, sailing to Spain in early 1536. With him were men who would later accompany him on the *La Florida* expedition.

While in Spain, de Soto used his riches to hire a number of servants and secure other trappings that befitted someone of his station. He was presented at court and, with the entourage of military aides who had accompanied him to Spain, must have created quite a stir. During this visit he married Isabel de Bobadilla, the daughter of the Castillo del Oro governor with whom de Soto had first traveled to the New World.

De Soto next attempted to persuade the crown to grant him the right to New World lands which he could govern (and exploit). He asked for lands either in Ecuador and Colombia (north of Pizarro's holdings) or failing that, Guatemala. Though these requests were denied, he was able to successfully negotiate an agreement to conquer and govern *La Florida*. The royal charter given to de Soto by Carlos V is dated April 20, 1537.

The Expedition into *La Florida*

De Soto's *La Florida* expedition was well planned and supplied. According to his contract, de Soto was to conquer, pacify, and settle 200 leagues of *La Florida*'s coast (taking with him 500 men and supplies for eighteen months), and he was to build three stone forts. In return he was to receive titles, lands, and a share of the colony's profits. De Soto funded the *La Florida* expedition with his own newly-acquired wealth. In addition to members of his army who had previously fought with him in the New World, the expedition included people with a variety of skills, such as tailors, shoemakers, a stocking-maker, notary, farrier, trumpeter, friars, servants, and at least two Spanish women.

While gathering supplies in Cuba prior to sailing for *La Florida*, de Soto sent a party ahead to reconnoiter the landing site, a large protected harbor called *Bahía Honda* (Tampa Bay). It is clear that he knew ahead of time that *Bahía Honda* was the best location along the Gulf coast for harboring and unloading his ships. He was probably aware of the information gathered by previous Spaniards who had visited the Florida Gulf coast, including Alonso Álvarez de Pineda, who sailed the entire Gulf of Mexico coast in 1519, and Pánfilo de Narváez, who, with 350 men, traveled overland from Tampa Bay to the coast south of Tallahassee in 1528. Maps and navigation information were widely available to New World Spanish explorers and pilots (*e.g.*, the Chaves *Espejo de Navegantes*, compiled prior to the de Soto expedition). While in Cuba, just prior to sailing for *La Florida*, de Soto wrote his will. He also left his wife Isabel de Bobadilla as governor of Cuba. She became the first woman to govern a colony of Spain in the New World. Isabel was assisted by lieutenants of her husband while she governed the island.

The expedition went ashore in Tampa Bay in late May 1539, established a camp, and unloaded the horses and supplies. They scouted the surrounding territory for six weeks, gathering information from various aboriginal groups. Then de Soto, about 500 men, and a number of captive Indian bearers moved inland, heading northward. Some men and supplies were left at the camp. The expedition crossed the Alafia, Withlacoochee, Santa Fe, Suwannee, and Aucilla rivers before reaching the territory of the Apalachee Indians near Tallahassee where de Soto and his men spent the late fall and winter of 1539-40.

Breaking camp in March 1540, the expedition, led by Indian guides, moved north-north-east across Georgia into South and North Carolina. From North Carolina, de Soto and his army headed northwesterly, crossing the Appalachian mountains into Tennessee. De Soto knew that great wealth had been discovered in mountainous regions of Peru (among the Inca) and central Mexico (among the Aztec). He apparently hoped to find similar wealth in the mountainous areas of *La Florida* as well.

The Appalachian Mountains did not, however, offer mineral wealth, and de Soto and his army proceeded southwesterly through the Piedmont across the northwest corner of Georgia and well into Alabama before turning northwest across Mississippi where they again wintered. In May 1541, they reached the Mississippi River.

The next year was spent in Arkansas, traveling from place to place, still searching for wealth. Finally, the army returned to the Mississippi River. De Soto, now sick with a fever, died on June 20, 1542. The expedition, led by Luis de Moscoso, then attempted to walk southwesterly across Texas to reach New Spain (Mexico). After traveling hundreds of miles, Moscoco decided that the effort was futile. The army retraced its steps to the Mississippi River, arriving in December.

During the first six months of 1543, they labored to build boats on which they could float down the Mississippi River and paddle along the Gulf coast to the safety of New Spain. The expedition set out down the river in late June 1543, and reached the Gulf twenty days later. On September 10, the 311 survivors reached a Spanish settlement on the River of Panuco in New Spain (near present-day Tampico, Mexico), ending their incredible journey.

Despite the hardships suffered on their four-year trek, a few of the survivors would accompany Tristán de Luna y Arellano in 1559 on his ill-fated attempt to establish a settlement at Pensacola Bay. Members of that colony went inland and found Indian towns in northeastern Alabama through which de Soto had passed nearly two decades earlier. Other of the Indian towns that de Soto had visited in North Carolina were also visited in the late 1560's by the Spanish expedition led by Juan Pardo.

Measured against the terms of the contract drawn between de Soto and the King of Spain, the expedition would be considered a failure. However, de Soto's *entrada* into *La Florida* provided Spain with valuable information about the interior of the southeastern United States. De Soto and his army were the first Europeans that most of the aborigines had ever seen. Unfortunately, exciting as this initial contact seems to us, in it lay the seeds of the destruction of the native cultures. Old World diseases spread almost unchecked through the Indian populations, killing hundreds of thousands of people. The rapid decimation of population led to many changes in the social and political organization of the indigenous cultures. As a result, the Indians encountered by Spanish missionaries in the seventeenth century and by English traders in the eighteenth century were very different from those alive at the time of de Soto.

De Soto and the Florida Aborigines

Just as important as the expedition was to Spain for the information it supplied on *La Florida*, is its importance to modern scholars. In many instances the descriptions of the Indians chronicled in the expeditionary journals, however fragmentary, are the only accounts we have about aspects of aboriginal life prior to the changes that took place later in the sixteenth and seventeenth centuries. It is important to be able to trace de Soto's route throughout the Southeast in order to apply that information to specific aboriginal groups, who can also be studied through archaeology and the interpretation of later documents.

After landing in Tampa Bay, de Soto and his men found themselves in the territory of the Ucita Indians, who apparently controlled the area from the Little Manatee River south-southwesterly to the Gulf of Mexico. Another Indian group, the Mocoso, controlled the eastern part of the bay to the north, encompassing the Alafia River. Each of these groups, as well as others in the Tampa Bay region, was composed of several villages under the overall leadership of one chief.

De Soto and his men set up camp in one of the towns controlled by Ucita. The Gentleman of Elvas described the town as consisting of "seven or eight houses, built of timber, and covered with palm-leaves. The chief's house stood near the beach, upon a very high mount made by hand for defense; at the other end of the town was a temple, on the top of which perched a wooden fowl with gilded eyes. . . ."

The Tampa Bay region Indians lived by fishing and collecting foodstuffs from the lands adjacent to the bay. Evidently farming was relatively unimportant to the Ucita and Mocoso, because it was only after traveling several days inland that the Spanish first encountered maize (Indian corn) fields. Perhaps the inland farmers maintained some military and political hold over the coastal dwellers, because the Ucita and Mocoso chiefs paid tribute to a powerful chief named Urriparacoxi who lived inland.

After leaving their Tampa Bay camp among the Ucita and passing through the territory of the Mocoso, de Soto's expedition headed for the territory of Urriparacoxi, 20-30 leagues from Tampa Bay. Although it is not certain from the narratives, Urriparacoxi may have controlled all of the inland area as far north as the Withlacoochee River. The main body of the expedition never reached Urriparacoxi's main village and it may have been situated well west of Tampa Bay.

Along the entire route, the treatment of the Indians by the Spanish was, by our standards, very cruel. Indians were enslaved to serve as bearers and were often placed in chains and shackles to prevent them from escaping. Mutilating or killing Indians and capturing leaders as hostages in order to command obedience were regularly practiced. The Spanish conquest of *La Florida* was by force, not diplomacy. As a result, when the opportunity presented itself, the Indians retaliated with quick, guerilla-like skirmishes.

Once across the Withlacoochee River the expedition entered the territory of the Cale Indians. Here de Soto had intended to spend the winter. The Ucita Indians had regaled de Soto with stories of the Cale's wonders. In a letter to associates in Cuba, written while he was still at Tampa Bay, de Soto described the town of Cale as being so large and so extolled by the Indians that he could not even repeat all of the things they said. He also reported that the Indians said there were food and gold, silver, and pearls in great abundance. Upon arrival, however, Biedma was little impressed: "We found it to be a small town. . . .We got some maize, beans, and little dogs, which were no small relief to people who came perishing with hunger."[1]

Cale, located just east of the Withlacoochee River (the River of Cale in the narratives), did not contain enough stored food for de Soto's army, and a foray was made to the Acuera Indians to the east to gather maize. The Florida Indians quickly understood the Spaniards' desires for food and wealth and often tried to steer them to sources located elsewhere, in the apparent hope that the Spaniards would leave them. At Cale, de Soto was once again told that what he was seeking was further north where, according to Elvas, there was a "large province abounding in maize, called Apalachee."[2] De Soto was unsure if he should winter in Cale or seek Apalachee. Eventually he decided to leave most of his army at Cale and take a smaller force northward to Apalachee.

North of Cale the expedition traveled through a region of relatively abundant foodstuffs (compared to the route from Cale south to Tampa Bay). Corn was easier to obtain, and de Soto and his smaller force could move rapidly from Indian town to Indian town, taking the aborigines' stored food for themselves. After their departure from Cale, they camped first at Itaraholata and then at Potano. The Potano Indians are well known from the seventeenth century when two Spanish missions and a ranch were established in their territory.

Next the Spaniards reached Utinamacharra and two other villages before crossing the Santa Fe River (River of Discords) and arriving at the town of Aguacaleyquen. While staying in this town, de Soto sent messengers back to his men in Cale to tell them to join him. De Soto found himself in a populous region inhabited by a well-organized people who posed a military threat. These were probably the ancestors of the Timucuan Indians who inhabited Columbia and Suwannee counties in the 1560's and were said to have 40 towns united under one chief. From the time the expedition reached Aguacaleyquen until they crossed the Suwannee River (River of Deer) they were in the territory of these Indians, who harassed the Spanish whenever possible.

After crossing the Suwannee River the expedition was among still another major Indian group, the Ucachile (probably the same people called *Yustega* by the Apalachee). Moving rapidly westward, the expedition reached the Aucilla River. This river formed the boundary between the Ucachile and the Apalachee Indians, the latter being the largest and most politically complex group in Florida.

After marching several days through Apalachee territory, the major town was reached. There de Soto decided to spend the winter of 1539-40. He had a camp set up and sent word back to Tampa Bay for the men and supplies he had left there to join him.

The journey to Apalachee that had taken less than three months and had covered about 300 miles was only the start of de Soto's odyssey through the Southeast. But it marked the beginning of the end for the aboriginal peoples who had inhabited the region for 14,000 years. Epidemics first brought by the Europeans in the sixteenth century continued for 200 years. By the early eighteenth century all of the aboriginal peoples had disappeared. Florida had been changed forever.

Tracing de Soto's Route Through Florida

How do we know about the expedition of Hernando de Soto and how can we be certain of his route through Florida? How do we know, for instance, that the expedition landed at Tampa Bay and not at the Caloosahatchee River as some scholars have claimed? The answers are provided by several humanities disciplines working together on the problem, including documentary/historical research, cartographic/geographical interpretations, and archaeological investigations.

Documentary sources include three first-hand narratives of the expedition written by participants and a fragment of a fourth narrative that was recently discovered by noted historian Eugene Lyon. The first of these narratives was written by a Portuguese knight from the town of Elvas. His account, published in Portuguese in 1557, was made available in English in 1866 and was reprinted and more widely circulated in the early twentieth century. A shorter, first-hand narrative is that of Luis Hernández de Biedma, the Spanish crown's representative on the expedition. Like the Elvas narrative, it was published in English in 1866 and reprinted in 1922.

The third first-hand narrative was written by de Soto's personal secretary on the expedition, Rodrigo Ranjel. It is the most complete of the three narratives and contains almost daily entries, especially for the Florida portion of the route. The original manuscript has been lost, but it was copied by the noted Spanish historian Gonzalo Fernández de Oviedo y Valdéz. It appears in his five-volume *Historia General y Natural de las Indias*, written in the sixteenth century and published in 1851. The Ranjel narrative was first published in English in 1904. It was reprinted in 1922 with the Elvas and Biedma narratives.

The fourth, most recently discovered first-hand narrative was penned by Father Sebastián de Cañete, a priest who accompanied the expedition. His account, by far the richest of the four, contains excellent descriptions of the Indian chiefdom of Cofitachequi located in South Carolina, but it is of no use for interpreting the Florida route.

A fifth account of the expedition that has been widely circulated was written by Garcilaso de la Vega (nicknamed "The Inca") several decades after it occurred. Garcilaso was not a participant, but based his account on interviews with survivors. About one-quarter of the manuscript apparently was completed by 1587. The work was not completed until 1599. By that time, fifty years after the initial landing, memories had faded and stories had become exaggerated. Published in Spanish in 1605 and in English in 1951, Garcilaso's version of the events is more literature than history.

Other documents and letters exist in Spanish archives and help to shed light on the route and the nature of the expedition. Some of these have been published in English as appendices to the accounts mentioned earlier, while others remain unpublished.

These expeditionary accounts give us descriptions of geographical features along the route which can be located on modern maps. For example, if the accounts say the expedition stopped at an Indian village by a lake, then crossed a very large swamp, bridged a swift river and came to another Indian village, we must locate the lake, swamp, and river. Several locations may satisfy the combination of lake, swamp, and river, but in the context of the whole route, it is usually not difficult to fit the pieces of the puzzle together.

Another line of evidence used in tracing the route is the use of old maps that show trails and paths which existed prior to modern roads. De Soto and his army usually traveled along Indian trails, many of which trails continued to be used into the 1830's and the Second Seminole War, when the first accurate maps of the interior of Florida were compiled. Using the 1830 maps in conjunction with modern aerial photographs on which the old trails can sometimes be seen, we can locate trails which de Soto's army might have taken.

Using the documentary and cartographic sources of information, the supposed route can be confirmed through the search for physical evidence. Because Florida has a long history of Spanish exploration and settlement (from 1513 into the nineteenth century), finding Spanish artifacts alone is not good evidence for the presence of de Soto. We must be able to show that the artifacts date from the 1530's and are not items salvaged from Spanish ships or given out by seventeenth century Spanish missionaries.

Recent archaeological investigation of an Indian burial mound in Citrus County has found quantities of such artifacts, more than have been found elsewhere along de Soto's route. In addition to Spanish artifacts of the right period, a mass burial of more than seventy Indians was found in the mound, possibly the victims of a Spanish-induced epidemic. Some of the bones exhibit sword wounds. Such dramatic evidence certainly seems to offer proof of de Soto's expedition.

In early 1987, archaeologists located the Indian village of Anaica where de Soto and his army spent the winter of 1539-40. Anaica, the major town of the Apalachee Indians, is in downtown Tallahassee very close to the trail de Soto was thought to have followed. Excavation of the site has thus far revealed beads, broken pottery, coins, and pieces of chain mail, all lost or discarded by expedition members. Evidence of a building has also been found; future excavations will show whether or not it was built by the Spanish. As archaeological investigations like these continue, we discover that there is still much to be learned about our Spanish past.

THE EXPEDITION OF
ALONSO ÁLVAREZ
DE PINEDA

The discovery of new land in 1492 by Christopher Columbus ignited the dreams, the imagination, the adventurous spirit, and the desire for riches among many an intrepid Spaniard. One of them, Francisco de Garay, who accompanied *Almirante Cristóbal Colón* on his second voyage, became governor of Jamaica in 1511. Garay became one of the wealthiest colonists in America.

Francisco Garay harbored a great ambition to conquer lands that were as yet unknown and to find a western passage through the Gulf of Mexico. To pursue these goals he sponsored and financed an expedition. He first obtained permission for the expedition from the Order of St. Jerome which governed La Española or, more commonly, Hispaniola (the island that consists of present-day Haiti and the Dominican Republic). He put in command of his dream a friend and experienced pilot, Alonso Álvarez de Pineda, who was also the chief pilot of an ill-fated exploration of the Yucatán.

In 1519 Pineda sailed with three ships, arriving at the coast of Florida nine months later. Álvarez de Pineda sailed easterly, trying to approach this land which had previously been discovered by Ponce de León. However, winds, currents, and shallow waters full of reefs prevented Pineda from accomplishing his objective. Instead, he decided to sail into the Gulf of Mexico. There, he painstakingly and extensively followed the shoreline westward to Mexico. There he disembarked, explored a bit, and claimed possession in the name of Spain.[1]

When Pineda reached Veracruz, Mexico, he found that it already had been claimed by Hernán Cortés. Disappointed, Pineda retraced his route along the Gulf of Mexico coastline.[2] It was at this time that he discovered a mighty river which he named "*Río del Espíritu Santo*" or the "River of the Holy Ghost." It is believed that this river, which Pineda sighted twenty-two years before Hernando de Soto, is now known as the Mississippi. The Chippewa Indians .had called it the Meact-Missipi which means "the Father of Running Waters."[3]

Although Pineda did not colonize any land, his accomplishments were of greater significance than he could imagine. He discovered that Florida was part of the North American mainland, and not an island.[4] He found that there was no passage west through the Gulf of Mexico, and discovered that Florida was connected to Mexico.[5] He sighted and mapped the coasts of what is now Texas.[6] He recorded the first sighting of the Mississippi River and charted the Gulf of Mexico.[7] And, Pineda fueled the spirit of discovery and the dreams of great riches.

Francisco de Garay's zest for exploration encouraged him to finance other expeditions, depleting his personal fortune. The last one was to Panuco, where Pineda had been four years earlier. Garay personally headed this expedition, traveling with eleven ships and 850 men. Fights with the natives were followed by disputes with Hernán Cortés who dominated the entire area. Garay later reached an agreement with Cortés on territorial limitations. The marriage between Garay's son and Cortés's illegitimate daughter seemed to solidify their accord. However, one day after the two conquerors had attended Mass, Garay took suddenly ill and died of a high fever. Some suspect that Cortés fatally poisoned Garay.

It was an inglorious end for one who dedicated his energies and fortune to the exploration of the New World. Yet his contributions, especially as financier of the Pineda voyages of exploration, paved the way for later explorers and settlers in the southeastern United States.

BARTOLOMÉ DE LAS CASAS AND THE *ENCOMIENDA* SYSTEM:
A STRUGGLE FOR HUMAN RIGHTS

The discovery of the New World by Christopher Columbus brought prestige and, eventually, riches to the kingdom of Spain. It also presented a new challenge to Queen Isabella and King Ferdinand. With the defeat of the Moors in Granada and the expulsion of Jews from Spain, Christianity had become the only acceptable religion in Spain. The discovery of America brought to the Crown of Castille non-Christian subjects who had to be converted to Christianity and introduced to Spanish life and customs.[1]

A zeal to spread the faith, a desire for adventure, personal ambition or simple escapism prompted individuals to join the groups of conquerors who volunteered to teach the Christian faith to the newly discovered people in the New World. Queen Isabella had no shortage of volunteers responding to her expectations and goals. Of course, not all of the "missionaries" were acting in good faith; some sought only personal gain.[2]

The Spaniards found the indigenous people to have totally alien values, with a culture and societal structure different from their own. The Indians were content with their simple agricultural life, preferring this to the demands being made upon them by the colonizers. In turn, the colonizers saw that a system of forced labor would be necessary to procure the output of work they sought.[3]

In letters to King Ferdinand and Queen Isabella, Christopher Columbus listed the advantages of domesticating the wild natives of the islands he had visited. In his opinion, educating the Indians would conform them more closely to "civilized" behavior and render them more servile and receptive to the Spaniards. He recommended further that the Crown consider the sale of Indian slaves. The Crown reacted forcefully against such a proposal,[4] stating that the Indians should be treated as free men, and that they should be rewarded for their work.

In constant conflict with the newcomers, however, the Indians saw no choice but to escape. The Spaniards examined, as a possible solution, the concept of *repartimiento*, which would permit the gathering and transporting of Indians from one region to another.

Instead, to overcome the shortage of laborers, the *encomienda* system was established. A grant of a specific number of Indians was conferred by the Spanish government to anyone desiring labor aid, whether a conquistador, official or other. The receiver of the grant, the *encomendero*, could then exact tribute from the Indians in gold, in goods, or in labor. On December 20, 1503, Queen Isabella ordered the governor of Hispaniola (now the Dominican Republic), Fray Nicolás de Ovando, to distribute Indians among the colonizers requesting them. The *encomendero* was responsible for instructing and Christianizing the Indians. He was also obligated to treat them well and to use them as servants, not slaves.[5]

Although the *encomienda* had been promoted by some of the conquerors in good faith, it became the principal tool of early Spanish exploitation. The system permitted appalling abuses by the *encomenderos*. The exploitation of the Indians as a means to acquire wealth entirely displaced the goals of instructing them and saving their souls. If the Indians resisted their master, they had to succumb immediately and became virtual slaves. The intensity of exploitation was intolerable. Indians, who were primarily engaged in working in the mines and on plantations, suffered and succumbed to disease, especially the fatal maladies introduced by the Europeans, influenza, measles, smallpox, and typhoid. The Indian population declined at an alarming rate, affecting the economy of Spain, which "had a period of economic and demographic decline."[6]

In 1510, a group of Dominican missionaries arrived in Hispaniola, and with them arrived the beginnings of desperately-needed reforms. The plight of the Indians prompted a group of priests to organize a protest in their defense. The missionaries roused colonial interest by exposing the abuses heaped upon the Indians. The first person to denounce the injustices, from the pulpit, was Father Antonio Montesinos, a Dominican priest. The news soon reached Spain. In the province of Burgos, a council of jurors and theologians sought a solution, reviewing the policies then in effect. Their answer was codified as the Laws of Burgos (1512). The purpose was to put an end to the *encomienda* system. The Laws stated that the Indians were in need of Christian guidance. Specifically, the Laws said that Indians could no longer be enslaved, that slaves without title had to be freed, and that existing *encomiendas* were to expire on the death of the holder. The thirty-five articles then became the fundamental law ostensibly governing Spanish-Indian relations for the ensuing thirty years.

The Laws of Burgos were far from perfect. They were idealistic and reflected the prevailing morality. Yet they also contained loopholes which allowed the *encomenderos* to disregard the spirit and even the letter of the laws. The *encomienda* system thus survived, continuing the maltreatment and decimation of the Indians.[7]

During this period, Bartolomé de las Casas took holy orders (in 1510). He had once been a conquistador, where he gained some experience in controlling the Indians, but he had since repented of his actions. As a priest and *encomendero*, he treated his Indians justly, instructing them in the teachings of Christ. He disagreed with the Dominicans, and was one of the colonists who refused to free the Indians he held in *encomienda*.[8]

Las Casas was born in Seville, Spain in 1474. At the age of twenty-four, he and his father, Antonio, joined Christopher Columbus's second expedition. He returned to Cádiz, Spain on November 25, 1500. Las Casas was ordained a Catholic priest by the first Bishop of Hispaniola in 1510. He became the first priest ordained in the New World.[9]

Las Casas was a close friend of Diego Velázquez, whom Diego Colón chose in 1511 to head an expedition to colonize the island of Cuba. A very wealthy man, with great experience and status, Velázquez asked Bartolomé to join the expedition as a chaplain. Las Casas's mission was two-fold: to provide pastoral care to the members of the expedition, and to evangelize the Indian population.[10] Once in Cuba, Las Casas was rewarded with an *encomienda*. His friendship with Velázquez was an asset in his struggles on behalf of the Indians.

In 1515, as a parish priest in the newly founded village of Sancti Espíritu, Bartolomé de las Casas claimed to have been enlightened. While preparing a sermon for Diego Velázquez's group of Spanish colonizers, he came across the Biblical lectures of Ecclesiastes. The verse, "He that sacrificeth of things wrongfully gotten, his offering is ridiculous, and the gifts of the unjust men are not accepted. . ." left him astounded.[11] It was a revelation that convinced him to change. Las Casas mentions this experience in his book *The History of the Indies*. He wrote that each passing day made him think about these verses, and he became truly aware of the injustices being committed against the Indians of the Indies.[12]

Embracing the principles of the Dominican priests, Las Casas became so convinced of their righteousness that he decided to speak publicly against Indian slavery and the inhumane system of *encomienda*. To denounce the system and demonstrate his strong convictions, he decided to free his own slaves.

Las Casas discussed his plans with his good friend Diego Velázquez. Anticipating the reaction of the Spaniards, Velázquez asked Las Casas to reconsider. Las Casas replied that the decision was final. He maintained that the *encomienda* was not the best method to teach the Indians, and that it existed to enhance the wealth and comfort of the settlers.[13]

On the holy day of the Assumption of the Virgin, August 15, he made a public announcement from the pulpit, giving the governor authorization to further publicize it. As expected, the Spaniards were astonished to hear him say that keeping the natives in slavery was sinful and that their obligation was to set them free. Las Casas did not stop there, however. He went on to say that all that had been taken from the Indians, including gold, silver, jewels, and land should be restored to them. Pedro de Rentería, a long-time associate of Las Casas, agreed fully with the decision.[14] Others reacted predictably.

From that moment, Las Casas began an arduous struggle for the rights of Indians throughout the newly-conquered lands. He joined the Dominican order, and in the fall of 1515, he left for Spain to personally discuss his concerns with King Ferdinand V. He wanted to expose the crude reality of the political developments in the Indies, and request more effective methods to control the oppression of the Indians by the Spaniards.

On December 23, 1515, Bartolomé de Las Casas was able to meet with the king. He was fully aware of the problems encountered by the Indians through the writings of Montesinos, which Montesinos had himself delivered to the king. But King Ferdinand was now very old and ill. Although his response to Las Casas was positive, it proved to be useless.

On January 25, 1516, King Ferdinand died, and with him, apparently died out Las Casas's plans. Although saddened by the death of the king, he quickly resolved to persevere. Cardinal Jiménez de Cisneros was now in charge of the regency until the arrival of Charles V. Las Casas arranged to meet with Cisneros to give him an account of the problem in the Indies. Cisneros promised to intervene. He directed Las Casas to draft laws to insure the liberation of the enslaved Indians, and to indicate how these laws could be implemented. A committee, which included Fray Antonio de Montesinos, was formed to draft the legislation.[15]

The committee decided to send three priests, with the full authority of the government of Spain, to the island of Hispaniola. Upon their arrival in the New World, they received little support from the colonizers; Las Casas himself believed that they were not sufficiently resolute in carrying out their mission.[16]

Las Casas, appointed Universal Procurator of Indians by Cisneros, continued his vigorous fight. Putting into practice his doctrine of peaceful persuasion, he obtained permission from Emperor

Charles V to allow him to settle some land with free Indian labor. There the Indians could be taught the Christian faith and paid according to their ability and efforts.[17] The area was mountainous, rough, and full of fierce animals. The natives of the region were savage. On three prior occasions, the conquistadors had tried to invade the region and had failed. The area had been called "Land of War." Las Casas and the Dominicans, with the full support of the Spanish crown, renamed the area, the "Land of True Peace."

Due to the constant efforts of the Council of the Indies, the New Laws were enacted in Barcelona in 1542. They prohibited the enslavement of Indians. The settlers, however, persisted in ignoring the laws.

In 1544, Las Casas was appointed Bishop of Chiapas, located in southern Mexico. His diocese included the region of Telizutlan (now Guatemala). The constant battle between the colonists and Las Casas continued. A group of investigators sent by the Crown to verify the colonists' ill-treatment of the Dominican priests found ample evidence. In May 1556, the friars reported to the Council of the Indies that the experiment in the province of Telizutlan had failed. They detailed the hardships they had encountered, including the fact that the colonists and *encomenderos* had united strongly against the Bishop of Chiapas, eventually forcing him to flee to Nicaragua. In that region, too, Las Casas found himself struggling against the cruelty and hostility of the conquerors.[18]

For forty-nine years Las Casas traveled unceasingly, facing constant dangers in the areas through which he passed. He crossed deserts, survived insurrections in Peru and Nicaragua, and was confronted by the avaricious colonizers in Venezuela. Hernán Cortés had established the *encomienda* system in Mexico, but the results were disastrous. In Paraguay, the system caused unrest and turmoil. Yet Cuba, Hispaniola, and Puerto Rico all wished to adopt it. The system had been enforced in nearly all of the Spanish colonies, though a few discarded it when it proved to be unsatisfactory. It is interesting to note that Florida never maintained the system. [19]

Fray Bartolomé returned to Spain in 1547 for the seventh and last time. Giving up his bishopric, he continued his struggle. Appearing before the Council of the Indies, he presented a manuscript he entitled *Apología* to the judges. He emphasized that the Indian conversion to Christianity must be accomplished through peaceful colonization, love, and true example. He also discussed the rich Indian heritage, accomplishments, and abilities.

Las Casas had many enemies who wished to destroy him and strip him of his prestige. When his new efforts to abolish the *encomienda* system came to light, the colonies sent representatives back to Spain to argue for the status quo, in the interest of alleged peace and economic prosperity. One of the most knowledgeable Spaniards of his day, a renowned Aristotelian scholar, Juan Ginés de Sepúlveda, chaplain and first historian to the King, was asked to appear before the Council. His objective was to refute Las Casas and to justify the Spanish conquest and subjugation of the Indians and their land by war. He contended that it was the only way that the natives could be Christianized.[20] The judges of the Council of the Indies, after hearing arguments on both sides, were unable to reach a final decision.

In the last few years of his life, Las Casas moved to Madrid, where he remained until his death in 1566. He continued to write prolifically, to expose the injustices committed against the Indians. The most powerful and thorough account of his activities and experiences, although somewhat exaggerated, is his *Very Brief Account of the Destruction of the Indies*. The book, translated into most major languages, gives an account of the atrocities that were being committed by the Spaniards in the New World. It gave origin to the "Black Legend" that Spanish settlers, soldiers, and administrators hindered, rather than helped, the missionaries in their efforts to win the souls and allegiance of the natives. The legend aroused even greater animosity among the French and English settlers to any Spanish encroachment in North America. By the latter part of the seventeenth century, the Spanish colonial regime was considerably humanized.[21]

With the passage of time, Las Casas has emerged as one of the most important personages of the sixteenth century, and the first one to dare to publicly denounce the abuses of Spanish colonialism.

His doctrines endured and were reflected in the Laws of the Indies in 1681.

The *encomienda* system was crude, abusive, and verged on absolute slavery. Though circumstances might have created a need for such a system, it was yet another striking example of man's abuse of his fellow man. In Bartolomé de Las Casas, the Indian population of the New World found an untiring advocate for their human rights. It matters little that Las Casas was unable to abolish the *encomienda* system. It matters greatly that one beacon of truth and goodness illuminated the sixteenth century with the love due to one's fellow men.

SAN MIGUEL DE GUALDAPE:

THE FIRST EUROPEAN SETTLEMENT
IN THE UNITED STATES

The first European settlement in North America was founded by the Spanish in 1526.[1] The first colony was not in Florida or in Virginia, but in Georgia.[2] The Indians referred to it as the land of Chicora. Its history unfolded almost forty years before Pedro Menéndez de Avilés founded St. Augustine (1565) and eighty-one years before the English established Jamestown (1607).

The first quarter of the sixteenth century had just come to a close. Hispaniola by then had developed into a prosperous colony, exporting such commodities as sugar, cotton, and timber. Gold mining was the dominant industry. Four times a year, the precious ore was melted down, cast into bars, and shipped to Spain. The native Indian population had been reduced by disease and forced labor. African slave trading was a thriving business, as was the slave trade of Caribs, as some of the native islanders were called. Jamaica, Puerto Rico, Cuba, and other islands in the West Indies had been settled. Spain had pushed its conquest into New Spain, the Yucatán, Central America, and parts of South America. These exploits had produced fabulous wealth in the form of silver and gold. Juan Ponce de León had already discovered Florida; the upper coast of the Gulf of Mexico had been visited and charted. Maps of that historical period graphically depict the Spanish conquest of *De Orbe Novo*.[3]

In this atmosphere of adventure and avarice, bold mariners discovered and explored new lands. Expeditions were sent out and financed by men of wealth and high position. The island of

Hispaniola was an ideal base from which to venture into new conquests.

Lucas Vázquez Ayllón

Lucas Vázquez Ayllón was one such man of wealth and position. A nobleman from Toledo, Spain, he arrived on the island of Hispaniola in 1502 with Nicholas Ovando who, several years later, would succeed Diego Columbus as governor of the island.[4] Of reputed intellect, education, and integrity, Ayllón received the appointment of *alcalde* of La Concepción and other towns. By 1520, the native from Toledo was one of the auditors of the islands, a judge for His Majesty in the Royal Council of Española. His duties were, in the language of Pietro Martire d'Anghiera, "to sit on the Council, examine the accounts. . .recompense the good, and punish the wicked."[5] Pietro Martire d'Anghiera (1457-1526), also known as Peter Martyr, was the first historian of the New World and a member of the Spanish Court who was attached to the Imperial Council of the Indies. He wrote his *Decades* in the form of epistles, comprehensively filled with events as they were reported to the Council. Unable to direct the affairs of his growing New World empire from such distance, Charles V conferred considerable power and authority on this Council. That Ayllón was a member of this powerful assembly attested to his privileged and trustworthy relationship to the king.

Ayllón was granted four hundred Indians in *repartimientos* or fiefs, and was considered rich. "He was, however, not so rich as not to care to become richer."[6] Countries of fabulous wealth, islands or a mainland, were said to lie to the west and north. Caught in the fever, like so many adventurers who discovered the riches of the new lands, Ayllón decided to participate in the expanded explorations of the North American continent at his own expense. He had participated in the development of gold mines and sugar plantations, and owned a half-interest in a large sugar mill, so Ayllón could finance his own expeditions.

Having obtained from Indians information about a land still farther to the north than the Lucayas, as the Bahamas were called, the

spirited nobleman hired Francisco Gordillo, a captain of high reputation, to explore the North American coast.

The First Voyage Sponsored by Ayllón

In 1520, the bold captain set out on his first voyage, always
keeping in mind his employer's and his king's command to find a
passage to the Spice Islands (China). Gordillo spent many months
exploring. It is believed, and fairly well substantiated, that he entered at possibly three places along the Atlantic Coast: Port Royal
(Santa Elena) and Winyah Bay (San Juan Bautista River), both in
South Carolina, and probably Chesapeake Bay. Gordillo and his
sailors erected stone pillars or cut crosses in trees and claimed the
places in the name of their employer Ayllón and his Emperor, Charles V of Spain. Returning in 1521, empty-handed except for the
maritime knowledge gained, Gordillo captured one hundred and
forty Indians off the South Carolina coast whom he intended to sell
as slaves.

Ayllón had given Gordillo strict orders not to "enslave any of
the native people with whom he might have contact."[7] Angered at
the capture of the Indians, Ayllón condemned the captain for his
disobedience. The whole matter was brought before a council presided over by Diego Columbus, governor general of the Indies. Ultimately, the Indians were set free and ordered to be returned to
their land of Chicora. Pending their return, the natives were left in
the custody of Ayllón and another nobleman, Matienzo, whose captain, Pedro de Quexos had met Gordillo on the high seas and had
conspired with him to capture and sell the Indians.[8]

Ayllón, with a reputation of "never having donned a corselet or
borne a sword to earn his wages therewith" was not a professional
soldier.[9] On the contrary, his sense of justice was widely known. A
learned scholar of the law, his eminence as a jurist and legal counsel
were a matter of record.

Royal Grant from Emperor Charles V

To secure Gordillo's discovery of the new lands of Chicora,
Ayllón hastened to Spain to obtain a royal grant from his Emperor.

Charles V readily acceded to the request, bestowed upon Ayllón the habit of Santiago, and granted him a *cédula* (patent) which conferred upon him and his son after him the titles of *adelantado* and governor.[10] The *cédula* entitled "our man of peace," as Ayllón was referred to by contemporary historians, to explore the coast for a distance of eight hundred leagues in vessels furnished at his own expense. He was also required by the Emperor to begin his journey the following year (1524) and to complete it within three years. Should a strait be discovered, Ayllón was to pursue it. The Spanish emperor was determined to find a passage to the Spice Islands, a dream that proved to be an illusion for nearly two hundred years. The explorer was also ordered to take silk worms to develop a silk industry and to take aboard his ship a surgeon, a doctor, and an apothecary with the necessary medicines for the physical well-being of his crew.

Charles V had additional demands of his eager adventurer. He reserved the right to name his treasurer, accountant (*contador*), and agent (*factor*) to accompany Ayllón's fleet in their official capacities and to supervise the administration of the province. Ayllón was encouraged to promote the agricultural development of his territory. He was also authorized to purchase prisoners of war held as slaves by the natives, to employ them on his farms, and to export them as he saw fit.[11]

Mindful of the spiritual needs of the new colony, as well as the conversion of the natives to Christianity, the emperor also required Ayllón to "carry with him monks and priests who were to establish churches and a monastery of St. Francis. . .and no Indians were to be made slaves except those captured in war."[12] Attesting to the overriding integrity and sense of justice of Charles V of Spain, the emperor stated in clear language that Ayllón was to be "truthful and fair in all his dealings with the natives."[13]

At last, Ayllón and his expedition were ready to establish the long-planned colony. However, upon his return to Hispaniola, he was faced with pressing official duties which he had to fulfill, lest his patent for further exploration and colonization be rescinded. Deeply dismayed at the postponement of his trip, Ayllón decided to secure his rights to the land of Chicora by asking for an extension of the expedition to 1525. Early that year, Ayllón had dispatched two caravels under his newly-appointed captain, Francisco Quexos, to explore further the discovered lands. Quexos not only revisited the places earlier claimed by Gordillo, but had the noble duty to return the Indians earlier captured by Gordillo and Pedro de Quexos from the first expedition.[14]

The Final Voyage

At last, in July of 1526, having overcome all the delays and hindrances of his official duties, Ayllón and his six-vessel fleet set sail. Five hundred able-bodied men, missionaries, some women and black slaves, and eighty-nine horses filled the proud caravels to their seams. Provisions well-planned by the chief mariner promised physical well-being in an unknown land, at least for some time. Pietro Martire d'Anghiera, upon hearing about Ayllón's patent from the Emperor had predicted:

> Associates will not fail him, for the entire Spanish nation is in fact so keen about novelties that people go eagerly anywhere they are called by a nod or a whistle, in the hope of bettering their condition, and are ready to sacrifice what they have for what they hope.[15]

According to Oviedo, "so large a number leaving the island of Hispaniola had a depressing effect on that colony."[16]

Ayllón himself was chief-in-command. The first-lieutenant was Francisco Gómez and Pedro de Quexos served as chief pilot. In those days of the sailing vessel, it was difficult for any mariner to land at an exact predetermined point. Driving winds and drifting currents tended to throw the vessels off their course. The Gulf Stream also held its power over sailing ships. The prefixed point of landing was approximately thirty-three degrees latitude north from the point of origin. However, gale winds pushed the caravels farther north, past the earlier-explored San Bautista River, near another river which was named the River Jordan by the explorers (currently known as Cape Fear River). On attempting to enter the river, the capital ship sank. Ayllón promptly set to work to replace the first vessel with a smaller flat boat to be propelled by oars or sails, referred to as a *gabarra*. With great joy after a tumultuous journey, the expedition settled temporarily at a "commodious haven." The eighty-nine horses were unloaded. While the cavalry surveyed the surrounding countryside, the caravels continued to sail west, gradually turning southward for some fifty leagues, until the mariners found themselves in the San Juan Bautista River. Sailing up the bay, they landed near the mouth of a larger river, which the Spaniards called "Gualdape." Thus, this is the very place that received the distinction of becoming the first European settlement along the Atlantic coast — founded by the Spanish prior to the colonies of St. Augustine and Jamestown.

The Colony of San Miguel de Gualdape

The colony of San Miguel de Gualdape was planted in the heat of summer of 1526 near the mouth of a river, referred to as the Gualdape by the Spaniards. According to the prominent historian Quattlebaum, the location was well-suited for settlement, and the river is said to have been "very powerful and to have had many good fish."[17] The entrance to it was shallow, and only passable at high tide. The countryside was flat and full of marshes, unhappily conducive to the breeding of malaria. The colonists encountered scattered towns in which the Indians lived in huts or large communal houses. These remarkable buildings, fifteen to twenty feet wide and over three hundred feet in length, were constructed of double intersecting rows of tall pine trees, of which the top branches united together and formed sufficient protection from the weather. Open places were interwoven with matting. Each structure could hold three hundred persons.[18] The Chicoras drank the juice of a plant called *quay*, which caused them to "feel good." In place of the cassava bread, popular in the Caribbean islands, they ate bread of maize.[19]

The Spanish also encountered Indian temples on certain islands which were constructed of stone and mortar. In the vicinity of the temples, burial houses differentiated between the bones of adults and children. The bodies of the "principal people" were buried directly in the temples themselves.[20] The natives were found to be very good archers and carried bows made with quivers of skin and chestnuts.

The newly-settled colony became a thriving town of some five hundred inhabitants who had made the long and arduous journey from Hispaniola on six vessels of varying sizes. A chief magistrate was appointed to direct the town's affairs. The settlers built their houses, with a storehouse for supplies being the first building erected.

San Miguel also has the distinction of being the first Spanish mission established in what today is the United States. In addition to the conquest of the new lands and their material wealth, Emperor Charles V, a devoutly religious man, also intended the conversion of the native population to Christianity. The Emperor stated in the clearest possible terms that:

> [O]ur principal intent in the discovery of new lands is that the inhabitants, who are without the light or knowledge of faith, may be brought to understand the truths of our Holy Catholic Faith . . . and to this end it is proper that religious persons should accompany you on your explorations.[21]

Indeed, the historian Oviedo mentions by name three Dominican friars who accompanied Ayllón as chaplains and missionaries. One of the three was the famous Father Antonio Montesinos who was the first to preach against the enslavement of the natives in Santo Domingo. It was the three Dominican friars who erected a house of worship.

The Tragic End

Unfortunately, the colony of San Miguel de Gualdape did not survive. With the approaching winter and its intense cold, many settlers became sick and too weak to catch their fish from an amply supplied river. Almost two-thirds of the original five hundred settlers died.

Ayllón himself succumbed to malaria. He died as a "good Catholic, having received the sacraments, repented of his sins, sorrowed for the plans and for his fleet. . . ."[22] Before death came on St. Luke's Day, October 18, 1526, the dying explorer named as governor his nephew Juan Ramírez.

Jealousy and treachery followed Ayllón's death. After a revolt was put down, the weary, sick, and despondent settlers decided to abandon the settlement. Ayllón's body was placed in the *gabarra*, with the intention of carrying him back to his former home, Hispaniola. The man of vision and determination, however, was denied such just reward. Along with eight others, "whose flesh was falling off from frozen bones, Ayllón was committed to the sepulchre of the ocean-sea, where have been and shall be put other captains and governors."[23] Of the five hundred settlers who sailed from Hispaniola with such high hopes, only one hundred and fifty reached home again, estimated to be early in the year 1527.[24] The promise of a permanent European colony vanished with the death of its founder and the unimaginable hardships the early colonists encountered.

One can only imagine how different the history of the United States might have been if this first settlement in our country had become a successful and permanent Spanish colony.

SEVENTEENTH CENTURY NEW MEXICO:

A STORY OF CONFLICT AND STRUGGLE

The history of seventeenth-century New Mexico is one of conflict and struggle; it is the story of persistent, opposing wills spanning an entire century. When the Spaniards conquered the province of New Mexico in 1598, they could not foresee the century of strife that lay ahead. Since the first venture of the conquistadors into their barren desert land, the Indians refused to accept domination. The various tribes of the northern country fought vainly to maintain their ancient ways of life. While such strife was played out against a backdrop of a harsh and unforgiving land, the Spaniards waged their own internal battles. Unrelenting friction between the leaders of church and state would nearly destroy the kingdom they sought to claim for the sovereign crown of Spain. In 1630, in good faith and will, both factions attempted a reconciliation in order to gain peace and unity in the province.[1] The attempts soon proved futile. They were but a hope that quickly faded under the glare of the desert sun.

Franciscan friars, returning from their missionary work in New Mexico, informed officials in New Spain (Mexico) that they had converted more than seven thousand Indians to the holy Catholic faith and wished to return to build a city.[2] The viceroy of New Spain, Don Luis de Velasco, had considered recommending that exploration in the province be abandoned, but King Philip III in Spain was not convinced. Informed of the impressive strides the friars had made in converting Indian souls, King Philip asked them to continue. He promised to fund the enterprise.[3]

A new governor would go to New Mexico King Philip decreed, "in order that those settlements and the people there who had been converted to our holy faith should be preserved and protected."[4] De Velasco accordingly appointed Pedro de Peralta the third royal governor of the province in 1609. He instructed Peralta to seek to maintain peace and order in the province. Peralta was told to settle or found a villa "in the shortest possible time in order that the settlers may begin to live in an orderly manner."[5] As compensation, Peralta was told that he would receive an annual salary of two thousand pesos in common gold. That was just one small part of the more than one million pesos it cost to maintain the province. Spain's world power was declining, but despite the considerable expense, it held steadfastly to its interests in religion and in the New World.[6]

In one of his first acts as governor, Peralta moved the capital of the province from San Gabriel, to a more central location farther south and closer to the Indian settlements along the Río Grande. From there the converted Indians could be more easily protected. It was in the winter of 1609-1610 that Peralta found the spot known to the Pueblo Indians as Kuapoga, or "the place of the shell beads near the water." Kuapoga once had been the site of a Tano Indian village.[7] To Peralta, Kuapoga was ideal. It was easily reached from the north, south, east, and west. It was located in a basin where water and arable land were abundant. Perhaps most importantly, its open fields allowed for horses to move about in wartime.[8]

Peralta named the site Santa Fe, the Royal City of the Holy Faith of Saint Francis of Assisi, or *La Villa Real de la Santa Fe de San Francisco de Asis.* He built a *palacio* (city hall) with Indian labor, and surrounded it and the city with a wall to protect it from hostile Indian attacks.[9] In this tiny town that more closely resembled the villages of the Pueblo Indians than one worthy of a royal monarch, the United States third-oldest town foundation and oldest state capital was established.[10] Santa Fe had become a symbol of European and, more specifically, Spanish presence in the New World. The act signalled a redirection on the part of Spain from exploration to missionary work and colonization.[11]

Governor Peralta then set about his next task, to establish a system of municipal government in the new city. The citizens, or *vecinos*, had relocated from San Gabriel to the new city. Those Spaniards who owned property held annual elections and voted for their town councilmen, or *regidores*. In turn, the *regidores* chose two civil and criminal judges, or *alcaldes ordinarios*, whose appointments were subject to the governor's approval. Peralta also approved and confirmed the offices of the town attorney, the municipal secretary, the royal standard bearer and the constable and court bailiff, whom the *regidores* recommended. Appeals were sent to Governor Peralta and then to the *Audiencia* of Guadalajara, except in cases of minor affairs for which the town council, or *cabildo*, rendered decisions. Cases regarding the Indians were referred to Peralta.[12]

It was by way of this system of government that the first conflict between the civil and church authorities was documented; the *cabildo* of Santa Fe prepared a signed statement in which they voiced their complaints about a Franciscan. Friar Isidro Ordóñez had presented Peralta with an order from the viceroy giving permission to all soldiers and colonists to leave the province if they so wished. It was an attempt by Friar Ordóñez, who had taken charge of the missions in 1612, to weaken Peralta's authority within the province. Peralta believed the order was a forgery and continued to carry out the duties of his office. To punish him, Friar Ordóñez excommunicated Peralta and threatened to do the same to his supporters. In July 1613, Peralta in his frustration, fired a shot at the friar, but missed. He fled to Mexico, but Ordóñez had him arrested.[13] Ordóñez held Peralta as a prisoner in the Sandia pueblo for nearly a year.[14] Eventually, the viceroy replaced both the governor and Ordóñez.

Peralta's length of term as governor would set a pattern for administrations to come. Throughout the decade, governors came and went; many were corrupt, and bitterly quarreled with the Spanish missionaries. Governors and other civil servants complained that the Franciscans were abusing and exploiting the Indians; the Franciscans accused the governors and their subordinates of the same crimes. Peralta had tried to limit the exploitation of the Indians, but there was much work to be done in building a new city and little food to spare for the laborers of the villa.[15] Subsequent governors forced the Indians to work for them and ridiculed the Franciscans' efforts to convert them.[16] Civilians who resided in Santa Fe did not improve relations between the friars and the governor's officials. They sided with each when it was convenient to do so.

With the building of Santa Fe, the Mission Supply Service was organized to carry supplies the distance of more than fifteen hundred miles to and from Mexico City. The service was run by the friars who sent hides, pinon nuts, and *mantas* (the blankets woven by the Indians). Eventually they would even send sheep and Indian slaves southward. These were traded for supplies for the missions and churches, as well as clothing and various luxury items. The original aim of the Mission Supply Service was to provide for the missions, but as it was the province's only connection to Spain and to Mexico City, it served a much larger purpose. The arduous journeys they made every three years were the only means of communication, seventeenth-century style. Ultimately the supply service was likely responsible for ensuring the survival of the brave settlers of the New World.[17]

While the Mission Supply Service was a material factor in the survival of the early Spanish settlers of New Mexico, equally important was the initial role played by the native Indians in developing New Mexican history. Later, that role would be reversed completely when the Indians sought to rid their land of any trace of Spaniards, because both the friars and the government officials had been guilty of exploiting the Indians. A common source of Indian labor was the *encomienda*, a system that assigned the natives to perform necessary tasks. The *encomienda* resembled the serfdom of the Middle Ages, under which serfs performed labor for feudal knights to free them for battle.[18] The Indians provided materially for both the Spanish settlers and the friars, but it was the missionaries who justified the exploitation, saying the Indians would be converted to Christianity.

As the years progressed and the Spaniards maintained their presence in the New World, the discontent of the native Indians grew. The struggle between church and civil authorities escalated until it verged on civil war in 1650.[19] At the same time, the Indians were beginning to retaliate against the Spaniards for the crimes against their people. For example, in 1640 forty Indians who refused to renounce their religion were whipped, imprisoned, and hanged. From 1645 to 1675, the natives waged a number of attacks on the settlers to regain their freedom. They fought for their religious beliefs and their ancient habits of living which the Spaniards were attempting to change or eradicate.[20]

Not all the Spaniards were guilty of such mistreatment of the native people of Mexico. From 1661 to 1664, Don Diego de Penalosa forbade the exploitation of the Indians by the friars during his term as governor. He told the friars they could no longer make the Indians weave the cotton *mantas.* For this reason, the Spanish Inquisition took its vengeance. At the end of his term, de Penalosa was forced to walk barefoot through the streets of the city, carrying a green candle.[21]

Because of the crimes that de Penalosa had attempted to abolish, in 1680 the Indians planned a surprise attack in which they would spare not even women and children. Popé, a San Juan Indian living in Taos, was to lead the revolt. The Indians planned to isolate Santa Fe from Río Abajo by occupying thirty leagues in the center of the province and ordering all escapees on their way to El Paso killed by the Mansos Indians. The attack was launched on Thursday, August 15, 1680, and lasted five days.[22]

Except for Santa Fe, the attack rid New Mexico of Spaniards. The Indians robbed and set fire to the *haciendas, estancias,* and churches. More than four hundred Spaniards were killed, men, women, children, and missionaries. Those who survived assembled in La Isleta and Santa Fe, isolated by the Indians. At the end of their five-day attack, the Indians fled. The colonists and animals together crowded into the *casas reales* for shelter and protection. On August 21, the survivors left for La Isleta. The Spaniards went to Fray Cristóbal on September 13. They were barefoot and half-naked. They had neither food nor horses.[23] Finally, they arrived at La Toma del Río del Norte, and sent word to the viceroy for aid. According to Governor Don Antonio Otermín, just under two thousand survived.

For the next twelve years, Indians would once again dominate the land of New Mexico. During that period, it was evident that the conversions of the pueblo people to Christianity were not genuine, but made solely to accommodate the Spaniards who gave the Indians little choice. Concerned with the events transpiring in the outlying villages, Fray Francisco de Ayeta encouraged Governor Otermín to attempt to regain a foothold in the province. Father Ayeta, a native of Pamplona, was ordained in Mexico City in 1659 when he was nineteen years old. Twenty years later he was elected *custos* of New Mexico by the Provincial Chapter, and the same year was elected procurator general of New Spain. It was Father Ayeta's hope that the missionaries could continue to perform the work of God in the New World.

Otermín's was the first attempt to regain New Mexico. Appealing to the fathers in El Paso for aid in making preparations, Governor Otermín received the necessary supplies. Otermín's army left El Paso on November 5, 1681. It crossed the Río Grande, known to the Spaniards as the Río del Norte, and went northward where it encountered hostile Indians.[24] Francisco Xavier, secretary of government and war, recorded notes of a stop in the pueblo of Senecu where the army arrived on November 26:

> They recognized many signs of the Apache enemies on horseback and on foot, and going to the said pueblo to see what people were there, and what was to be done, they found the said pueblo deserted and depopulated, the holy temple and convent burned, only the walls having remained, and these badly demolished in parts. In the towers of the church they found two bells, and another fallen in the cemetery without a clapper. . . .Also in the cemetery was a holy cross of pine which in former times was in the main plaza. They entered the place where the sacristy had been and found there the hair and crown from a crucifix, thrown on the ground, and an altar and two pieces of another. They saw many signs of the apostates having deserted the place from fear, being oppressed by the heathen Apaches. The reverend father *visitador*, Fray Francisco de Ayeta, ordered them to gather up some crosses which were found in the houses of the pueblo—all

of which were standing and without a sign of being burned—and he ordered them burned, together with the crown and the hair and other things from the altar made of wood and directed that the altar and the other two pieces of one be thrown in the current of the Río del Norte.[25]

The secretary noted that once this work had been finished, Father Ayeta ordered the pueblo burned.

The men continued their journey, reaching the passages of la Vuelta del Socorro on November 30, advancing through rain and sleet to the pueblo of Alamillo on December 1, to Las Vueltas de Acomilla the following day, and to the depopulated pueblo of Cebolleta by December 4. On December 5, Governor Otermín and seventy Spanish soldiers rose at dawn, and forming four squadrons, advanced from all directions on the pueblo of La Isleta. More than five hundred Indians of the pueblos of La Isleta, El Socorro, Alamillo, and Sevilla, and of the Piro nation were living as they had before the Spanish domination. They laid down their arms and surrendered to the Spanish, and gathered in the plaza. Soon after the Spaniards found that the holy temple and convent had been burned and ruined. Crosses had been thrown down throughout the pueblo, and a cow pen was housed inside the church.[26]

Father Ayeta had remained behind at the camp because of illness. Governor Otermín sent word to him that the Indians were peaceful. Now encouraged by that news, Father Ayeta rode on horseback to the pueblo to speak to the Indians waiting in the plaza.[27] Francisco Xavier, secretary to the government and war, recorded what Father Ayeta told them:

> He gave them to understand how gravely they had offended in committing so many kinds of crimes, admonishing them to return to the holy faith, telling them the things which please God and are to His service and those by which His Divine Majesty is offended, and explaining the divine commands to them, and saying that they should come with a clean heart, accepting the holy doctrine.[28]

Father Ayeta then baptized the infants of the village, ordered the people to ask God's forgiveness and "ordered that they bring out of their houses and from any other place the idols, feathers, herbs, powders, masks, and everything concerned with superstition and idolatry."[29]

Despite the efforts of the Spanish soldiers and of Father Ayeta to bring the natives back to Christianity, the attempt at reconquest was not successful. No record was made of the remaining twenty-eight leagues back to El Paso from Estero Largo after Otermín closed the record books. No great military achievement had been made or noted. Otermín's most notable accomplishment was bringing three hundred eighty-five Indians to El Paso, but that only served to complicate the Indian situation there.[30]

In August 1683, Domingo Jironza Petriz de Cruzate became the province's newest governor, and served for four years until he was deposed by the viceroy over a political controversy. Upon his appointment, Petriz de Cruzate immediately petitioned the viceroy for two years' salary in advance in order to reconquer the province. In addition, Petriz de Cruzate sent survival petitions for supplies. His requests were unsuccessful until Father Ayeta interceded. Still, it was not until the arrival of Don Diego de Vargas that the reconquest would be successful.[31]

Don Diego José de Vargas Zapata y Luján Ponce de León y Contreras was appointed governor and captain general of New Mexico on June 18, 1688. Vargas was from a wealthy family of noble lineage. The families of both his parents possessed large landed estates. Vargas had served the Spanish sovereign at court in Madrid and in campaigns in Naples and other parts of Italy. Eventually he migrated to the Indies. In the Indies, Vargas served as the *alcalde mayor* of Teutila, the state of Oaxaca, during the viceroyalty of the Marquis of Mancera from 1665 to 1673. Later he served as the *justicia mayor* of the mining camp of Tlalpujahua, the state of Michoacán. With a great amount of wealth, Vargas hoped to reconquer New Mexico thinking he would win favor with the crown and rewards of new titles and higher appointments. Although he was appointed governor in 1688, Vargas did not assume the responsibility of the office until February 22, 1691. At that time he planned to set about his task immediately and at his own expense. However, he became greatly disillusioned when he arrived in New Mexico to find most of the soldiers did not even possess leather hackets or swords.[32]

In his report to the viceroy, Vargas told him that in El Paso one hundred and thirty-two soldiers lacked the proper equipment for such a campaign as he was planning. There were approximately one hundred twenty *vecinos*, and no more than two hundred horses and mules in El Paso, the four adjoining pueblos, and the Suma missions, and no more than one thousand Christian Indian men. Between these economic problems, Indian wars on the settlers, and administrative "red tape" with Spanish officials, Vargas's reconquest was delayed one and a half years. Meanwhile, the shortages of food and supplies continued. The only cattle in the province were six hundred steers that belonged to the missions.[33]

By the summer of 1692, the poverty and suffering had grown so unbearable that the settlers appealed to Vargas to allow them to move to the state of Chihuahua. Vargas, fearing a loss of his purpose, denied the petition,[34] and the Indians continued their raids on the Spanish settlements.[35] It was at this time that reports began to circulate of silver in the province. The government was then faced with a decision, to proceed with the reconquest or to search for the Sierra Azul. The officials decided that the reconquest was of greater importance. Vargas wanted to dispatch the first unit on July 12, 1692, but he was ordered again to delay.[36] The governor finally left El Paso on August 21.[37]

Governor Vargas set out on a preliminary expedition, and with three hundred men, captured the lower pueblos. Confident as a result of his initial success, he marched on to Santa Fe, through eerie, deserted country, accompanied by only forty Spaniards and fifty Indian allies, entering the city of September 13. Bravely, he met and reached an agreement with his Indian adversary El Picuri, and went with him to subdue the outlying pueblos, whose allegiance he had lost.[38] Except for an outbreak in 1696, the seventy-seven pueblos of New Mexico remained under the control of the Spanish empire.[39] It was a feat Vargas had accomplished peacefully without loss of life or blood. With the exception of an encounter with hostile Apache

Indians, Vargas did not fight a battle in his effort to free New Mexico from Indian domination.

After 1693, Vargas escalated his campaign to further colonize New Mexico. Now free from strife with the Indians, Vargas was able to begin to rebuild and extend Santa Fe. New growth also included the establishment of Villa Nueva and the building of churches and convents in Indian pueblos throughout the province. The efforts to Christianize the Indians were so successful that religion has become a dominant part of Indian culture of today. Meanwhile, the Spanish were giving their presence in New Mexico greater permanence. Vargas instituted a new land-grant program for the colonists. The policy was a reinstitution of a program that had been disrupted during the twelve years of Indian rebellion against the Spaniards. Vargas's ability to adopt New Mexico's earlier policies and adapt them to current conditions, demonstrated the great success of his administration. The "Napoleon of the Southwest" thus closed a significant chapter in the history of New Mexico and Spain's campaigns in the New World.[40] Vargas brought permanence, and thus laid the groundwork for new ventures and exploration at all points north, east, and west of the province, opening a new chapter in the history of the Southwest.

PEDRO MENÉNDEZ DE AVILÉS

Pedro Menéndez de Avilés is credited with establishing the first permanent European settlement on the shores of the United States in September 1565. What personal qualities and circumstances led this Asturian seaman to such a momentous achievement is, alone, a tale worth the telling.

From his portrait by Titian, of which engravings still exist, we may catch a glimpse of the man. He had reddish hair and a full beard. His face expressed his keen intelligence and supreme confidence. He was a man to whom others naturally turned for leadership. A would-be naval strategist and skilled tactician on land and sea, he was also deeply pious and fond of instrumental music. Although ambition drove him to pursue adventure at sea and to seek preference at the Castillian court, Pedro Menéndez was grounded firmly in his home region of northern Spain.

He emerged from a proud and vigorous people, rooted deeply in the green, mountainous land of Asturias. These closely connected families, fiercely loyal among themselves, were gathered near their chief shrine, that of San Pelayo at Covadonga. They were strongly committed to the Christian reconquest of Spain from the Moors, begun by Pelayo, and had offered their swords in that cause down the centuries. From their shoreline base, they readily became seaborne on the Bay of Biscay and in northern waters. Later, after the Columbian discoveries, Asturian seamen were active in Spain's Indies trade.

Pedro Menéndez's own career followed this pattern. While still a youth, he sailed out with a small craft to fight his life-long enemy, the French, off their own coasts. Menéndez, who embodied all a sailor's clear-thinking self-reliance, came early to the favorable attention of the Court. Granted royal letters-of-marque, he later was appointed fleet commander for the Indies convoys. He was a ship owner in the American trade, but chose as his principal ladder to success a militant opposition to his sovereign's enemies wherever they might be found. Thus he also participated in the supply of the Spanish armies in Flanders prior to the victory at St. Quentin. He pleased Prince (shortly King) Philip by serving Queen Mary Tudor, and escorted Philip himself to safety on his return to Spain.

The European world of Pedro Menéndez was rent by religious and dynastic wars, fought out in Italy, Germany and in the Mediterranean. As the sixteenth century advanced, these conflicts and tensions were reflected in the New World. France challenged Alexander VI's donation to Portugal and Spain and the resulting division of the Western Hemisphere between them. The French sent explorer Giovanni di Verazzano to explore the North American coasts in 1524.

In the meantime, Spanish expansion had proceeded apace. After Columbus's first discoveries, the tide of Spanish conquest spread outward from the Caribbean islands. After seizing Montezuma's golden kingdom, which Hernán Cortés named New Spain, it was inevitable that Spanish adventurers should reach for Central and South America. They had already begun to seek to conquer eastern North America.

Juan Ponce de León named the land he discovered in 1513 "La Florida," but was killed by Indians in attempting to conquer it. After the unsuccessful expedition of Lucas Vázquez de Ayllón in 1526, legends of rich lands and exotic inhabitants continued to draw Spaniards and Frenchmen toward the coasts of the present Carolinas. They were particularly attracted to the area of the Cape, or Point, of Santa Elena (near today's Hilton Head).

One would-be conqueror of Florida followed another: Pánfilo de Narváez, Hernando de Soto, Fray Luis Cáncer, Tristán de Luna y Arellano, Angel de Villafañe. By 1560, all their attempts had occasioned large expenditures, but had resulted neither in a lasting settlement nor in the religious conversion of the native Americans. Rather, they had spread European disease and promoted hostility toward the Spaniards among the Indians.

By far the most useful outcome of the previous Florida explorations was the intelligence their leaders and chroniclers had gathered. This information was passed along from one would-be conqueror to the next. Thus a map of the Southeast made during the overland journeys of Hernando de Soto was furnished to Tristán de Luna; Pedro Menéndez de Avilés knew the details of the de Luna fiasco and studied the "Cañete relation" of the de Soto journey. He also received, but discounted, rumors arising out of Mexico: the legend of "gold-crowned kings, far inland" — a reflection of the Seven Cities which Coronado had sought. The later Spaniards were therefore inheritors of all the explorations which had gone before. They all hoped to pierce the mysteries of North American geography and to find the fabled "Northwest passage" through the continental mass, reaching the Pacific and thence the Orient.

By 1560, the latest war with France had ended with the Treaty of Cateau-Cambrésis. The agreement left both Spain and France in a state of misapprehension about the issue of New World settlement. While Spain continued to claim her exclusive rights under the Papal donation, the French felt quite free to settle North America at will. Jean Ribault, a Huguenot captain, therefore explored the east coast of the continent and made a settlement at Port Royal, near present Beaufort, South Carolina, in 1562. It did not endure, but Spaniards from Cuba eventually explored the place and captured one French survivor, from whom they heard the story of the French failure.

When, in 1563, Philip II learned of Ribault's colony, he pressed the latest *Florida Adelantado*, the second Lucas Vázquez de Ayllón, to fulfill his contract and depart for *Florida*. Vázquez never sailed for *Florida*; the way was cleared for another Spanish try at preventive settlement on the North American coasts.

In the meantime, René de Laudonnière left France in 1564 to establish a French settlement near present-day Jacksonville. The French leader built Fort Caroline, became acquainted with nearby

Indian groupings, and sent an expedition up the St. John's River, which Ribault named the River May. The existence of this colony was unknown to the Spaniards until events brought it to their attention, many months after its establishment.

Late in the year, mutineers seized three small craft and deserted the French settlement; they set sail for the Spanish West Indies, where they began a career of piratical depredations.

Philip II had already opened negotiations with Pedro Menéndez de Avilés for the *Florida* conquest and settlement; he signed their contract on March 20, 1565. It was a standard agreement of its type. Menéndez would act as a surrogate for his King. In return for certain privileges, Pedro Menéndez agreed to underwrite most of the expense and risk of the Florida enterprise. He would be civil and military governor of *Florida* for two lifetimes, receive exemptions from some taxes and the rights to certain monopolies. The Crown granted him a number of ship licenses in the Indies trade, and the right to 500 slave licenses. He was to receive the title of *Adelantado* and that of Marquis, with a 25-league squared land grant in *Florida*. He was required to bring 500 private soldiers. Menéndez was obligated to build two cities, and to foster the evangelization of the native Americans into the Roman Catholic faith.

Now the acts of René de Laudonnière's deserters resulted in their arrest and capture in Jamaica and Cuba, and the existence of Fort Caroline was revealed. Word of it did not reach Philip II until March 30, ten days after Menéndez's contract to settle *Florida* had been signed. The effort then became more of a fiscal joint-venture in conquest, as King Philip II added three hundred soldiers and their supplies to those the *Adelantado* carried on his own account. Still, Menéndez had to strain his resources to the limit to charter and outfit ships, raise and embark his own private soldiers, and purchase arms and supplies for the *Florida* enterprise. In so doing, he called upon a whole network of relatives, friends, and associated families from Asturias.

Each person and family had a very real advancement in mind. Menéndez himself sought the status of grandee and the lands promised for his future estate. His noble supporters would also receive land in the new colony. Menéndez's soldiers signed agreements which promised them rations and passage-money to Florida, and town, farm, and pasture-lands, should their services merit it. This was, then, an enterprise of settlement and establishment. But the purposes of the *Florida* enterprise were larger than the motives of a King and his *adelantado* or other participants; they represented a cultural transfer from Castile to America, full in the mainstream of a Spanish conquest. When, on June 28, 1565, Pedro Menéndez sailed with his main force from Cádiz bound for *Florida*, a battle was about to be joined for large personal and dynastic stakes.

When it came, the Franco-Spanish clash in *Florida* developed rapidly to a dramatic and decisive conclusion. Throughout a stormy and difficult voyage to *Florida*, Menéndez had attempted to arrive in time to forestall the French reinforcements, but he lost the race. Jean Ribault anchored first off the River May. The naval battle which followed on September 4, 1565 was a standoff. Ribault, with his fleet at sea, then launched an unsuccessful assault upon the Spaniards' new base at St. Augustine.

When a strong windstorm lashed the Florida coasts a few days later, it wrecked the French ships southward from Mosquito Inlet (present Ponce de León Inlet) to Cape Canaveral. Instinctively, Menéndez felt that the French had weakened their land garrison to strengthen their fleet. Under the cover of the storm, he led an overland attack on Fort Caroline. There Menéndez overpowered the enemy garrison, killing most of them. Later, at a little inlet south of St. Augustine, he encountered groups of stragglers from the French shipwrecks. There he killed Jean Ribault and most of his followers who had voluntarily surrendered themselves to him. To this day, that place has borne the name of Matanzas, "place of slaughters."

As elements in a growing "Black Legend" about Spain in the sixteenth century, Pedro Menéndez's acts in Florida have been portrayed as those of a religious fanatic, the massacres he carried out at Matanzas characterized as sectarian murders. Of course, Menéndez was a devoted partisan of the Catholic faith, but this interpretation overlooks his supply situation; he would have been unable to feed his own men while burdened with such large numbers of French prisoners. More significantly, it underemphasizes the dynastic component of the conflict. It was apparent that the Franco-Spanish clash had arisen out of the final maturing of long-held French plans to colonize North America. When Menéndez took Fort Caroline, he found a small chest containing Ribault's patents and other papers, which appeared to confirm those plans. These convinced the *Adelantado* and his King that they had been correct in believing that the French saw "New France" as an extension of a policy of national outreach.

Once Menéndez's military victory had been won, he could return to his enterprise of preventive settlement and evangelization. Now the *Adelantado* confronted a continent. It was not for nothing that Menéndez's contract projected a *Florida* writ large — from Newfoundland to the Keys.

Menéndez had a grand design, a continental vision. He would, he told the King, patrol the Newfoundland fishing banks, levying tribute upon foreigners using them. At the same time, his coastal settlements in Florida would protect the Gulf Stream passage for the homebound Spanish treasure fleets. Menéndez also expected to locate a two-pronged waterway which he believed traversed the continent. One branch, he thought, debouched near the mines of Guanajuato and Zacatecas in New Spain. The other led directly to the Pacific and the riches of China. Near the mouths of these passages, Menéndez would settle and fortify; along their route, he projected a line of inland fort-missions. To begin the exploitation of his wide provinces, the *Adelantado* built two cities — St. Augustine and Santa Elena, the latter on present-day Parris Island in South Carolina.

Pedro Menéndez's outreach continued with the expedition of Pedro de Coronas, sent to the Chesapeake, the "Bay of Santa María" to establish an outpost. He commissioned Captain Juan Pardo to explore westward from Santa Elena; in two lengthy journeys, Pardo reached and passed the Appalachian Mountains. Pardo's orders were to examine and describe the character of the lands and waters he explored, and to find the route to New Spain, believed to be only five hundred leagues away. The Captain reported the finding of "land. . .good for bread, wine and all kinds of livestock. . .many fresh rivers and good groves. . . ." It was, he believed, a land as good as the best in Spain. Pardo built several inland fort-missions. It was expected that settlers from Santa Elena would soon move to their vicinity, to practice agriculture.

The *Adelantado* also dispatched his nephew Pedro Menéndez Marqués to explore the coasts up to Newfoundland, and turned his logs over to the Royal cosmographer, Juan López de Velasco. Encouraged by the reports of his expeditions, Pedro Menéndez applied to King Philip II for another contract for settlement and conquest, this time in the area of Pánuco. That province, adjoining the boundary of New Spain, would complete his territories and make possible the desired link-up with the mines.

In the peninsula where French incursion had accidentally placed him, Pedro Menéndez quickly established a network of Spanish bases. He renamed the French fort San Mateo and built forts with Jesuit missions at Tequesta on Biscayne Bay, at Carlos (believed to have been on Mound Key in present Estero Bay), and at Tocobaga on Tampa Bay. In 1566, Menéndez had discovered the Cuchiaga passage through the Florida Keys, thus shortening the route for ships sailing from Vera Cruz to Havana and Spain. But, as he explored and gleaned intelligence from native Americans and French prisoners, Menéndez evolved another idea: the notion of an inland waterway system. He believed that the St. Johns flowed from the "great lake" now called Okeechobee, and that waterways leading to the Gulf and Biscayne Bay also entered there. In a curious foreshadowing of the Cross-Florida Barge Canal projected almost four hundred years later, Pedro Menéndez envisioned the exploitation of the interior peninsula and safer Spanish shipping to and from Spain and Vera Cruz. Late in 1566, he sent an expedition to the Mosquito Inlet and thence inland to Mayaca in Central Florida, to seek escaped Frenchmen and bring the natives there to his purposes.

Almost immediately, serious threats to Pedro Menéndez's colony arose. One came from within: his unruly soldiers mutinied in a series of full-scale revolts. The cause of the mutinies was rooted in the haste in which the *Adelantado* had come to defeat the French forces: supplies were short, and Menéndez had to absent himself to seek food in Cuba. While his vital leadership was removed from *Florida*, the garrisons at St. Augustine, San Mateo, and Santa Elena rebelled. The mutineers seized several ships and deserted *en masse*. The rebellions of early 1566 almost destroyed Pedro Menéndez's *Florida* enterprise. But he returned to reassert authority over his remaining men, and built a viable supply line to Cuba and Yucatán.

Another perceived menace was that of a French-Indian coalition. The long-term effects of the former French occupancy were not erased as easily as their military presence had been. Menéndez continued to believe that the French had built, or would shortly build, other forts on the Florida coasts or in the Keys. He also found himself caught in a web of problems with the native Americans tied directly to their former relations with the French. Saturiva and many other Timucuan leaders who had been Laudonnière's friends could be counted as enemies of Menéndez, while those natives who had opposed the French might more easily befriend the Spaniards.

That Menéndez's fears vis-à-vis the Indians and the French were not entirely imaginary was proven by the raid of Dominique de Gourgues in 1568. The damage inflicted was transitory, but the Spaniards in *Florida* remained in a continual state of alert. Menéndez had to alter his methods of warfare to conform to the rapidity of Indian arrow firepower, requisitioning crossbows and padded cotton armor.

Indeed, from the very beginning, the most difficult and enduring problem of the *Florida* conquest was that of the native Americans. Spanish Indian policy wore two conflicting faces. The rhetoric of good treatment was backed by Royal edict. The New Laws of 1542 were founded upon the pressure of religious authorities back to Bartolomé de Las Casas; the treatment of the Indians had touched the consciences of Spanish rulers since Isabella.

Through the use of interpreters, Pedro Menéndez exercised his charismatic personality and made treaties of friendship and fealty with many Indian groupings. These required loyalty to Philip II and the payment of tribute to his Spanish governors. But, in *Florida* as in the other Indies, officials, soldiers and settlers often changed drastically the terms of dealing with the native Americans. They required the Indians to trade for Spaniards' private enrichment, levied heavy food supply requirements upon them, and set up forced labor arrangements. Much mutual misapprehension and tension arose over the evangelistic efforts of the Spanish missionaries. The Indians realized that the imposition of Christianity threatened not only their own religions but their whole cultural structure. Moreover, the Spaniards often assumed the right to interfere in the selection and deposition of native leaders, arousing Indian hostility.

Due chiefly to these tensions with the Indians, the Jesuit missionaries failed to win converts in South Florida. After three years, Spanish *Florida* began a shift in emphasis to the northward impulse, as Santa Elena became the new capital of the colony. All the forts and missions in South Florida, and San Mateo, were abandoned. The provinces were now reorganized along a north/south axis between St. Augustine and Santa Elena. This route was anchored at Cumberland Island by a new fortification at San Pedro de Tacatacuru.

Pedro Menéndez de Avilés now began his major *Florida* colonization effort. In 1568, he sent 225 settlers and families under contract to him. Most of these colonists went to Santa Elena. By the end of 1569, there were 327 persons in the city, and the Jesuit mission had moved there. Menéndez's Royal contract was extended, and the King promised, but did not immediately begin, a Royal subsidy for *Florida*.

After sending the settlers, Menéndez's resources were thin. By 1570, the King had still not established the subsidy. Moreover, high Jesuit officials were unhappy with their lack of success in *Florida* and the restrictions Menéndez had placed upon them. The *Adelantado* forced a crisis by removing almost all his troops, and four Royal Councils — State, Exchequer, Castile, and Indies — met in Madrid with Pedro Menéndez and Jesuit leaders for high-level deliberations about *Florida*. The outcome was that the King decreed the payment of the subsidy should begin. For their part, the Jesuits determined to make one last mission attempt in *Florida*; they built and staffed a mission outpost at Chesapeake Bay.

Armed with the new Royal commitment, Pedro Menéndez began a new undertaking of settlement. In 1571, he also brought his wife and household to Santa Elena with rich personal goods. Because his son had been lost at sea, the *Adelantado* had to entrust the government of Spanish *Florida* to his sons-in-law. To one of these, Don Diego de Velasco, he gave a dower contract to persuade him to serve as his lieutenant and govern *Florida*. Menéndez intended to establish his eventual estate, and the Royal land-grant, at Guatari, in piedmont Carolina.

There was much economic activity at Santa Elena. Menéndez imported equipment to begin whaling from the port. Vineyards and wheat-fields were planted, and the raising of hogs (pork being always vital in the Spanish diet) began. Using Indian labor, the Spaniards gathered and exported sassafras root, believed to be a remedy for syphilis. Corn, brought in from the Yucatán and from the *Florida* Indians, began to replace wheat, which did not immediately succeed. Sugar cane, planted in Guale (present Georgia coast) did not grow well. Squash, melons, and other vegetables thrived. Shipments of lumber and naval stores were made from both ports. Menéndez also built two small vessels in *Florida*. Noting how the French had established a bustling fur trade in Newfoundland, Menéndez began the commerce in furs and hides with the *Florida* Indians.

Unfortunately for the Spanish settlements in *Florida*, Indian relations did not generally improve. While Pedro Menéndez was absent from *Florida*, serving as Governor of Cuba and Chief of the Royal Indies Armada, his *Florida* subordinates were often harsh, cruel, and venal in their dealings with the Indians. Hostilities at the Chesapeake led to a massacre of the Jesuit missionaries, and led to their final removal from *Florida*. The inland Carolina forts were abandoned. Indians on the seacoast often captured and killed shipwreck survivors and even seized small vessels.

By 1573, Pedro Menéndez asked the Crown to allow him to capture hostile Indians and sell them into Caribbean slavery. Although the King refused his request, it evidenced the *adelantado's* basic failure as a colonizer. Neither the Spaniards or their missionaries could evangelize or otherwise acculturate sufficient numbers of Indians to bring the kind of order which they sought. This in turn made it impossible for Spanish settlers to penetrate to the more fertile inland areas.

Philip II ordered Pedro Menéndez to undertake, in 1574, the arming and direction of a mighty armada at Santander in Spain. Its purpose was similar to that of the Invincible Armada of 1588 — to support Spain's armies in Flanders and possibly seize a foothold in England. While engaged in this venture, Pedro Menéndez was stricken ill and died, in September 1574.

Even though Hernando de Miranda, another Menéndez son-in-law, succeeded him as *adelantado* and governor, he lacked the abilities of his father-in-law. After a major Indian uprising, Santa Elena fell, and Miranda fled *Florida*. When, in 1577, the King's Council of the Indies picked a successor, they chose nephew Pedro Menéndez Marqués. But *Florida* was no longer a proprietary government; rather, it had become a Crown colony. Despite great cost in blood and treasure by King and *adelantado* alike, the full vision of Pedro Menéndez de Avilés, that complex, powerful man, had failed of realization. The Spanish settlement, evangelization and prosperity of a continent had not occurred, but an enduring mark had been left: the founding of St. Augustine, the first permanent European settlement in what is today the United States of America.

SAINT AUGUSTINE

Juan Ponce de León discovered Florida on March 27, 1513. The land that de León discovered was named Florida, not because of the numerous flowers present, but because it was discovered on Easter Sunday ("*Pascua Florida*").[1] Here St. Augustine, the oldest city in the United States was founded in 1565.

The establishment of St. Augustine was made possible by a joint venture between Philip II, the King of Spain, and Pedro Menéndez de Avilés, a Spanish conquistador.[2] Philip II was concerned about the French settlement at Fort Caroline, near present-day Jacksonville, which encroached upon the Spanish New World. Fort Caroline had been established by the French Protestant Huguenots, under the command of Jean Ribault. While they may have been motivated more to flee religious persecution than to challenge the fledgling Spanish empire, it was enough that Philip II perceived a threat to spell their doom.

Philip II had claimed *Florida* for Spain on the basis of earlier expeditions of discovery by de León, Hernando de Soto, and other Spanish conquistadors who explored the interior of *Florida*. Menéndez was commissioned by Philip to expel the French from *Florida*. The expedition was funded by the King and Menéndez himself. Menéndez and his force landed at the Indian village of Selooe, near where St. Augustine now stands, on September 7, 1565.[3] The city of St. Augustine received its name because the date on which Menéndez sighted the Florida coast coincided with the day (August 28) that is celebrated as the feast day of St. Augustine by the Roman Catholic Church.[4]

On September 19, Menéndez and his troops attacked and captured Fort Caroline, massacring all but seventy of the French.[5] The commander, Ribault, had previously left the fort with a small fleet of ships in the hope of surprising and capturing the Spanish fleet, thus cutting off supplies to St. Augustine. Ribault's plan failed, however, because his ships encountered a violent storm off the coast and were wrecked between the Mosquito and Matanzas Inlets. After securing his hold on the fort, Menéndez, a pious Catholic, located the shipwrecked Ribault and his troops, and ordered them to surrender to him. The Huguenots did so; then they were all massacred by the Spaniards, except for a few who claimed they were Catholic.[6]

During and after the conquest of the French Huguenots, St. Augustine's defenses were fortified. The danger of a counterattack by the French still existed. Menéndez also set up a government for the settlement, with military as well as civil officials, and a hall of justice.

In April 1568, Dominic de Gourgues, a French soldier of fortune, landed at the mouth of St. Johns River, near St. Augustine, to try to avenge the bloody massacre of the Huguenots by Menéndez and the Spaniards. The Spanish fort received de Gourgues's fleet of ships warmly, believing that de Gourgues was sympathetic to the Spanish.[7] De Gourgues took the opportunity to attack the Spanish fort with the aid of Indians under the leadership of Saturiva, who was as friendly toward the French as he was bitter toward the Spanish. The garrison, led by de Gourgues, captured the two forts on the St. Johns River and massacred almost all of the Spaniards.[8] When Menéndez returned from a voyage to Spain, he found his troops in a wretched condition.

By 1586, nine years after Menéndez's death, St. Augustine had developed into a small town. Its prosperity was short-lived. Sir Francis Drake and his fleet, on a return voyage from South America, destroyed St. Augustine. After the devastating attack, attempts to rebuild the city and increase its population were headed by Pedro Menéndez's nephew, Don Pedro Menéndez Marqués. Other disasters in the sixteenth century, such as floods, hurricanes, and land fires, further hindered the redevelopment of the area. Rebuilding was slow. The economic resources of St. Augustine and the surrounding area were not abundant. There were no valuable metals or stones. The sandy soil was not conducive to agriculture. No large, agricultural Indian tribes were native to east Florida. Also, the *encomienda*, a plantation system in which the natives of a certain area were bound to a Spaniard who could extract forced labor and tribute for life, was illegal by the time that St. Augustine was settled. Therefore, a profitable *encomienda* system did not develop in St. Augustine. It became a self-sufficient colony from its own labors.[9]

During the seventeenth century, St. Augustine's population grew to over one thousand people, and a cattle ranching industry was started. Attacks by the pirate John Davis and troubles with the English resulted in the construction of the Castillo de San Marcos, a fort that still stands today.

In 1702 and 1704, James Moore, the governor of South Carolina, raided St. Augustine. The Castillo protected the townspeople and prevented Moore from capturing the colony. Moore's second raid on Florida in 1704, and other English attacks, such as the siege of St. Augustine by Oglethorpe, resulted in the desertion of the interior of Florida and the reduction of Spanish control over St. Augustine. After 1702, however, St. Augustine was almost completely rebuilt by the Spanish settlers.[10]

Integration with the British colonies, as well as increased population growth and immigration to St. Augustine, took place during the eighteenth century. In 1763, Florida was given to England under the Treaty of Paris which ended the French and Indian War. Then, for twenty years, until the second Treaty of Paris (1783), England occupied, colonized, and settled Florida. In St. Augustine, they built large structures in the Roman style of architecture and public roads, known as the king's roads, which still remain.[11]

During the American Revolutionary War, St. Augustine served as a depot for English troops. The city was also used to hold prisoners of war who were captured by the British. June 1784 marked the end of the British colonial rule in Florida, which had been returned to Spain as result of the Treaty of Paris of 1783. Spain controlled St. Augustine and Florida for nearly forty more years. On July 10th, 1821, Florida was transferred to the United States of America, thus ending the colonial era of St. Augustine.

Just prior to the outbreak of the United States Civil War, Florida became the fourteenth state to secede from the Union, on January 10, 1861. During the war, St. Augustine was captured by Lieutenant S.F. DuPont, and the entire state was "returned" to the United States.[12]

In the twentieth century, the city of St. Augustine has emerged as a tourist destination. The city still has a Spanish ambience. The narrow, twisting streets and old Spanish-style buildings have been retained. The Castillo de San Marcos remains a historic site and a tourist attraction. Most of the streets bear Spanish names. Modern-day St. Augustine, however, is also characterized by skyscrapers, large stores, and spacious hotels. Thus, the city, though retaining and exhibiting its past proudly, keeps moving ahead with history.

BLACKS IN SPANISH FLORIDA

African-Americans played significant roles in Florida's history, yet they remain invisible in the literature. However, the sources for the Black history of Spanish Florida are amazingly rich and varied. The Spanish were meticulous bureaucrats and African-Americans appear everywhere in their records. These records are preserved in the Archive of the Indies in Seville, Spain, the University of Florida's P.K. Yonge Library, and elsewhere.

Black Slaves

Beginning in 1565, Black slaves were brought to Florida to labor for Spaniards. Some of these slaves led lives of unceasing toil and misery. Others lived fairly comfortably in the homes of their Spanish owners.

The royal government was the main employer of slaves in Spanish Florida. Slaves served as auctioneers, town criers, and messengers. They worked in the royal hospital and barracks, and served the military by cutting firewood, maintaining weapons, tending mounts, and providing their music. Royal slaves worked on public construction projects, in the stone quarries, and at lime kilns.

In the countryside, slaves were the cowboys, field hands, and lumberjacks. They also hunted, trapped, fished, and grew food to sustain themselves and the large white community.

Urban slaves were the artisans, domestics, musicians, sailors, and soldiers of St. Augustine. They were included in dowries, bequeathed in wills, traded and exchanged, and even posted as bonds.

In short, slaves were a critical component of both the economic and social structure of Spanish Florida.

Legal and Social Status

What was the legal and social status of African-Americans in the Spanish world? Long before Africans were enslaved by Europeans, slave codes were incorporated into Castilian law by King Alfonso X. When African slaves began to reach Spain in the fifteenth century, these codes were applied to them. As the New World discoveries were considered a kingdom of the Crown of Castile, Spanish laws governed slavery in Florida.

The *Siete Partidas* of King Alfonso held that slavery was *contra razón de natura* (against the laws of nature). Man was a noble and free creation of God. Slavery was an accident of fate and an aberration in nature, not a preordained or perpetual condition.

Unlike slaves belonging to the English, Spanish slaves were never merely chattel property. Spanish legislation specifically granted slaves rights and protections. Slaves had the right to personal security and had legal recourse against a cruel master, including being released from the control of an abuser.

Slaves had the right to hold and transfer property and to initiate legal suits. They had the right of self-purchase and the ability to pursue it.

Spanish tradition encouraged owners to practice charity towards their slaves and to treat them well. Owners were responsible for teaching their slaves the rudiments of the faith, so that they might be admitted to the Church. Before God, masters and slaves were considered brothers-in-Christ. Slaves enjoyed all the sacraments of the Church, including marriage. The sanctity of the family was protected by requirements not to separate family members. Owners often became part of a slave's extended family by serving as godparents at slave marriages and baptisms.

However, the ideal represented in Spanish slave codes cannot be accepted at face value. Some laws were observed. Others were not.

Nor were the Spanish free of racial prejudice. In the New World, Iberian anxieties over religious orthodoxy became a preoccupation with racial purity. African-Americans were assigned to the bottom of the social hierarchy. Blacks and mulattoes, even if free, suffered penalties for having descended from slaves.

Free Blacks

Nevertheless, the emphasis on a slave's humanity and rights, and support for manumission in Spanish slave codes and social practice, made it possible for a significant free Black class to exist in the Spanish world. A few were manumitted by owners. Others were already free when they came to Florida from Cuba or other areas of the Spanish empire.

Another group of slaves became free by astutely manipulating the contest between Britain and Spain.

In 1670, England challenged Spain's claim to exclusive sovereignty in *La Florida* by establishing the colony of Carolina. Soon after, slaves from the English plantations began to seek refuge among the Spanish. The runaways received baptism in the Catholic faith and were welcome additions to Florida's labor and military force. In 1693, the Spanish king freed the converted slaves, "granting liberty to all. . .the men as well as the women. . .so that by their example and by my liberality. . .others will do the same." He cited religious principles, but clearly understood the diplomatic and political implications of his action.

The English complained of the Spanish sanctuary policy, considering it "a flagrant provocation." In fact, slaves continued to seek asylum in Florida. They frequently were aided in their escape by Indians. The Spaniards sent parties of escaped slaves and Indians back to raid Carolina plantations. In turn, frustrated British planters launched an unsuccessful retaliatory raid against St. Augustine in 1728. African-Americans fought bravely in the town's defense.

Francisco Menéndez

The case of Francisco Menéndez illustrates the sometime dilatory nature of Spanish racial justice. Menéndez, a Mandingo born in West Africa, was enslaved and taken to Carolina. He escaped and joined the Yamassee Indian war against the English. Three years later he made his way to St. Augustine in the company of the Yamassee chieftain, Jorge.

In St. Augustine, Menéndez intended to claim the freedom promised by the Spanish Crown, but was betrayed by a non-Christian Indian named Mad Dog and sold back into slavery. Menéndez did not give up. Again and again, he petitioned the Spanish governors and the Bishop of Cuba for his liberty and that of other escaped slaves.

Finally, in 1738, Governor Manuel de Montiano investigated and found for Menéndez and his fellow slaves. He freed the petitioners and established the first free Black town in the present-day United States, *Gracia Real de Santa Teresa de Mose* (commonly known as Fort Mose), about two miles north of St. Augustine. Menéndez, his wife, María, and some thirty-seven other families became homesteaders in Mose. In gratitude the freedmen vowed to be "the most cruel enemies of the British" and to spill their last drop of blood in defense of the Great Crown of Spain and the Holy Faith."

Fort Mose

Mose, strategically located on the major land and water routes to St. Augustine, was a walled fort which enclosed a church, the priest's house, a lookout, a well, and guardhouses. A moat, with vicious Spanish bayonets growing from its top, surrounded the fort.

The villagers lived outside the walls of the fort, near their planted fields. Twenty-two thatched huts, resembling those built by Indians, sheltered at least forty-four men and twenty-three women, according to a village census.

Governor Montiano referred to these people as the "subjects" of Menéndez. Menéndez's character and military skills led the Spaniards to regard him as a natural lord, much like an Indian *cacique.* He commanded the Black militia from 1726 until at least 1763.

The first settlement at Mose was short-lived. In 1740 General James Oglethorpe, the English governor of Georgia, led an attack on St. Augustine. His vastly superior forces overwhelmed Mose. The Blacks retreated to St. Augustine. From there Captain Francisco Menéndez led his military on dangerous reconnaissance missions.

When the time came, they joined in the surprise attack which re-took Mose, devastating the enemy. The governor commended Menéndez's bravery in two letters to the king.

Mose's original structures were destroyed in the fighting. The displaced settlers had to live in St. Augustine until a second Mose was rebuilt in 1752. The new settlement was occupied until the Spanish were forced by treaty to evacuate Florida in 1763.

For twenty years Florida was British.

The Second Spanish Period

After the victories of the Spanish Captain General Gálvez at Pensacola and the American General George Washington at York-town, the Spanish were able to regain control of Florida in 1784. They did their best to re-establish Spanish hegemony and culture as it had been, but this time they found themselves a minority in their own colony. In 1790 Spaniards, including troops and dependents, accounted for only about one-sixth of the total population, making Florida unlike any other Spanish colony in the New World.

During their brief tenure in Florida, the English had established flourishing plantations worked by slaves. Many of these Britishers remained, after swearing loyalty to the Spanish Crown.

The American Revolution forced those loyal to George III to evacuate Charleston and Savannah. Many headed for Florida. Refu-gee planters from the Carolinas and Georgia brought more than 8,000 slaves with them to East Florida.

Some of the slaves took advantage of the situation. Amidst the disorder they escaped. Many of them requested and received relig-ious sanctuary and freedom.

Governor Zéspedes doubted the religious motives of these refu-gees but honored the seventeenth-century sanctuary decree. More than 250 slaves were granted liberty.

Runaway ads placed by their English masters describe a family which sought sanctuary: Prince Witten and his wife, Judy, were born in "Guinea" around 1760. Their children were slave-born in South Carolina. Prince was "negro, six feet, strong built and brawny. . .talkative, with a large mouth." A skilled carpenter, he

risked several escape attempts "to avoid separation from his family.
. . .to which he is much attached." Judy was 5'7". . .a smart, active
wench." Glasgow was about eight years old and a "well-looked boy
of open countenance and obliging disposition." Polly, age six, possessed "lively eyes" and was "gently pitted with small pox."

In St. Augustine, the Wittens found freedom. They underwent
religious instruction, were baptized, and Prince and Judy conse-
crated their twenty-one year union. Prince provided for his family
by doing carpentry. The Wittens acquired a home, had prominent
white neighbors, and even became slave owners themselves.

Prince went on to a heroic career in the free black militia.

Black Militia

Blacks enjoyed a long tradition of military service in Spanish
Florida. The earliest records for Black troops date back to 1683.
Blacks proved to be loyal and fierce warriors against Spain's ene-
mies: Indians, French, English, Georgians, and even the United
States Marines. They had a vested interest in maintaining the sover-
eignty of the government which had freed them.

In 1796 General Jorge Biassou, *Caudillo* of the Black Auxiliaries
of Carlos IV in Santo Domingo, arrived in St. Augustine. One of the
most important leaders of the Haitian revolution, he commanded an
army of 4,000 and outranked the more famous Toussaint L'Ouverture. The Spanish king honored his army with proclamations, med-
als, uniforms, and pensions. But at war's end, he ordered them to
disband and disperse.

Jorge Biassou led the remnants of his "family" into exile in St.
Augustine. Shortly after their arrival, Biassou's brother-in-law and
military successor married the daughter of Prince Witten. Whether
or not it was a whirlwind romance, this enabled the two refugee
groups to combine forces and consolidate their status. Thereafter
many marriage and godparent ties linked their members. Together,
the Biassous and the Wittens served in joint military expeditions on
the northern and southern frontiers of St. Augustine.

Spain Departs

In 1821 Spain ceded Florida to the United States and the Spanish community of St. Augustine was once more evacuated to Cuba. Most African-Americans joined the exodus. Many of those who stayed behind were relegated to the category of chattel.

The Georgians who flooded into the colony had no intention of permitting a propertied and armed free Black class to encourage their slaves' aspirations toward freedom. When they gained legal control of Florida they legislated white supremacy, and opportunities for free Blacks declined.

THE SAINT AUGUSTINE SCHOOL:

THE FIRST INTEGRATED SCHOOL
IN THE UNITED STATES

Two hundred years ago, as our Founding Fathers were drafting our Constitution in Philadelphia in 1787, the first public integrated school in the United States opened its doors in St. Augustine, Florida. A school for white children had been founded in St. Augustine in 1606. It is not known how long this school operated. If it survived, it was probably closed in 1763 at the end of the first Spanish period.[1]

Spanish explorer Juan Ponce de León discovered Florida in 1513. Several other Spanish explorers unsuccessfully attempted to settle Florida in the years that followed. Finally, Pedro de Menéndez de Avilés founded the first permanent settlement in the United States at St. Augustine in 1565. Spain governed Florida from that date to 1763. In 1763, Spain was forced to cede Florida to England in order to regain Havana, which had been captured by the British during the Seven Years' War. In 1783, Spain regained possession of Florida pursuant to the Treaty of Paris, which had also brought independence to the thirteen colonies. Spain and France had fought Great Britain and had provided decisive assistance to the American Colonies. After a twenty-year interlude, the Spanish flag flew over Florida once again.

St. Augustine was in a state of flux as thousands of British subjects made preparations to leave the province. The new Spanish governor, Vicente Manuel de Zéspedes, had arrived from Havana in June 1784 with five hundred soldiers. Two Catholic priests accompanied the new governor to St. Augustine, and soon a third arrived. Two of these priests would lay the foundation of the first integrated public school in the country.

One of them, Father Thomas Hassett, a native of Ireland, was a graduate of the Irish College in Salamanca, Spain. This college had been founded by King Philip II in 1593, as a place where young seminarians could study for the missions in Ireland at royal expense. Many Irish priests were graduated from Salamanca and some went to the Spanish colonies in America. A royal order in 1778 commissioned Father Hassett to Florida to assist the Minorcan colony which had settled in New Smyrna. The Minorcans, as well as some Greeks and Italians, in all 1,400 men, women, and children, had been brought to Florida by Dr. Andrew Turnbull, a wealthy Scottish physician, then living in London. The offer of free land in Florida had encouraged him to establish a settlement near Mosquito Inlet, just south of St. Augustine.

Father Hassett arrived in Havana in April 1779, eager to begin his assignment in Florida. However, three months later, Spain declared war on England, and he could no longer go to Florida. Instead, Father Hassett was sent to Philadelphia to take charge of a school for children. After the war ended in 1784, Father Hassett was sent to St. Augustine as a parish priest.

Like many urban areas in the country today, St. Augustine was a multilingual, multicultural city. It was not unusual to hear six or seven languages and many dialects spoken in the streets of St. Augustine. The diverse population of St. Augustine comprised Spaniards, Minorcans, Greeks, Italians, Swiss, Canary Islanders, Germans, French, Scots, Irish, Americans, and English, in addition to Blacks from different countries, and Indians.[2]

Perhaps in an effort to have a common language that could be understood by all, Father Hassett presented a proposal to the governor, requesting that a school be constructed. In January 1786 a royal order was given from Spain to build one or two schools. At the request of the governor, Father Hassett prepared twenty-six detailed school rules for students and teachers.[3] These rules remained in effect until Spain ceded Florida to the United States on July 10, 1821.

Two teachers were selected, and their appointments were approved by the King of Spain. Father Francisco Traconis, a native of Santiago de Cuba, was chosen first and, thus, had the distinction of being the first teacher of an integrated public school in the United States. Father Traconis was in charge of the primary grades. He received a salary of eight pesos a month above his regular annual salary of three hundred pesos as chaplain of a hospital. José Antonio Iguíñiz, the school's second teacher, was in charge of the upper grades. The school was furnished with benches and desks, and opened in September 1787. Governor Zéspedes summoned the two teachers before him and read them Father Hassett's rules. Together with other historical documents, these rules provide some knowledge of how the St. Augustine school operated.

The school was public and supported by funds from the royal treasury. It was open without charge to all children, including Blacks. Attendance was compulsory for whites and optional for Black children. Teachers were told to treat Black and white children the same. However, Black children were placed apart in seats near the door.

The school was to be open from seven o'clock in the morning until noon, when students were dismissed for dinner. Classes resumed at two o'clock and ended at sunset during the winter and one-half hour before sunset during the summer. Upon arrival, students were required to greet their teacher with respect, hang their hat in the proper place, sit down, bless themselves in the name of the Blessed Trinity, and begin to work.

Attendance was taken at eight o'clock in the morning and at 2:15 in the afternoon. If a student were absent, one or two boys were sent to find the truant. Students had to come with their hair combed and with their face, hands, and feet (if barefoot) clean. It is hard to imagine how barefoot boys would have clean feet, but that was the rule.

As in modern-day Japan, students were responsible for cleaning the school. Teachers rotated the cleaning assignments. When a child had to go to the bathroom, the teacher issued the student a ruler as a pass. A pendulum that hung from the ceiling of the classroom was set in motion by the student as he left the room. He had to return to the classroom while the pendulum was still in motion. Only one student could leave at a time.

Students were told that upon leaving school, they were to go directly home without loitering on the streets. Furthermore, they were to be respectful in greeting adults on the way to and from school.

The rules for the teachers were also very specific. They were admonished to be moderate in punishing students; it was suggested that moral suasion was preferred to corporal punishment. Teachers were asked to learn the character and disposition of each child, and were told to treat each student with impartiality and with love. Teachers were not to be verbally abusive to the students, nor could they criticize the parents of their students. Teachers were told to teach the alphabet, reading, writing, arithmetic, and the catechism of Father Flaure (or similar catechism). Homework was to be assigned in order to prevent students from being idle at home.

Students were to be seated in class according to achievement. The most capable student was to sit in a special seat, and was given the title of *"Emperador."* Every month, students would be tested in all subjects before the parish priest to determine class rank.

Students were also required to participate in a variety of religious observances: Masses, processions, rosaries, and even funerals. Finally, a copy of Father Hassett's regulations was to be kept in the classroom as a reminder of each student's duty to follow the rules at all times. When New Orleans Auxiliary Bishop Cirilo de Barcelona visited the school, he was pleasantly surprised with the quality of education in St. Augustine, especially because neither Louisiana nor West Florida had schools.

An exact record of the number of students attending the St. Augustine school does not exist. One can extrapolate, however, from a census that Father Hassett conducted in 1786. He found that there were 940 people living in the community, excluding the soldiers in the garrison. Father Hassett divided the population into four groups. The first, composed of foreigners, for the most part British and American, numbered 85. They owned 126 slaves. The second group were the Minorcans, although a few Greeks and Italians were included among them. These were the survivors of Turnbull's New Smyrna Colony who had come to St. Augustine after enduring great hardships in their original settlement. There were 469 "Minorcans," and attached to them were 70 blacks, most of whom were probably slaves. He designated the third group *"Floridanos."* These individuals (fifty in number) had lived in Florida prior to 1763, during the first Spanish period. Some had remained during the twenty years of British rule in St. Augustine; others had gone to Cuba as "exiles," returning to their former home after the Spanish regained control. With them were 82 blacks: some slaves, some freemen. The fourth group consisted of 46 Spaniards, with 12 slaves.

The total population of St. Augustine (excluding the soldiers) was, thus, 940: 650 whites and 290 blacks. There were 69 boys and 74 girls, ages seven to fifteen. It is believed that the school admitted boys only. During this period some boys were employed as apprentices at the age of fourteen. We can therefore assume that the number of students was less than the number of school-aged boys (69 white plus an unknown number of black boys).

Very little is now known about the Cuban-born priest, Father Traconis. He accepted the assignment at St. Augustine hoping to impress his superiors and thereby obtain a sinecure in the cathedral of Havana. Father Traconis was also in charge of the hospital. It is a matter of record that he objected to the rule requiring teachers to attend rosary services at night because he felt that it conflicted with his duties at the hospital. Father Hassett, however, refused to excuse Father Traconis from this obligation. Instead, he submitted the matter to the governor. Poor in health and working long hours at school and hospital, Father Traconis had reason to complain. As chaplain of the hospital, he had to visit patients and provide sacraments. He also had to be present whenever a terminally ill patient was nearing death.

Father Traconis repeatedly asked to be relieved of his assignment at St. Augustine, but the governor refused. He was finally permitted to leave in 1791, after four years of service. The second teacher, José Iguíñiz, left after ten years to become auditor of war. The parents of the students complained after the teachers were gone, and the governor brought the matter to the attention of the court in Madrid. A substitute teacher, Dimas Cortés, was then hired; yet, when Rafael Saavedra y Espinosa, the second teacher, resigned along with Cortés, the school temporarily closed.

In 1797 a layman, José Monasterio, was hired at a salary of eight pesos monthly for both the primary and the grammar school. He soon asked for an increase of seven additional pesos per month. Another teacher, Juan Nepomuceno Gómez, was hired in Havana in 1799.

One of the greatest difficulties in operating the St. Augustine school, as well as dealing with other public matters in this small frontier post, was the rigidity of control of the Spanish administrative system. The refusal to delegate detail work to subordinate officials complicated and compounded problems. On one occasion, in order to hire a new teacher, letters were sent to the Spanish court, the Archbishops of Seville and Zaragossa, and the rector of the Irish College of Salamanca.[5] The delays in communication and the slow pace of decision-making in the court of Spain hampered the functioning of the school.

Nevertheless, the St. Augustine school of 1787-1821 was ahead of its time in its rules and regulations. In other southern States during that period, any form of education was denied by law to Blacks. Public support for education and the acceptance of Black and white students under one roof made the St. Augustine school unique. Today, most Americans, even in the state of Florida, are unaware of the important contribution of the Spanish in St. Augustine in laying the foundation for integrated public schooling in the United States.

REGULATIONS AND INSTRUCTIONS FOR THE SCHOOLS OF ST. AUGUSTINE

Regulations and instructions to be observed in the government and administration of the schools which are to be established by order of His Majesty and at his expense in the city of St. Augustine, East Florida, the said regulations and instructions being prepared in accordance with the Royal will and at the suggestion of Señor Don Vicente Manuel de Zéspedes, Brigadier of the Royal Armies and Commandant General of the aforementioned City and Province, and of Don Thomas Hassett, Parish Priest, Vicar, and Ecclesiastical Judge of the same City and Province. Year of 1786.

The rules were:

1. In accordance with the devout intentions of his Majesty, no one shall be qualified to teach except upon examination and approval of the ecclesiastical and civil superiors of the province and every teacher shall be bound to observe these rules and such other orders and resolutions or any part of them, as the said superiors may see fit to communicate from time to time in the interest of the fullest advancement of the pupils.

2. The schools shall be designated as first and second. Children who are beginners and others who are more advanced, but not yet ready to begin writing, shall alone be admitted to the first school. When they are ready to begin writing they shall pass from the first to the second school where they shall be taught writing and arithmetic, while being perfected in reading, etc. Only children of this higher grade shall be admitted to the second school unless the superior authority determines otherwise.

3. His Majesty having assigned to the teachers an income sufficient for their decent maintenance, no one of them shall demand of the parents any recompense whatever for the instruction of their children.

4. Every year at Easter the teachers shall prepare a list of the children based on the parish register and, informed of the place of residence, ages, etc. shall request the parents to send their children to school. If this request does not have the desired effect, whether by reason of the culpable neglect of the

parents or the indolence and indifference of the children themselves, the teachers shall report to the parish priest, who will determine the just and proper procedure in the matter. The teacher shall make like reports in the cases of pupils kept away from school as a result of idle complaints made by their parents.

5. Throughout the year the schools shall be opened at seven o'clock in the morning and at two in the afternoon. At no time shall the pupils be dismissed in the morning before twelve o'clock, nor in the afternoon in winter before sunset. In the rest of the year the dismissal in the afternoon may be a half hour before sunset.

6. As each pupil enters school in the morning and in the afternoon he shall greet with proper courtesy first his teacher and then his fellow pupils. He shall then hang up his hat in the (proper) place and then seat himself in all modesty. After blessing himself in the name of the Blessed Trinity, he shall take up the book with which his study is to begin.

7. Each teacher shall keep in the school a list of pupils under his instruction from which, every day at eight o'clock in the morning and a quarter past two in the afternoon, he shall call the roll, designating each pupil by both his christian and his family name. In case anyone fails to answer, the teacher shall immediately send one or two of the boys to the home of the parents to learn the cause of his absence and if necessary bring him to school. If the information obtained warrants it, the teacher shall apply appropriate punishment to the delinquent.

8. In reproving and punishing the pupils, the teacher shall endeavor to be moderate; and as for the same moral suasion is better than corporal punishment, the teacher shall take special care to learn the character and disposition of each child. In the case of such children the teacher shall not break out into imprecations or epithets, much less throw in their faces the faults of their parents or relatives, nor permit them under any circumstances to talk to one another in this manner in the school or out of it. Each and all should be treated impartially as faithful christians worthy of love and charity.

9. The children shall present themselves in their respective schools mornings and afternoons with all possible cleanliness, with their hair combed and with their faces, hands and feet (if they come barefoot) clean. The teachers shall not permit children in the school with contagious diseases, such as the itch and other diseases of like nature, the parents being first informed in order that they may not be offended at having their children kept out of school while they are being cured.

10. The school rooms shall be swept at least once a week by the pupils themselves, and the teacher shall appoint a sufficient number of pupils for this purpose, treating all alike beginning with the highest class and continuing to the lowest so that each class in turn shall fulfill this obligation.

11. No pupil shall leave the classroom except when necessity demands without the express permission of the teacher; and in order that not more than one shall go out at a time, the teacher shall deliver a ruler which he shall have on his desk for the purpose, to the one being excused, and a second permission shall not be given until the said ruler is returned. The length of the Pupil's absence shall be measured by the movement of a pendulum hung from the ceiling of the classroon, which pendulum the pupil himself will put in motion at the time of his going out, the teacher taking note whether the pendulum is still in motion when the ruler is returned.

12. The schools shall be divided according to the capacity and advancement of the pupils, by numbers and separate seats into distinct classes, and to the first or most capable of each class shall be given some title, reserving for the first of the highest class the title of Emperor of the whole school, and these titles shall prevail over others more striking can be found.

13. At the beginning of every month there shall be a general examination before the parish priest and the teachers to determine the advancement the pupils may have made during the previous month in writing, reading, arithmetic, Christian doctrine, etc., and as a reward of merit for the advancement shown in the examination when he shall be awarded it again,

provided no one excels him in merit. In this latter case he shall descend to occupy the place corresponding to his merit.

14. From pupils studying the alphabet, the syllabary, and reading, the teacher shall hear four lessons a day, two in the morning and two in the afternoon. The teacher shall instruct these pupils at the same time, morning and afternoon, in Christian doctrine and prayers and litanies. He shall endeavor (by his own efforts and not those of some other person) with consummate care and attention to inculcate a clear and distinct pronunciation and understanding in their reading, requiring the commas, semicolons, etc., to be observed. The teacher of the second school shall proceed by the same method in the teaching of writing with the sole difference that the pupils in this school shall write only two exercises a day. The teacher shall instruct the pupils in the correct position of the hand and how to hold the pen; and after the exercises are finished, he shall point out the faults and reprove the pupils for making them.

15. Pupils in arithmetic or counting shall solve two problems a day, write one or two exercises, read two lessons and receive instructions in Christian doctrine once in the afternoon; and the teacher shall never allow his pupils to pass on to new matter until the old is thoroughly learned. It shall be the duty of the teacher to correct and reprove as provided in the rule immediately preceding.

16. The teacher of the second school shall require his pupils, as they advance, to memorize the tables of arithmetic; in order that this may not interfere with other tasks in the school, the pupils may take the tables home and learn them at night, reciting them to the teacher the next morning; and provided the pupils of reading are not occupied with matters of this sort the teachers may assign in the afternoon to each one according to his capacity, a portion of the historical catechism of Father Flaure, or of some other author, to be memorized at night, thus preventing the pupils from being idle at home.

17. The teachers shall instruct their pupils how to assist at Mass, and every Saturday night and on the eve of the other feasts of the year when there is to be a congregation in the church, they shall name by turns two of their pupils to assist the sacristan in the conduct of divine services.

18. On nights when the Procession of the Rosary leaves the parish church and passes through the streets, the teachers shall attend with their pupils, no exception being allowed and no excuse being valid. The teachers shall take care that the pupils comport themselves with proper modesty and devotion.

19. The teachers shall attend with their pupils the Salve on Saturdays, the Vespers of Sundays, and other principal days, and at all the services of the church when there is preaching of the Gospel.

20. Whenever God may be pleased to call to judgment any of the children, the teachers shall go with their pupils in procession to the funeral, and if necessary the remains shall be borne by four of the pupils to the burial place.

21. During each of the four Ember Seasons of the year, all pupils of seven years of age and above, shall go to make confession in the presence of their teachers, to which and the teachers shall notify their pupils a day or two beforehand, in order that they may examine their consciences. The teacher shall instruct the pupils in a manner appropriate to their age, how they should prepare themselves, the method they would observe to avoid, by negligence or other culpable reasons, omitting sins that ought be confessed, and the teachers should inform the pupils also of the necessity of repentance to make the sacrament valid, etc. The teachers shall give these same instructions to the pupils who are of an age to receive the Holy Sacrament of the Eucharist; and in order that everything may be done with system, the pupils shall be divided into three equal divisions and each teacher shall assign one division of his school for each of the ember days, in order that by this means the pupils may be attended to with dispatch in the church and sent back promptly to school.

22. The teacher shall endeavor to obtain the most instructive books to be read by their pupils. They shall not permit any other language than Spanish to be spoken in the school.

23. The pupils shall ask with most profound humility that the blessings of their parents accompany them on their way to and from school, and whenever they meet any of their elders in the street, they should salute them with proper courtesy.

24. On leaving school the pupils shall go directly home without loitering, or shouting or committing mischievous pranks in the streets.

25. If any negroes or mulattoes should attend the schools, they shall be placed near the door in seats apart; but in matters of instruction, spiritual and temporal, the teachers shall do to them the same justice as to all the rest.

26. The teachers shall have in their respective schools a copy of these regulations in order that everyone may be promptly informed of their provisions and in order that they may be invariably and duly observed as his Majesty desires.

Library of Congress, East Florida Papers, 41 B 4, Reglas y Instrucións. q. se deben observar p. el Gobierno y Dirección de las Escuelas que se van a Establecer por orden y a cuenta de S.M. en esta Ciudad de S. Agustín de la Florida Oriental, formadas con arreglo a dha. orn. ya instancias de S.S. el S. D. Vicente Manuel de Zéspedes, Brigadier de los R. Ex. Gov. Com. de dha. Plaza y Prov. por D. Thomas Hassett, Cura Beneficiado, Vicario y Juez Ec. de Esta referida Ciudad y Provincia. . .Año de 1786. A copy of these regulations may be found in Joseph B. Lockey, "Public Education in Spanish St. Augustine," Florida Historical Society Quarterly, XV (1937), 147-168, and in Michael Curley, Church and State in the Spanish Floridas (1783-1822), Washington, D.C. 1940, 78-82.

SEPHARDIC ROOTS IN AMERICAN HISTORY

The first Jewish settlers arrived at what is now New York Harbor aboard the *St. Charles*, later nicknamed the "Jewish Mayflower." The twenty-three immigrants had fled Brazil where they feared Portuguese persecution. On their return voyage to Holland, they were the victims of a storm and then of pirates. A French vessel, the *Saint Charles*, rescued them and brought them safely to the colony of New Amsterdam on the tip of Manhattan. It was 1654, a few days before the Jewish New Year, "Rosh Hashana."

More than 150 years after the expulsion edict of Ferdinand and Isabella, these oldest of Jewish settlers in America were still fleeing the Inquisition, a part of the Sephardic ("Spanish" in Hebrew) diaspora. They viewed themselves as a remnant of the people of Israel, alone in a distant land; and as such, they called their congregation of twenty-three members of Spanish and Portuguese origin, Sheraith Israel, "remnant of Israel."[1] They prayed following the Sephardic rites, just as generations before them had done in the Iberian Peninsula. Sheraith Israel provided more than a synagogue; it was a communal center. The original members were soon joined by other settlers. Together they constituted about half of the estimated 2,000 Jews living in the American colonies.[2]

Sephardics grew and prospered within the scheme of American life, yet they retained a close link with ancestral traditions. Sheraith Israel members, it has been said, were willing to make any sacrifice to provide Jewish education for their children, kosher meats for the community, and welfare for the needy.

Families intermarried and they all became interrelated. Abraham de Lucena who arrived in 1655, is a common ancestor of families such as the Nathans and the Hendricks. It was the Nathan, the Hendricks, the Seixas, the Gomez, and other families who became "connected," and they all contributed men of stature to diverse areas of American life. Abraham de Lucena had come from Holland; as an escapee from the Spanish Inquisition, he spoke Spanish, not Dutch. He started out by trading with the Indians for pelts, and soon became one of New York's most important fur merchants.[3] Among his more prominent descendants are New York State Justice Edgar J. Nathan, Jr., who was also Manhattan borough president under Mayor La Guardia, and U.S. Supreme Court Justice Benjamin Nathan Cardozo. Mendes Seixas Nathan was a banker who helped draw up the constitution of the New York Stock Exchange. The founder of Barnard College, Annie Nathan Meyer, was a granddaughter of Isaac Mendes Seixas Nathan. And then "the patriot rabbi," Gershom Mendes Seixas, also related, is said to have closed his synagogue in New York and moved the Congregation to Philadelphia "rather than ask his flock to pray for George III.[4] On July 8, 1788, when Philadelphia celebrated the ratification of the new Constitution by the requisite number of states, this rabbi, leader of the Congregation Mikveh Israel in Philadelphia, marched along with the Christian clergymen. When it came time for refreshments after the march, there was a kosher table set out for the Jewish paraders.[5]

Another noteworthy descendant of the Nathan family is Emma Lazarus, who wrote the poem which is engraved on the base of the Statue of Liberty:

> Give me your tired, your poor,
> Your huddled masses yearning to breathe free,
> The wretched refuse of your teeming shore.
> Send these, the homeless, tempest-tost to me.
> I lift my lamp beside the golden door.

The Hendricks — Henriques in Spain — are credited with founding the first copper-rolling mill in the United States. Before the eighteenth and nineteenth centuries, copper, "the poor man's metal," was abundant, easily mined, easily milled, and used for the cheapest coins, kitchen pots, and utensils. The time came when copper was needed in New England and in the West Indies for the bottoms of huge stills that turned out hundreds of thousands of gallons of rum. A few years after Harmon Hendricks founded his enterprise, most of the rum produced in America came from stills made of Hendricks copper. In the process, the Hendricks became "America's earliest millionaires, in fact, before there was such a word."[6]

Daniel Gomez was the first to realize how native Indians could be effective in the fur business as trappers and skinners. In 1710 he began buying land in what seemed to be wilderness. He was able to buy inexpensively land that nobody else wanted on the west bank of the Hudson River. He soon acquired 2,500 acres where he built a massive stone fortress. It was there that Indians gathered to negotiate prices on mink, beaver, and black fox, among other pelts. Gomez's fort became known as "the Jew's house," and the stream, once navigable, that ran by his home was until recently designated on local maps as "Jew's Creek." When the Naturalization Act was passed, Daniel Gomez was one of the first to take advantage of it and become a voter.[7]

One of the twenty-three aboard the *Saint Charles*, Asser Levy, built a successful slaughterhouse and established a tavern as well, known as Levy's Tavern, where he was known to have extended credit as well as cordiality to his customers. When he teamed up with a non-Jewish partner, in the first partnership of its kind on record, Mr. Levy was granted special permission not to kill hogs, since this was forbidden by his religion. Asser Levy is known to have lent the Lutherans enough money to build their first church in America. He then supported it by not charging rent for the use of the land (which he owned) on which the church was built. A relative of his, Moses Levy, also a philanthropist, was one of the seven Jews who contributed to a fund to build a steeple for the original Trinity Church, today rebuilt and a Wall Street landmark.[8] Of the Levys, Moses Levy is the one remembered for having turned down an appointment as U.S. Attorney General by President Thomas Jefferson.[9]

Isaac Touro, the first of the Touro family to arrive in America, came to Newport by way of the West Indies. He was among those who drew up the plans for Newport's famous synagogue. This synagogue has a secret escape tunnel, leading from the desk where the Torah scrolls are laid for reading through the basement to the courtyard.[10] The quaint architectural detail is a reminder of the fear of persecution and the need for secrecy that were a part of Jewish life in the Spanish middle ages. After 100 years of holding services in the homes of members, the Newport Congregation requested financial assistance from Sheraith Israel in New York so that they could build a synagogue. The resulting contribution represented one-tenth of the total construction cost.[11]

Judah Touro, Isaac's son, spent his life in New Orleans. He became a legend among Jewish philanthropists after his death because he left $483,000 to charities in his will. In Boston, the Touro name is associated with Massachusetts General Hospital, the Asylum for Indigent Boys, and the Female Orphan Asylum, among others. To New Orleans, he left funds to combat yellow fever — endemic in those days — and for a hospital, the Touro Infirmary, which was established to help fight the disease. For the City of Newport, funds were donated to create a public area around the Newport Tower, saving it from demolition. That plot is now known as Touro Park. Judah Touro's benefactions to Christian causes are remembered. When the First Congregational Church of New Orleans was having financial difficulty and risked demolition, Judah Touro bought the church for $20,000 and then gave the building back to the congregation.[12]

Some say that Haym Salomon actually "financed the American Revolution," by providing George Washington with a large personal loan at a crucial moment.[13] It is a fact that, at a time when Washington's men would fight no longer without wages, a messenger on horseback was sent at night to Philadelphia with instructions to obtain $400,000 from Haym Salomon. When the message arrived, Salomon was at the synagogue. He talked to some friends and raised the immense sum needed to pay Washington's troops. According to some accounts, Haym Salomon himself contributed $240,000 of the money.[14]

It is known that he also extended personal loans to many prominent individuals of the Revolution, as well as to members of the Continental Congress. Presidents Thomas Jefferson, James Madison, and James Monroe all borrowed from Salomon when they needed cash.[15] Madison's records attest to Salomon's generosity — the "Jewish financier" often lent him money without requesting a note or charging him interest.[16] Today a statue stands in Chicago, depicting Haym Salomon between George Washington and Robert Morris.

Francis Salvador is another Sephardic Jew worthy of mention. He was the first Jew to die fighting in the American Revolution. He also fought in many of the battles against the Indians. History tells us that he saved the life of his comrade-in-arms Hugh Williamson, a delegate from North Carolina, when he raced to warn him that the British fleet was nearing Charleston. John Rutledge, a delegate from South Carolina, thought so highly of Salvador that he appointed him to the commission designated to establish the South Carolina Provincial Congress of 1775.[17]

Among the Sephardics involved in the judicial system, Benjamin Cardozo is the most admired. With "clarity of thinking" and "lucidity of judgment," Cardozo brought a particular and individualistic style with him to American justice. Armed with a photographic memory that allowed him to cite cases and chapters without looking them up in the law books, he was an early champion of the little man against the giant corporation. He was also one of the first to spell out that the concepts of "moral wrong" and "legal wrong" are not interchangeable. He was the type of jurist who attempted to inject fairness into laws which had been written as too vague or too broad (as when he ruled in favor of a man fatally injured while working after hours). Yet despite his remarkable contributions to the development of American jurisprudence, Cardozo remained an exceedingly modest man who often expressed a low opinion of himself.[18]

Some American Sephardics had German-sounding names, a result of having fled from Spain first to Germany, before reaching the United States. Among them, Isaac Franks deserves mention. George Washington rented Franks's house in the Germantown section of Philadelphia on November 17, 1793 for himself and his troops, as protection against a yellow fever epidemic.[19]

Colonel Isaac Franks, only sixteen when he enlisted, was called the "boy hero of the Revolution." Once, captured by the British, he managed to escape across the Hudson River.[20] He rose in the ranks until he was attached to headquarters as General George Washington's aide-de-camp. By 1793, when Washington was a guest in his home, Isaac Franks was a successful merchant and businessman.

Another member of the family, Colonel David Salisbury Franks, was Washington's emissary to Paris, carrying dispatches between Washington and Ambassador Benjamin Franklin. David Franks was also the individual who delivered copies of the 1784 peace treaty with England to the American embassies in Europe.[21]

The Gratzes were another family that had escaped the Spanish Inquisition by the German route, changing the name which originally may have been "Gracia" or "Garcia."[22] The Gratzes became prominent traders and land speculators,[23] and in more recent generations, became connected through marriage with the non-Jewish Rockefeller family.

That was not the case for Rebecca Gratz. Her love for a Christian man left her unmarried, despite beauty and kindness that impressed all who met her. She devoted her life, instead, to good deeds. She founded the Philadelphia Orphan Society in 1815, became Secretary of the Female Association for the Relief of Women and Children in Reduced Circumstances, and founded as well, the first Hebrew Sunday School Society. Thomas Sully, who painted her portrait, said that he had

> never seen a more striking Hebraic face. The easy pose, suggestive of perfect health, the delicately turned neck and shoulders with the firmly poised head and its profusion of dark, curling hair, large, clear, black eyes, the contour of the face, the fine white skin, the expressive mouth and firmly chiselled nose, with its

strength of character, left no doubt as to the race from which she had sprung.[24]

The man she had loved had died young after an unhappy marriage. Her presence shocked many of those who attended his funeral and saw her place a small object under the coffin. It was a portrait of herself with three white roses, crossed to form a six-point star. She may have been, as some claim, the model Sir Walter Scott used in the characterization of Rebecca in *Ivanhoe*.[25]

Sephardic Jews from other countries have since joined the community in America. Latin American Sephardics (among them, Cubans) and Ashkenazi Jews who have lived in Hispanic countries for generations are welcome additions to this community. *Ladino*, the language of medieval Spain spoken by Sephardim, was passed down through generations as a link to their Spanish heritage. The Sephardic newspaper, *La vara*, was published in New York until 1947. In its pages, news, commentaries, ads, and poems were written in Spanish scripted in Hebrew characters.

As to whether the twenty-three Jews aboard the *Saint Charles* were the first Sephardim to arrive in the New World, there may be room for some speculation. The Sephardic scholar Sol Beton has suggested the possibility that Christopher Columbus was of Jewish descent — that his family had fled Catalonia after a pogrom in 1390. Beton points to Columbus's fluent Spanish which, however, reflected some of the archaisms peculiar to the preceding century. It is also known that in a letter to his son Diego, the Jewish letter "beth" and "hai" appear in one of the top corners of the stationery, the initials for "Baruch Hashem," a benediction which was common practice in correspondence among Jews.[26] Other sources suggest that Columbus was the son of Spanish Jewish parents living in Genoa.[27] And if Columbus himself was not Sephardic, he certainly surrounded himself with many who were and who helped him in his efforts. It is known that Columbus used Judah Cresque's sailing charts in order to prepare for his voyage. Cresque was known as the "map Jew," the head of the Portuguese School of Navigation in Lisbon. From Abraham Ben Zacuto, a Jewish professor at the University of Salamanca, came the almanacs and astronomical tables. The bankers who financed the expedition were all Jews, first Isaac Abravanel, then Luis de Santangel, Gabriel Sanchez, and Abraham Senior, and to them, not to Ferdinand and Isabella, was Columbus's first word back to Spain.[28]

Columbus's crew was loaded with Marranos (crypto-Jews who had only converted to appease the Inquisition, but who never abandoned their heritage). Aboard the *Santa María*, both Mestre Bernal, the physician, and Marco, the ship's surgeon, were Jews. The official interpreter of the expedition, Luis de Torres, had been brought along since they expected to reach the Orient. De Torres was the first man ashore in the New World.[29]

Many have been the successes and the contributions in America, with a new golden era for Sephardic Jews, comparable perhaps to the one enjoyed by their ancestors. No wonder Steven Birmingham says in his work, *The Grandees*, that "Jews can be said to have found their greatest successes and their fullest freedoms within the context of the two civilizations of modern America and medieval Spain."[30] When, in 1924, General Miguel Primo de Rivera issued an edict in Spain that special permission be granted for Jews to return to Spain, and a letter of invitation was written by Dr. Angel Pulido Fernández to the Sephardic student society, "*Esperanza*," directed to Jews "who bear the illustrious Spanish names, who speak the Castilian language," only a few Sephardim were interested in regaining Spanish nationality.[31] By then, they were looking far across lands and seas, some toward their ancient Palestinian homeland that would later become Israel, and others, perhaps, to the community their brothers had built in America.

SPAIN AND HISPANIC AMERICA:
FORGOTTEN ALLIES OF THE
AMERICAN REVOLUTION

Americans who have studied United States history are generally aware of France's role in the American Revolution. Textbooks describe the contributions of the French Marquis de Lafayette, Count de Rochambeau, and Admiral de Grasse. The assistance of other Europeans, Casimir Pulaski and Thaddeus Kosciusko of Poland and the German Baron von Steuben, for example, is often noted. You will search textbooks in vain, however, for recognition of the valuable service Spain and its colonies rendered to the thirteen colonies. During this period, Spain and Hispanic outposts from Venezuela to California generously committed money, matériel, and naval and military forces. Many Hispanics made the ultimate sacrifice, fighting and dying in battles in the Mississippi Valley and along the Gulf of Mexico. Textbooks refer to scores of major and lesser battles, but one can find no reference to the many battles fought by soldiers from Spain, Cuba, Mexico, Puerto Rico, Dominican Republic, and Venezuela. In the words of Miami banker Luis Botifol, it is a "conspiracy of silence."

There are many possible explanations for these glaring historical omissions. One reason may be that American historians have inherited the traditional British dislike of Spain. It may stem from the fact that Spain declared war on Great Britain in June 1779 as an ally of France but not of America. The United States invasion of Florida, the Texas conflict and the war against Mexico and Spain during the nineteenth century may account for the biased reporting. One wonders if the "Black Legend," propagated by Great Britain to discredit Spain at the peak of its glory in the sixteenth century, persists to the present. Or it may just be a case of simple historical neglect. Regardless of the reason, this historical injustice must be corrected.

Hispanics are entitled to know that their ancestors contributed to the establishment and growth of the first democracy in the modern world. This is especially true for the students attending schools and institutions of higher learning. This knowledge can serve to increase the self-esteem and cultural pride of Hispanic students, and give them a better appreciation of their heritage. It may also increase their love for the American institutions which their ancestors helped to create.

Hispanic Aid Considered Vital

It was enormously difficult in 1776 for the thirteen colonies to wage a successful war against Great Britain, the strongest naval and military power in the world. American colonists themselves were not unified in their willingness to fight for independence. Historians estimate that only one-third of the American colonists wanted independence, while another third actively opposed it and the rest remained neutral. Without the considerable diplomatic, financial, naval, and military support of France, Spain, and to a lesser degree, the Netherlands, the American Revolution may have foundered.

Even after the entry of France into the war, it is worth noting that General George Washington believed Spanish assistance was critical to success. In a letter to Robert Morris dated October 4, 1778, General Washington stated, "If the Spaniards would but join their fleets to those of France, and commence hostilities, my doubts would all subside. . . . Without it, I fear the British Navy has too much in its power to counteract the schemes of France. . . ." To the President of Congress, the General wrote on November 11, 1778, "The English are now greatly superior to the French by sea in America; and will from every appearance continue so unless Spain interpose. . . ." To Henry Laurens, Washington wrote on November 14, 1778, "The truth of the position will entirely depend on naval events. If France and Spain should unite and obtain a decided superiority by sea, a reunion with England would avail very little. . ." After Washington received the news of the Spanish declaration of war against Great Britain, he wrote on September 3, 1779 to John Sullivan, "I have the pleasure to inform you that Spain has at length taken a decisive part. . . . It is hoped that this formidable junction of the House of Bourbon will not fail of establishing the Independence of America in a short time. . . ."[1]

Textbooks fail to explain adequately the importance of foreign assistance, both military and monetary, to the War of Independence. It is as if acknowledging foreign assistance would somehow detract from the courage and sacrifices of American troops during the Revolution and the superb leadership of General Washington.

Financial Assistance to the American Revolution

Prior to the Declaration of Independence in 1776, the Spanish Ambassador to France, the Count of Aranda, met with the French Minister of Foreign Affairs, the Count of Vergennes, to discuss how each nation could assist the American colonies. Louis XVI, then King of France, was a nephew of Carlos III, the King of Spain. Both monarchs were bound by the Bourbon Family Pact and viewed the rebellion as an opportunity to punish their ancient adversary, Great Britain.

France and Spain had suffered great losses during the Seven Years' War, also called the French and Indian War. From France, Great Britain had won Canada and all the land east of the Mississippi River, excluding the city of New Orleans. Spain had lost Havana to England, and was forced to cede Florida to regain the Cuban capital. No longer interested in keeping Louisiana, France ceded it to Spain. Now both nations saw a unique opportunity, although intervention was not without certain risks. If Spain were on the victorious side, an independent United States would set an undesirable precedent for Spain's vast colonial empire in North, Central, and South America. If defeated, Spain could lose more territory in Europe or the New World. Weighing in favor of entry was the desire of King Carlos III to regain Gibraltar, the island of Minorca, Florida, and perhaps even Jamaica which had been lost to England in previous wars. He hoped that by entering the war he might accomplish all this. Under the reign of Carlos III, Spain was experiencing a renaissance in all areas. Carlos III, one of the greatest monarchs in Spanish history, prepared his country well for the war against Great Britain.

The first tangible assistance from France and Spain was a gift of two million *livres tournois* (the tournois pound was a French currency equivalent to four *reales de vellón*), one million from each nation, to the thirteen colonies. Soon afterward, according to a letter from the Spanish ambassador in Paris to the Spanish Prime Minister, the following items were delivered to the Americans: 216 brass cannons, 209 gun-carriages, 27 mortars, 29 couplings, 12,826 shells, 51,134 bullets, 300,000 boxes of gunpowder, 30,000 guns with bayonets, 4,000 tents, and 30,000 suits.[2]

A Spanish corporation, Rodríguez, Hortalez y Cía., was formed to handle the shipments. This corporation also financed the voyages of Baron von Steuben and General Lafayette, both of whom would render invaluable services to General Washington.

Wishing to obtain yet more help from Spain, Benjamin Franklin dispatched Arthur Lee to Spain. In a meeting at Burgos on March 1, 1777, Lee gave the Marquis of Grimaldi a list of needed supplies. Acting as interpreter at the meeting was Diego de Gardoqui, a wealthy Bilbao banker. Lee received 50,000 gold pesos from Spain at once, in April 81,000 tournois pounds, and in June another 100,000.[3] Through Gardoqui and Sons Corporation, Spain continued to help the American colonies until the end of the war. Diego de Gardoqui later served as Spain's first ambassador to the United States from 1785 to 1789.

The Spanish colonies also provided financial assistance to the Americans. For example, Louisiana governors Luis de Unzaga and Bernardo de Gálvez provided gunpowder, guns, food, medicine, and other vital supplies to General Charles Lee, second-in-command under General Washington and to General George Rogers Clark. The Spanish aid was critical to the Continental Army and the successful campaign of General Clark in the Ohio Valley.

Fray Junípero Serra, the founder of the Spanish missions in California, requested that each Spaniard in California contribute two pesos and each Indian one peso. The proceeds of the collection were sent to French General Rochambeau who was leading an army on American soil.

In the spring of 1781, Washington and Rochambeau were desperate for money to buy food, weapons, clothing, and supplies, and to pay their soldiers' salaries in arrears. Rochambeau wrote a series of letters to Admiral de Grasse whose fleet had recently arrived in Santo Domingo. He informed de Grasse that the Americans were at the end of their resources and funds to launch an attack against the British. De Grasse was unable to raise that considerable sum in the Colony of Santo Domingo, so he sent three of his best frigates, among them the *Aigrette* under Saint-Simon, to Havana. Upon arrival, Saint-Simon contacted the Governor of Cuba, Juan Manuel de Cagigal, and his aide-de-camp, Francisco de Miranda.

Historians differ as to how the money was collected in Havana. Some say that Cagigal and Miranda persuaded the ladies of Havana to donate their jewelry. Other historians, James A. Lewis for example, state that this romantic version of events is untrue. In an article published in *Americas*, in July 1980, Lewis claims that the origin of the legend was an anonymous pamphlet, published at the end of the war, regarding Admiral de Grasse and Francisco de Miranda's testimony during his trial for treason in revolutionary France. According to Lewis and the historian Reparaz, the unsung hero was a Spaniard named Francisco de Saavedra. Arriving in Havana aboard the *Aigrette* on August 15, 1781, Saavedra asked Governor Cagigal and other officials to appeal to the public for an emergency loan. The Spanish officials obtained the loan in just six hours. Twenty-six individuals, among them Barbara Santa Cruz, Marquesa de Cárdenas, lent 4,520,000 reales. The money was repaid in a month or two from a shipment that came from Mexico.[4]

All historians agree that the treasure brought to America by Admiral de Grasse helped finance the Yorktown campaign which ended with the surrender of the British troops on October 31, 1781. The Cuban financial assistance proved crucial. American historian

Stephen Bonsal writes, "the million that was supplied Saint-Simon to pay the troops by the ladies of Havana, may with truth, be regarded as the bottom dollars upon which the edifice of American independence was erected."[5]

Quite apart from financial aid, Havana assisted the American patriots in other significant ways. Spain permitted American privateers to use her own and her colonies' ports. During the conflict, American ships found a safe harbor, and were repaired and supplied at no cost at the shipyards, in Havana. For example, the small fleet of seven ships of Alexander Gillon from South Carolina was repaired, armed, and given food and other supplies in 1778 at a cost of 64,424 pesos. Juan de Miralles, the future Spanish agent in the colonies, assumed financial responsibility for the repairs of Gillon's ships.[6] The "Arsenal de la Habana" shipyards were the best in the world. Naval and merchant ships of all sizes were built and repaired there from 1724 to 1796.[7]

The total financial contribution by Spain and her colonies is difficult to calculate. At the beginning, aid was covert. Financial assistance came from various countries in Europe, as well as from Louisiana, California, Mexico, and Cuba. From Spain alone, 7,944,806 reales and sixteen maravedís vellín were contributed during 1776, 1777, and 1778.[8] Without the significant financial assistance of Spain, and also of France, it would have been very difficult, if not impossible, for George Washington to defeat the British Army.

The Diplomatic Mission of Juan de Miralles and Francisco Rendón

Although Spain did not officially recognize the independence of the United States until after the war, and therefore the countries were not formal "allies," it did send two diplomatic representatives to the thirteen colonies. The Council of the Indies, headed by Minister José de Gálvez, uncle of Bernardo de Gálvez, accepted the recommendation of Diego José Navarro, captain general of Cuba, and named the Havana merchant Juan de Miralles the first diplomat to the colonies.

Born in 1715 in Petrel, Province of Alicante, Spain, Juan de Miralles arrived in Cuba at a young age. He later married María Josefa Eligio de la Puente, a member of a prominent Cuban family. Miralles became a respected and wealthy merchant and raised a large family. He spoke English and French well. When he was already in his sixties, Miralles was asked to undertake an important diplomatic mission in the American colonies. He was not an ambassador, but rather a royal commissioner, serving as an agent or observer between Spain and the colonies. His instructions were to look after the Spanish interests and report to the captain general of Cuba and the minister of the Indies in Spain.

Miralles and his secretary, Francisco Rendón, born in Jerez de la Frontera, Spain, arrived in Charleston, South Carolina on January 9, 1778. There they were treated with great respect by Governor Edward Rutledge and other important leaders. Miralles stayed in Charleston for a few months; he bought a ship and started trade between the two countries. He then traveled to North Carolina and held conversations with Governor Abner Nash. On May 28 he arrived in Williamsburg, Virginia, where he was welcomed by Governor Patrick Henry and the House of Burgesses. Miralles discussed with the three Southern governors the possibility of a joint attack on British Florida. Soon Miralles met the important revolutionary leaders Henry Laurens, Charles Lee, and Edmund Randolph. Stopping in Baltimore, Miralles initiated further trade with Cuba. In July, Miralles arrived in Philadelphia where he moved into a house at 242 South Third Street.

As the new Spanish royal commissioner, Miralles at once started a series of conferences with members of the Continental Congress. He also coordinated his efforts with Sieur Conrad Alexander Gerard, the French Ambassador, and later with his successor, the Chevalier de la Luzerne. His pleasant personality, elegance, culture, generosity, and ability to speak English and French in addition to his native tongue, made Miralles a highly popular individual in Philadelphia. Together with Robert Morris, the "financier of the American Revolution," Miralles also established commerce between Philadelphia and Havana. Like the Spanish Ambassador in Paris,

Count de Aranda, Miralles became a strong supporter of the American revolutionary effort.

In addition to fostering commercial activities between Philadelphia, Charleston, Baltimore, and Havana, Miralles interceded on behalf of Spaniards captured by the British in New York and by American privateers.

The efforts of Miralles to persuade Congress to raise an army to attack British Florida were dashed, however, as the American forces were defeated by the British at Charleston.

It was not long before Miralles met Washington and the two became great friends. The *Pennsylvania Gazette* reported on November 12, 1778 that Miralles had purchased forty-eight reproductions of General Washington's portrait by Charles Wilson Peale[9], and that he sent these portraits to high officials in Havana and Madrid, along with letters praising General Washington. Later he bought five reproductions of another Peale portrait of Washington painted after the battles of Trenton and Princeton.

Miralles's friendship with Washington was no doubt reinforced by the gifts the general frequently received from the Spanish diplomat. Miralles sent wine, chocolates, granulated sugar, guava paste, lemons, medicine, turtle meat, and jewelry received from Cuba to General Washington, his staff, and their wives at a time when Congress could not or would not assist the army. General and Mrs. Washington showed their high regard for Juan de Miralles when the diplomat became seriously ill while visiting the General at Morristown with the French Ambassador la Luzerne. Both General and Mrs. Washington cared for the terminally ill diplomat. Miralles died on April 28, 1780 and General Washington presided over the magnificent funeral. General Washington wrote to Marshall Diego Navarro, the Captain General of Cuba, on April 30, 1780:

> Your excellency will have the goodness to believe, that I took pleasure in performing every friendly office to him during his illness, and that no care or attention in our power was omitted towards his comfort or restoration. I the more sincerely sympathize with you in the loss of so estimable a friend, as, ever since his residence with us, I have been happy in ranking him among the number of mine. It must however, be some consolation to his

connections to know that in this country he has been universally regretted. . . .[10]

Miralles's secretary, Francisco Rendón, succeeded him to head the diplomatic post. He continued to work closely with General Washington, exchanged military information, and expanded trade between Cuba and the colonies. Rendón lived in the same Third Street house as did Miralles. At the end of 1781, Rendón offered his house to General Washington who gladly accepted the invitation.

In 1967 the Spanish government placed a plaque on the house that replaced the original Miralles/Rendón residence at 242 South Third Street in Philadelphia. It reads:

> On this site stood the home, 1778-1780, of Juan de Miralles (1715-1780), the first Spanish diplomatic representative to the United States of America. He died on April 28, 1780, while visiting General Washington at his Morristown Headquarters. The same home became the residence of his successor, Francisco Rendón, who lent it to General Washington for the winter of 1781-1782. Through these officials Spanish military and financial assistance was channeled to the American Patriots. Tribute from the Government of Spain, 1967.[11]

After traveling extensively through the United States, Rendón became *Intendente de Hacienda*, a treasury official, in Zacatecas, Mexico where he spent the rest of his life. The final resting place of Juan de Miralles is the crypt of the Iglesia del Espíritu Santo in Havana, Cuba.

Diego Gardoqui, the Bilbao merchant who channeled so much military and financial assistance to the colonies was named the first Spanish ambassador to the United States in 1785.

Military Contributions by Individual Hispanics

The number of Hispanics who served in the Continental Army or fought in countless battles for American independence cannot be calculated precisely. There were approximately one hundred Spaniards alone captured by the British in New York for whom Juan de Miralles interceded. The military exploits of two Spaniards, however, are well documented, although little mentioned in textbooks.

Jorge Farragut, (anglicized from Ferragut) and Bernardo de Gálvez served the cause of American independence with great distinction.

Jorge Farragut was born in Ciudadela, Minorca. This island had been wrested from Spain by the British under the Treaty of Utrecht. It was given to France in 1756 and ceded back to England in 1763. Possibly unhappy with the British domination of his country, Farragut left Minorca when he was seventeen years old. He became a merchant marine captain and commanded a small boat that traded between Havana, Veracruz, and New Orleans. At the outbreak of the American revolution, Farragut became a first lieutenant, and later a captain, of a ship in the South Carolina navy. He fought the British at Savannah and was captured at Charleston. Later, after he was exchanged, Farragut joined the forces of General Francis Marion and fought at the battles of Cowpens and Wilmington. By the end of the war, he had attained the rank of major in the cavalry.

After the war, Farragut moved to Tennessee where he married Elizabeth Shine, a woman of Irish descent. At the age of fifty-seven, Jorge Farragut and his young son David participated in the War of 1812. Farragut ended his army career in 1814 and died three years later. Young David grew to become a great hero in the Civil War, Admiral David Glasgow Farragut. Admiral Farragut spoke fluent Spanish and visited Latin America and Spain frequently. On one visit to Spain, Farragut went to Ciudadela and read the baptismal records of his father.[12]

The Military Campaign of Bernardo de Gálvez

Bernardo de Gálvez, a forgotten hero of a forgotten ally, contributed significantly to the success of the American patriots in their war for independence. He was born on July 23, 1746 to a prominent family living in the village of Macharaviaya, near Malaga, Spain. His father, Matías de Gálvez, served in many important posts, among them captain general of Guatemala and viceroy of New Spain. Bernardo's uncle was José de Gálvez, minister of the Indies and an influential person in the court of Carlos III. At the age of sixteen, Bernardo began his military career as an infantry lieutenant, and he fought in the war with Portugal. Spain fought both Great

Britain and Portugal during the conflict known as the Seven Years' War (1756-1763). After the war, he was promoted to captain. In 1769 he accompanied his uncle, José de Gálvez, who had been given an important post in the Viceroyalty of New Spain, to America. Captain Gálvez participated in several expeditions against the Apache Indians. He was seriously wounded in two encounters. His experiences on the northern frontier of Nueva Vizcaya were of great value to him when he served as military and political leader. Years later he would write a guide on dealing with the Apaches, entitled *Instructions for the Interior Provinces.*

Gálvez returned to Spain in 1772 and spent the next three years with his regiment in France. There he learned French, a skill which proved useful to him in later years. He participated in the unsuccessful war against Algiers, during which he was seriously wounded and was promoted to lieutenant colonel. One year later he became a colonel and was assigned to New Orleans. On July 19, 1776, Colonel Gálvez succeeded Luis de Unzaga as interim governor of Louisiana. On January 1, 1777 he became governor. Once in office, the twenty-nine year old governor began helping American revolutionaries by opening the port of New Orleans to them. In April he confiscated eleven British ships which had been smuggling goods. He then ordered all British subjects to leave Louisiana, thereby curtailing British trade with the region. Governor Gálvez also sent 10,000 pounds of gunpowder up river to Fort Pitt. He worked closely with Oliver Pollock, the Continental Congress agent, and gave $74,000 and supplies worth 25,000 doblones to the army of General Washington and General Lee.[13] Gálvez's aid in the form of gunpowder, blankets, rifles, medicine, and bullets assisted the Continental Army in retaining control of the territory west of the Allegheny Mountains. Governor Gálvez also assisted George Rogers Clark with money and supplies. Clark captured Kaskaskia, Kahokia, and Vincennes, thus driving the British from the Ohio Valley.

The Mississippi Valley Campaign

On June 21, 1779, Spain declared war against Great Britain. When the news reached New Orleans in July, Gálvez held a *junta de guerra* or council of war. The majority of the officers in attendance recommended that New Orleans be fortified. They agreed to request military aid from Havana. Gálvez decided to attack the British immediately. As he was about to depart on August 18, a hurricane struck New Orleans, sinking all his ships. After refitting his army, he set out on August 27. His force was comprised of 170 veteran soldiers, 330 recruits from Mexico and the Canary Islands, 20 *carabineros*, 60 militia men, 80 free Blacks, and 7 American volunteers, including Oliver Pollock who acted as aide-de-camp to Gálvez. The small force of 667 marched to the German and Acadian coast. There 600 soldiers and 160 Indians joined the force, raising his command to 1,427 soldiers.[14]

On September 7, Gálvez captured Fort Bute in Manchac. On September 21, he captured Baton Rouge. Gálvez also demanded the surrender of Fort Pammure in Natchez. With forces from Pointe Coupee, Carlos Grand Pre seized the British posts on Thompson's Creek and the Amite. Additionally, eight British ships that were bringing reinforcements from Pensacola were captured. In a few weeks, Gálvez had captured five British forts and had taken over 1,000 prisoners.

The campaign then shifted to the upper Mississippi Valley. Captain Ferdinand de Leyba repulsed a British and Indian attack on St. Louis on May 26, 1780, even though the Spanish garrison was vastly outnumbered. On February 12, 1781, a small band of Spaniards and Indians captured the English port of St. Joseph on Lake Michigan. The Spanish commander, Pourre, read a proclamation which stated:

> I annex and incorporate with the domains of his Very Catholic Majesty, the King of Spain, my master, from now on and forever, this port of St. Joseph and its dependencies, with the river of the same name, and that of Illinois, which flows into the Mississippi River.[15]

Thus, British rule was ended along the length of the Mississippi River. In recognition of his achievement, the King of Spain promoted Gálvez to Brigadier General.

When Juan de Miralles informed General Washington of Gálvez's successful campaign in the Mississippi Valley, Washington responded in a letter to Miralles dated February 27, 1780:

> I am happy in the opportunity of congratulating you on the important success it announces to the arms of his Catholic Majesty which I hope is a prelude to others more decisive. These events will not only advance the immediate interests of his Majesty, and promote the common cause, but they will probably have a beneficial influence on the affairs of the Southern states at the present juncture. . . . It would not be surprising if the British general, on hearing of the progress of the Spanish arms in the Floridas should relinquish his first design [an attack by British General Clinton of South Carolina], and go to the defense of their own territories.[16]

The Capture of Mobile

The first time that General Gálvez requested reinforcements from Diego Navarro, the Captain General of Cuba, he was refused assistance. He then sent Colonel Estevan Miró as his personal representative to ask the Captain General for 2,000 soldiers. He received only 567 men of the Regiment of Navarra. In late February 1780, they arrived in Mobile Bay. Gálvez's army of 754 men left New Orleans for Mobile on January 2, 1780. His army consisted of 43 men of the Regiment of Príncipe of the Second Battalion of Spain, 50 of the Fixed Regiment of Havana, 141 of the Fixed Regiment of Louisiana, 14 artillery men, 26 *carabineros*, 323 white militia men, 107 free Blacks, 24 slaves, and 26 Americans.[17] On March 13, after a twenty-one day siege, he captured Mobile.

It should be noted that General Gálvez was always a gentleman. Before the attack, he shared food and wine with the British commanding officer, Elias Durnford, and tried to work out a plan to protect civilian lives and property. Further, as in Louisiana, he treated the captured soldiers with compassion. After this victory, the King of Spain promoted Bernardo de Gálvez to field marshal in command of Spanish operations in America, and he was given the new title, Governor of Louisiana and Mobile.

The Siege of Pensacola

Field Marshal Gálvez then began immediate preparations for the capture of the most important British stronghold in the Gulf of Mexico, Pensacola. The city was the capital of the British colony of West Florida and was defended by a British and Indian army of approximately 2,500 soldiers.

Gálvez encountered numerous difficulties in this enterprise. These included the reluctance of the captain general of Cuba to assist him and unfavorable weather. Three unsuccessful expeditions were launched against Pensacola. Two, in February and March 1780, were withdrawn by Navarro for various reasons. The third left Havana in October 1780 with about 4,000 men. After two days at sea, a hurricane struck, scattering the ships, some of which were carried by the winds to Mexico.[18] In January 1781, Colonel José de Ezpeleta was able to repulse a British-Indian attack upon Mobile. Gálvez recognized the danger that British Pensacola posed to Mobile.

The final expedition left Havana on February 28, 1781. Gálvez's army, with additional reinforcements from Mobile, New Orleans, and Havana eventually numbered over 7,000 men. It was truly an international army of Black and white soldiers born in Spain, Cuba, Mexico, Puerto Rico, Santo Domingo, Haiti, Venezuela, New Orleans, and Mobile. A Cuban-born general, Juan Manuel de Cagigal, who would later become Governor of Cuba, led the Spanish troops and the Cuban-born militia from Havana that were brought in as a relief expedition by Admiral José Solano y Bote. The Spanish admiral was later given the title Marqués del Socorro for his crucial assistance to General Gálvez.

Gálvez's bravery was demonstrated time and again. Admiral José Calbo de Irazabal refused to risk his ship entering Pensacola Bay. Great guns were mounted to protect the entrance of the British fort. Gálvez led three small ships past the guns and penetrated the bay successfully. All of the other ships followed his example, except that of Admiral Calbo who returned in disgrace to Havana.

Gálvez was often on the front lines leading his soldiers. He was again wounded at Pensacola. After two months of heavy fighting, on May 8, 1781, the British surrendered Pensacola. Gálvez had now succeeded in driving the British out of the Mississippi Valley and the Gulf of Mexico. For his great victory, Bernardo de Gálvez received many honors. He was promoted to lieutenant general, named governor and captain general of Louisiana and Florida, made a count, and he was given a coat of arms by King Carlos III of Spain, depicting him on a ship with the inscription "Yo Solo," *i.e.,* "I Alone."

General Gálvez was later appointed governor of Cuba and, upon the death of his father, became viceroy of New Spain. He died in Mexico at the age of forty, after a brief but highly successful administration.

Historian Orwin Rush has called the Battle of Pensacola "a decisive factor in the outcome of the Revolution and one of the most brilliantly executed battles of the war."[19] This is also the only battle of the American Revolution about which the commanding officer wrote a contemporary account. Gálvez's *Diario* is a remarkable day-by-day account of the battle. Cuban historian Herminio Portell Vilá stated that Gálvez's campaign broke the British army's will to fight. Significantly, the Spanish army's attacks on the British at Pensacola prevented the British from gathering a strong army at Yorktown. Consequently Yorktown became the final battle of the American Revolution.

Other Spanish battles indirectly assisted the cause of the colonies because the British were under siege all over the world and could not commit more resources to fight in the War of Independence. Gálvez's father Matías attacked the British along Central America, General Cagigal captured the Bahamas, and Spanish forces attacked Gibraltar.

It is indisputable that Spanish and Hispanic-American soldiers played a significant and decisive role in the American War of Independence. Their story needs to be told. A statue of Bernardo de Gálvez by Spanish sculptor Juan Avalos was presented by King Juan Carlos I of Spain to the American people during his bicentennial visit to the United States in 1976. This statue of Gálvez mounted on horseback is located in front of the State Department in Washington, D.C. There is an identical statue in New Orleans, and a different statue of Gálvez in Mobile, Alabama. On April 18, 1985, a United States stamp was printed from a reproduction of the Mobile sculpture. The Texas Legislature adopted a resolution on April 18, 1985, acknowledging the important contributions of Spain and General Gálvez to the American Revolution. A similar resolution prepared by this writer was approved by both houses of the Florida Legislature in May, 1990. Efforts like these may persuade historians and textbook publishers to give greater prominence to the role of Hispanic soldiers during the American Revolution.

DON JUAN DE MIRALLES:
EMINENT *DE FACTO* AMBASSADOR

Don Juan de Miralles was already in his sixties and a respected merchant when he was chosen for a sensitive and historically decisive mission, one that no career ambassador in the whole Spanish Empire could perform. As the representative of his Catholic Majesty Carlos III of Spain, Miralles was called upon to represent Spain's interests in the New World while the North American colonies were fighting for their independence from the British Empire. This task had to be accomplished without making it appear that Spain was a true and effective ally of the colonists. Accomplish it he did — brilliantly.

Don Juan de Miralles was born in 1715 in Petrel, in the Alicante Province of Spain. His father, Monsieur Juan de Miralles (or Mirailles) and Tizner, and his mother, Grace Trailhon (or Troyllon), migrated to Spain either from the frontier region of Bearn, France or possibly from the Saintonge Region a little farther north, in the late seventeenth or early eighteenth century.[1]

Young Don Juan de Miralles acquired considerable commercial experience working for Aguirre, Aristegui & Company, a Cádiz firm that traded with the British and with North Americans. He travelled frequently and added fluency in English to his command of Spanish and French. The trading activities eventually led him to Havana, where he established himself with a co-worker from Jerez de la Frontera, Francisco Rendón, who worked as Miralles's secretary. Here, in 1744, Miralles married Doña María Josefa Eligio de la Puente, a member of an important Cuban family.

The couple was quite prolific; they had one son and seven daughters. Don Juan survived a serious illness in 1752, but continued to prosper in business, particularly in the field of maritime shipping, where he represented various European shippers.

He invested in real estate, and eventually became a very wealthy man. Miralles frequently visited St. Augustine, various colonies in North America, and the Spanish possessions. He also maintained contacts in Savannah, Charleston, Baltimore, Philadelphia, and other North American ports. One of his colleagues in these activities was Robert Morris, later renowned as the "financier" of the American Revolution. Interestingly, European authorities did not permit this type of international commerce. They considered it smuggling.

Such activities occupied Miralles's life up to 1756 when the Seven Years' War broke out between the British Empire and the Franco-Spanish alliance. The war came to involve nearly every European nation and to extend to America and India. At its end in 1763, England drove France out of North America and Spain lost Havana, Cuba (in 1762).

The battle for the Cuban capital was preceded by a British build-up in Jamaica which, despite its secrecy, had been detected by Spanish intelligence. More detailed information concerning the preparations was needed, and Don Juan de Miralles was chosen by the Spanish government of Cuba to go to Jamaica on the pretext of a business trip. Unfortunately, the British fleet had already sailed. Its vanguard intercepted Miralles's ship and kept it seized during the passage to Havana. The siege and conquest of Havana was an intense and bloody operation. Don Juan was released when it ended. He behaved discreetly during the year that the city was occupied. Given his socio-economic stature and his knowledge of the English language, he was able to assist those residents who had to deal with the British conquerors. Although he provided detailed explanations concerning his capture and brief imprisonment by the attacking force, some Cubans, resentful of their mistreatment by the invaders, questioned his loyalty. Some historians express the opinion that Miralles was under suspicion during this period because his parents migrated to Spain from a region of France in which Protestant Huguenots abounded. Many Huguenots had fled to Catholic Spain to avoid persecution by Louis XIV of France. Miralles apparently was considered to be not a very devout Catholic, at least by contemporary standards in Havana. The unpleasantness persisted even after the British left Cuba. It reached a climax when a lawyer accused Miralles of treason and Don Juan retaliated by striking him with his cane. The police had to intervene, and Miralles was labelled as "foreign" in the procedures, without any specific nationality being mentioned. Political tensions finally eased when the Treaty of Paris was signed in February 1763; the peace terms included the withdrawal of the British from Cuba in exchange for Spanish Florida.

Having lost Canada, France secretly ceded Louisiana and the "Isle of Orleans" to Spain in 1762. This territory included New Orleans and all the vast areas west of the Mississippi River. It was granted to Spain as a compensation for the loss of Florida. All the French forts and ports on the eastern bank of the Mississippi were taken by the British. Some were renamed, for example, Fort Vincennes became Fort Pitt (now Pittsburgh). England now controlled the territory between the great river and the Atlantic Ocean, while Spain had absolute sovereignty over the immense area between the Mississippi River and the Pacific. In addition, Spain controlled the Caribbean, with the exception of Jamaica and a few small islands, as well as the rest of the South American continent (except Brazil), and offshore islands, including the Malvinas, South Georgia, and Sandwich. Spain was strong enough to exert sovereignty and control over fishing and other activities even in remote areas. Britain recognized the Spanish claims by treaty. Havana was the strongest base on the Continent. Its shipyard was the largest and was reputed to be the best in the world. It was also the largest arsenal in the Americas.

Louisiana was administered by a governor under the authority of the Captain General of Cuba, as Florida had been, until given to the British in exchange for Havana. The rest of the western territories, from Oregon to California, and all the Southwest, were governed by the Viceroy of *Nueva España* (New Spain), from its capital in Mexico City.

Louisiana was in a difficult situation under the Spanish governor, Alejandro O'Reilly. French colonials expressed discontent with the change to Spanish rule. Yet he succeeded in restoring and maintaining the peace, until Brigadier General Luis de Unzaga replaced him in 1770. Unzaga handled himself very discreetly, according to instructions from Havana and Madrid. His effectiveness was evidenced by the prosperity and compliance of the French settlers. He also made contact with influential persons such as Oliver Pollock, an Irish-American who was the most important merchant in Louisiana. Pollock had operated from Havana during the British occupation (1762-1763), and for some time afterwards. Unzaga was now trading with Cuba, Saint Augustine, and even Philadelphia, where Robert Morris was established, using Pollock as his agent.

This was the situation when the North American colonies rebelled against their British rulers in 1775. Under instructions from Havana and Madrid, Unzaga secretly supported and supplied North American operations without inciting retaliation from the British across the Mississippi, or from their strong garrisons and naval forces in Mobile and Pensacola. The cooperation of the Spanish grew, as did the Spanish preparations for war. Oliver Pollock decided to cooperate early in 1776. He began trading with the thirteen colonies despite the fact that they had no money, or even products, to exchange. Much of the time, Spanish merchants or the Spanish government would provide solid credit to enable Pollock to effectively aid the patriots. Don Juan de Miralles himself backed more than one of these transactions.

Colonel Bernardo de Gálvez, who had previously been in charge of the garrison of New Orleans, replaced Governor Unzaga. He was an experienced, brilliant officer who revealed himself as a remarkable political leader. His appointment was an additional step taken by Madrid in feverish preparation for war. The same can be said of the appointment of Don Diego Navarro, a remarkable military man, who replaced the Marquis de la Torre as Captain General of Cuba.

These were the circumstances in which Don Juan de Miralles was appointed Royal Commissioner between Madrid and the thirteen colonies, through the Captain General of Cuba. He was to report directly to the Governor of Cuba on all matters, and take orders from the minister of the Indies, the highest colonial authority in Madrid. Miralles had no direct channel with the Governor of Louisiana, but he had access through the Captain General in Havana.

Miralles's mission also included the establishment of friendly relations with the members of the Continental Congress, with General Washington, and with state governors. He was ordered to learn about their future plans in reference to Spain and her dominions. He was to obtain North American cooperation against the British both in Florida and in the forts bordering Louisiana on the eastern bank of the Mississippi. Finally, he was asked to secure certain food supplies, particularly the supply of wheat flour, for Louisiana and Cuba because Spain would not be able to maintain them on a regular basis once war was declared against Great Britain. This aspect of his mission made Miralles the founder of regular trade between the United States and Cuba, using whatever transportation he could find. His task was complicated by the fact that he sought recognition as the representative of Spain from a nation whose existence had not yet been officially recognized by his own government.

Miralles equipped himself with everything one could purchase in Havana that was calculated to make a good impression before the government in Philadelphia. Accompanied by his secretary, he departed from Havana on December 31, 1777 on board the Spanish brigantine *Nuestra Señora del Carmen*, sailing under Captain Anastasio de Urtetegui. Miralles left his family and his comfortable home behind. The *Nuestra Señora del Carmen* sailed without incident past St. Augustine and Savannah where British naval forces were stationed, and was able to sail up the Ashley River on January 9, 1778, where it simulated an emergency landing due to bad weather. She anchored at Charleston as expected, according to the messages from Havana that were delivered by Florida Indians, probably working with a brother-in-law of Miralles. The ship then continued its jour-

ney to Cádiz, Spain without Don Juan. British intelligence had no
way to detect this irregularity. The Spanish precautions were well-
founded, because a previous attempt to take an agent into the thirteen colonies had failed. Miguel Antonio Odoardo, also from
Havana, had been intercepted by the enemy.

Long after France had declared war on Great Britain, Spain continued to support the thirteen colonies only in secrecy, until its necessary war preparations were complete. This policy was formalized
by the Council of State (*Junta de Estado*) in Madrid, early in 1777,
when Benjamin Franklin presented a request for an alliance to the
Spanish court. However, the Spanish intentions to declare war had
been evidenced a year earlier, when Spain advised France that both
nations should strengthen their military and naval forces and inte-
grate an initial Franco-Spanish squad of twelve warships.

Simultaneously, the shipyards of Bilbao, Cádiz, Sevilla, Barcelona, and the *Arsenal de la Habana* worked feverishly to build warships. Ammunition filled storehouses in Havana, Veracruz,
Cartagena de Indias, Santo Domingo, and San Juan, Puerto Rico,
with gun powder from the large factories in Mexico and the smaller
ones in Cuba. Spain reached record levels in manufacturing military
supplies and weapons. Cloth from factories in Castilla, Cataluña,
and Valencia were used to make uniforms, blankets, and army tents.
Never before had Spain prepared so thoroughly for war. She had
learned a valuable lesson during the recent Seven Years' War when
she had been defeated by Great Britain.

Juan de Miralles had often been made welcome in Charleston
where he had personal and business acquaintances, particularly
among the French Huguenots who settled there after their persecution by Louis XIV. These Huguenots and their children, many already married in the British colonies, were among the leaders
during the administration of Governor Edward Rutledge. When
Miralles travelled to Charleston in 1777, they rushed to welcome
him and discuss political and military issues with him. During a
banquet, the Saratoga victory was celebrated, along with the new
treaty of alliance with France. Miralles himself was the subject of an
enthusiastic toast. The news of his arrival reached North Carolina,

Virginia, and the Continental Congress at Philadelphia. The event was interpreted everywhere as conclusive proof that Spain was also entering the war, although this fact would be announced only after another full year had passed. Miralles enjoyed a semi-official status during this initial period, enabling him to make contacts at many levels. He was able to gather information, such as the plans to attack the British in Florida.

Shortly after his arrival in Charleston, Miralles sent a letter to Don José de Gálvez, the Madrid minister of the Indies, stressing the need for his official royal appointment, apart from the designation he had been given by the Captain General of Cuba. The appointment had, in fact, already been granted by *real cédula* (royal decree) dated January 21, 1788. It would take several months, however, to reach Don Juan. The difficult communications of the times were made worse by war. He spent several months in Charleston, developing regular communications and commercial trade with Havana, as well as making contact with the French diplomats accredited before the Continental Congress, the North American leaders, and later on, with Washington in particular. At this time, General Washington was enduring the harsh winter of Valley Forge and the British were occupying Philadelphia.

George Abbott Hall, a seaman from Charleston, South Carolina, carried Miralles's first messages to Havana in February and March 1778. Hall was serving on board a schooner loaded with merchandise to be sold in Havana. He brought the return mail and also Cuban products, which might be regarded as the beginning of regular trade between Cuba and the United States. Miralles bought his own schooner in Charleston and named it *San Andrés*. He hired Andrés Pueyo, a Cuban seaman from Havana, to command it. The ship departed with a cargo of rice at the end of March 1778. The first dispatches Miralles sent aboard the *San Andrés* were so optimistic concerning the thirteen colonies that they even predicted that Canada would separate from Great Britain to join the united colonies.

On May 16, 1778, Miralles asked Governor Navarro to communicate with him through North American "merchant and corsair vessels arriving in [the] port [of Havana]."[2] His request is evidence of the fact that the North American colonists took advantage of Spain's neutrality, and that Cuban-American commerce was already very active.

Miralles participated with South Carolinian patriots in preparing a plan for a joint Spanish-American operation to attack eastern Florida, Pensacola, and Mobile. To that effect, Lieutenant Colonel John B. Hernant, an officer of French ancestry, was sent by the governor of South Carolina to Havana on board the schooner *Eagle* to try to convince the captain general of Cuba to initiate such an enterprise. Patrick Henry had already tried to convince Bernardo de Gálvez in Louisiana to undertake this project. Henry now cooperated with Miralles because he considered Don Juan to have greater influence on the authorities in Madrid than any other messenger. South Carolina was acting independently of the wishes of the Continental Congress. The colony went so far as to send Spyres Singleton to act as consul of South Carolina in Havana. His status was not accepted by either the captain general or the Continental Congress. Another display of independence was the creation of a state navy, complete with corsair ships commissioned in Charleston. The most notorious act of all, however, was that of the French-born Alexander Gillon who went across the Atlantic and tried to compete with the famous John Paul Jones in Europe. Gillon gathered a flotilla of seven ships, including his own and captured vessels. He had to take refuge in Havana, chased by a powerful British squad that was denied entrance to that port by the Cuban colonial government. Gillon and his ships were quite welcome. Those ships, including the frigates *Carolina* and *Medley*, were repaired, armed, and supplied with ammunition and food at the Royal Arsenal. The bill surpassed 100,000 pesos. Gillon could not pay, but the Treasury of Havana took care of it because the signatures of sympathizers of North American independence, including Don Juan de Miralles and his brother-in-law, Eligio de la Puente, served as collateral. This financial assistance was never reimbursed to those who provided it; in fact, Gillon's default contributed to his later break with the Spanish authorities of Cuba. Until that time, however, he was even allowed to sell some of his captured ships while waiting for an opportunity to escape from his British pursuers.

Miralles soon coordinated a route between Philadelphia and Havana with the help of Robert Morris. Don Juan travelled North in mid-May, even though he had not yet received the commission signed by Carlos III on January 21. This delay did not interfere with Miralles's plans for a combined military action against the British to expel them from Florida. To this end, he notified the French diplomatic representative in Philadelphia through Sieur de Pombard, French general consul in Charleston, of his departure for the North American capital, Philadelphia.

On his way north, Don Juan stopped to confer with Governor Abner Nash in North Carolina. The talks included a discussion of a joint plan to defeat the British in Florida and in the Mississippi valley. Miralles sincerely wished to implement such a project, but unilateral military action by Spain was outside his authority to direct. Spain would surely have to act alone because the thirteen colonies lacked the necessary military and naval forces to participate decisively. Furthermore, according to his orders, Don Juan did not have direct communication with Bernardo de Gálvez. Gálvez later took the initiative to defeat the British before they could attack his army from Canada to the Gulf of Mexico, as they were preparing to do.

On May 28, 1778, Miralles was received by Governor Patrick Henry and by the members of the House of Burgesses with all the solemn ceremony due an accredited diplomat. At that time, Patrick Henry handed him a plan prepared in Virginia, calling for Spain to capture Mobile, Pensacola, and St. Augustine with forces from Havana, Georgia, and South Carolina. This was essentially the same proposal which he had earlier presented to Gálvez. It overlooked the fact that Virginians, Carolinians, and Georgians lacked the resources to carry out an offensive in Florida, even if assisted by the Spaniards. This fact was demonstrated by the British success in the South, not only in open battle, but in the colonists' failure to recapture Savannah, and by the ill-fated defense of Charleston. The British capture of Charleston which occurred soon after Miralles's meetings with Governor Henry, unquestionably secured Georgia and the Carolinas until the end of the war.

Miralles continued his journey to Philadelphia in mid-June 1778. He travelled under escort to Yorktown, where he was warmly received. The last leg of the journey was probably by ship, landing at Alexandria, and then overland to Philadelphia, after surmounting the risks related to the presence of loyalist corsairs in these waters. Wherever he stopped, he was the object of honors corresponding to the representative agent of the King of Spain. In Baltimore, he took time to implement trade with Havana. When he arrived in Philadelphia on July 1, 1778, that city had just been recaptured from the British.

Miralles and Rendón moved into a house located at 242 South 3rd Street, which from that time was known as the official residence of the royal commissioner of Spain, even after Don Juan died and was succeeded by his secretary Francisco Rendón. The house is no longer standing; only a plaque remains, placed there by the Spanish government in 1967 to commemorate its existence.

Once settled in the house, Miralles began holding conferences with members of the Congress, still on an unofficial basis; Spain had not yet recognized the independence of the thirteen colonies, nor was she ready to begin regular diplomatic relations. Thus, Miralles's position was not as powerful as that of Sieur Conrad Alexander Gerard, the First Minister of France to the United States, or his successor, the Chevalier de la Luzerne.

His first contact was with Robert Morris, with whom he had maintained business relations since the year the British occupied Havana, (1762-1763). With Morris's support, the doors to offices, storehouses, military quarters, and residences of the most influential persons were opened to Don Juan. Again, with Morris, he established maritime routes between Philadelphia and Havana similar to those which he had earlier established in Charleston, South Carolina. In a few months, Robert Morris's schooner *Grey Hound*, with its master Wolman Sutton, departed from Philadelphia with Miralles's correspondence as well as a cargo of flour and other North American products destined for Havana. By October 1788, brigantines and schooners such as the *Buckskin, Don Miralles, Stephen, San Antonio*, and *Havana*, chartered by Miralles and Morris, were trading between Havana and Philadelphia. By this time, Don Juan de Miralles had become a definite sympathizer of the colonists' cause. Even though he was a Catholic, and thus considered a papist by the Anglican orthodoxy, he gained more and more friends.

On November 12, 1778 the *Pennsylvania Gazette* announced that painter Charles Wilson Peale had made an engraved picture of General Washington, and that "generous Miralles" had acquired four dozen copies at five dollars each, a sizable sum at that time. Miralles used his own funds to buy the pictures (he had no allotment for such purposes) and promptly began to give them away to Spanish officials, relatives, and friends. This action was the equivalent of a public relations campaign and was extremely effective as warm praise for the American leader accompanied each portrait. Miralles sent one of the portraits as a gift to the captain general, with a letter in which he expressed "no doubt that it will be received with great satisfaction since I know your Lordship is most fond of him."[3] Other copies were sent to the Army Intendent, the Head of Engineering, to Juan Josef Eligio de la Puente, and Ramón del Valle. The minister of the Indies in Madrid, Don José de Gálvez, was another recipient. In acknowledging Miralles's gift, the captain general Navarro confirmed his admiration for Washington, and commented on the appreciation of all the Cuban recipients for their portraits of "High Excellency Mister Washington whose great talent demands that his memory be kept in future centuries."[4]

A friendship between Miralles and Peale was shown in other ways. For example, on one occasion the painter had to go to Baltimore (on December 11, 1778) and was permitted to borrow Miralles's excellent horse for the trip. In January 1779, the Supreme Executive Council of Pennsylvania ordered from Peale his famous oil painting of George Washington after the battles of Trenton and Princeton, a work considered a masterpiece of the period. Again, Miralles bought copies, five in number, and again sent them to Cuba and Spain. He was known to have said that this portrait was so fine that there was "no difference with the living original [that it depicted] such a memorable man who. . .earned his well-deserved reputation."[5] He also stated that the presents were justified because the recipients were among those who had in their hearts "a prominent place for all those talents, virtues, and heroism that have been commendable and remarkable, as it [was] in the case of General George Washington whose fame is highly admired in the civilized world."[6] It is interesting to note that such admiration for Washington was not common at that time. These Spaniards, overlooked and forgotten during the celebration of the Bicentennial of the North American Revolution, were the first foreign persons who recognized Washington as the greatest figure of the fight for independence, as well as a universal man of his time.

General Washington was aware of Miralles's support. Although Miralles attempted to get close to him, the general had to move cautiously until the Spanish position became more definite. Thus, the first meeting was delayed for several months. Meanwhile, Miralles was kept busy handling the trade between Havana, Philadelphia, Baltimore, and Charleston. He also dealt with complaints from Spanish seamen who were often victimized by New England corsairs or imprisoned by the British. More than one hundred Spanish seamen died in captivity in New York. In addition, he responded to requests by the Continental Congress for Spanish military and financial assistance.

It appears that Miralles was never given the regular instructions given a country's plenipotentiary, but instead received directives as to how he was to deal with the Americans. The first and most important point with which he had to deal was the expulsion of Britain from North America. The military and political situation in late 1778 was reflected in the correspondence of George Washington.

To Governor Morris on October 4, 1778, Washington wrote:

> If the Spaniards would but join their Fleets to those of France, and commence hostilities, my doubts would all subside. Without it, I fear the British Navy has too much in its power to counteract the schemes of France.[7]

Washington addressed a letter to the President of Congress on November 11, 1778, in which he observed:

The English are now greatly superior to the French by sea in America; and will from every appearance continue so unless Spain interposes, an event which I do not know we are authorized to count upon. However, as I am destitute of information with respect to the present state of European politics, this is a point upon which I can form but an imperfect judgement.[8]

Again, in a letter to Henri Laurens, dated November 14, 1778, Washington reiterated:

The truth of the position will entirely depend on naval events. If France and Spain should unite and obtain a decided superiority by sea, a reunion with England would avail very little and might be set at defiance.[9]

A second objective of Miralles was to help with the British defeat in Florida. Despite Washington's victories in New England, the Ohio Valley, and the Great Lakes, he was unable to extend hostilities south to Florida, lacking the manpower, supplies, and the funds to do so. Thus, the clearing of the Mississippi Valley and of Florida was left to Spain. If successful, it meant the elimination of the British threat to the rear and southern flank of the thirteen colonies, as well as the eventual defeat of the British.

Another directive given Miralles was that he encourage the colonists to attack St. Augustine. Don Juan complied with this order from his very arrival in Philadelphia. He used his contacts with Patrick Henry, and spoke with as many members of Congress as he could. As soon as the Continental Congress accepted and responded with a formal proposal of a joint offensive against St. Augustine, Marshall Navarro wrote to Miralles, on March 10, 1780, that his instructions did not authorize him to participate in such an operation, and that the North Americans would have to conduct the offensive on their own. However, as mentioned earlier, they did not have the resources for such action. A new plan was then proposed by Miralles to Washington during their initial conversations. The leader favored it, and therefore issued pertinent orders to General Benjamin Lincoln, designated head of the American Army's South Department. On December 7, 1778, Philip Schuyler and Henry

Marchant, members of the Congress, approved the plan. On the 16th of the same month, there was a favorable vote on the proposal along with Congressional praises for Carlos III. Unfortunately, General Lincoln was defeated and captured by the British at Charleston, South Carolina. There was no way to concentrate the necessary military and naval forces in Florida, together with Spanish forces from Cuba. Still, Miralles asked General Washington and the Continental Congress to contribute four thousand troops. He was told that even this was not feasible.

In spite of Miralles's enthusiasm, Madrid had reservations about the formula for cooperation chosen by the North Americans. John Jay proposed that Spain should cede to the thirteen colonies all territories between the Appalachians and the eastern bank of the Mississippi River, and allow free trade on that river, down to its mouth. He presented this formula first to the Continental Congress, and then to Madrid in his role as plenipotentiary. In essence, Jay's plan gave the Americans all the territories controlled by the British west of the Appalachians, without their having to take part in any of the offensives conducted against the enemy in the area. Rather, it was Spain and her colonies that conducted the operations that ended in victory. Despite the lack of agreement on this point by Spain and the North Americans, Miralles was able to accomplish an important goal — becoming acquainted with the most important personalities in the American government.

The initial conversations held between Miralles and Washington occurred at the end of 1778, when Miralles was introduced to the general during the Christmas season. His arrival on December 22 was the impetus for parties, banquets, and other official events that Don Juan attended in order to become acquainted with the leader. In fact, Miralles organized a banquet at his residence on December 31, 1778 at which the Washingtons were honored guests. They attended not only because Miralles was the royal commissioner of Carlos III, but also because he was likely to become one of the most influential hosts in the capital. Washington had been apprised by Marshall Navarro, captain general of Cuba, of Miralles's stature and mission and of the six ships in regular commerce between Philadelphia and Havana. Each man was favorably impressed with the other, as evidenced in a letter to the captain general of Cuba, dated March 4, 1779, in which Washington said:

> Sir,
>
> A journey to Philadelphia in the winter procured me the honor of your Excellency's favor of the 11th of March last, by Don Juan de Miralles, and the pleasure of that gentleman's acquaintance. His estimable qualities justify your recommendation, and concurs with it to establish him in my esteem. I doubt not he will have informed you of the cordial and respectful sentiments, which he has experienced in this country. On my part, I shall always take pleasure in convincing him of the high value I set upon his merit, and of the respect I bear to those, who are so happy as to interest your Excellency's friendship, can only express my gratitude for your polite offer of service, by entreating you to afford me opportunities of testifying my readiness to execute any commands with which you shall please to honor me. With my prayers for your health and happiness, and with the greatest respect, I have the honor to be, &C.[10]

The visits exchanged by Miralles and Washington in Philadelphia were quite friendly. The merchant from Havana never overlooked the opportunity to show courtesy and be helpful to the American revolutionary leaders and their wives. His ships brought the wines, liquors, candies, and delicacies for which Havana was known. His Cuban rum and cigars were as welcome as the chocolate, colored sugar candy crystals, and the guava marmalade that were served at the parties given by Mrs. Martha Washington and the wife of General Nathaniel Greene. Miralles distributed Cuban limes generously among Washington's troops, recommending the fruit's ability to prevent scurvy. He also maintained a large quantity of quinine, a valuable medication for which Spain had the monopoly. For gifts, he imported items made of green-turtle shell, especially jewelry and combs.

Don Juan's generosity and good relationship with Washington caused the latter to ask him to import two of the famous Spanish jackass stallions to be used for breeding mules at Mount Vernon. Spain had export restrictions on these animals, the best in Europe, and only one had arrived at the end of 1785 (six years after Miralles's first request for them and long after his own death).

On May 2, 1779, General Washington ordered a military parade at his camp at Middlebrook with himself at the head, accompanied by Generals Von Steuben, Greene, Knox, Wayne, and others, as well as Alexander Hamilton as aide de camp, followed by the royal commissioner of Spain, representing Charles III, King of Spain, of whom so many things were expected. All were luxuriously decorated, and all were on horseback. The viewers, including the wives of the generals, enthusiastically applauded the colorful display of the renewed liberating army, after the terrible days of Valley Forge. On that occasion, Miralles was toasted as Carlos III's representative. He had just recently notified the Americans of the imminence of Spain's declaration of war against the British.[11]

On May 4, 1779, Miralles wrote to the captain general of Cuba, Marshall Navarro, of all the details related to his trip to Middlebrook, as well as the United States' pleasure in learning of the proposed Spanish attack against the British in Florida. The first official news of Spain's declaration of war was written in Havana on August 6, 1779 and sent to the North Americans via Charleston on one of Don Juan's ships. News of the letter was published in the Philadelphia newspapers. This information encouraged the Congress to pay closer attention to the requests of Miralles for a joint Spanish-American operation against the British. Thus, on September 17, Congress approved a bill committing itself to guaranteeing the Spanish possession of Florida, as long as Spain conquered it and made an alliance with the thirteen colonies and France against Great Britain. At the same time, Congress asked for a guarantee of free navigation on the Mississippi River. This was something Spain could not guarantee, but Congress asked for it anyway. John Jay, the ex-president of Congress took these demands to Carlos III in Madrid in the hope of negotiating a treaty.

Neither Madrid nor Havana waited to resolve Jay's intemperate demands. They took the necessary action to start an offensive against the British. Miralles officially communicated the Spanish decisions to General Washington, and accompanied his message with a valuable gift from Havana, a one hundred-pound turtle and a crate of limes.

Washington wrote to Miralles, grateful for the information, and in a letter to Lafayette, then in Paris, stated:

> The declaration of Spain, in favor of France has given universal joy to every Whig [pro-independence patriot]; while the poor Tory [loyalist] droops, like a withering flower under the declining sun. We are anxiously expecting to hear of great and important events on your side of the Atlantic. At present, the imagination is left in the wide field of conjecture. Our eyes one moment are turned to an invasion of England, then of Ireland, Minorca, Gibraltar. . . .[12]

This letter is particularly significant because the Americans and the French previously had made a commitment to Spain that neither country would sign a treaty with Britain unless Gibraltar were returned to Spain. In a letter to Field Marshall John Sullivan, Washington wrote from his headquarters at West Point, on September 3, 1779:

> I have the pleasure to inform you that Spain has at length taken a decisive part. In the enclosed paper, you will find her Manifesto delivered to the Court of Great Britain on the 16th of June last, with the message of the King to Parliament thereupon. It is to be hoped that this formidable junction of the House of Bourbon will not fail of establishing the independence of America in a short time.[13]

In another letter to Field Marshall Sullivan, dated February 27, 1780, in Morristown, Washington reveals the close cooperation with the royal commissioner and the importance assigned to the Spanish participation:

> In addition to the advices you were obliging enough to communicate, I have just seen official accounts from the Governor of Havana of the success of the Spaniards in the Floridas. If the remaining posts fall it will be a very important stroke; and in all probability the operations there will have a favorable influence upon our affairs in your quarter. Though perhaps it may not be probable, it is not impossible, the British General, if he has discre-

tionary power on hearing of the progress of the Spaniards in the Floridas, may suspend his original plan and turn his attention that way, and endeavor to defend their own territories rather than attempt conquests. Don Juan de Miralles, the Spanish agent, in a letter of the 18th communicating the foregoing intelligence has the following paragraph:

By Royal Order, I am very strongly charged to influence your Excellency to make the greatest diversion with the Troops of the United States against those of the enemy in Georgia, to the effect of attracting their attention and disabling them from sending succours to Pensacola and Mobile, which the Governor of Louisiana is to attack auxiliated with Sea and Land Forces, which were prepared in Havana with all the needful and ready to sail when the season would permit.

This I transmit to you for your government, satisfied that you will do everything to effect the diversion desired, which the situation of your force and that of the enemy combined with other circumstances will permit. If they act offensively against the Carolinas your whole attention will necessarily be engaged at home; but if they should direct their force elsewhere, you may possibly have it in your power to pursue measures favorable to the operations of the Spaniards and the immediate interests of the United States.[14]

Washington answered Miralles from Morristown on February 27, 1780:

Sir:

I have the honor of your letter of this 18th instant, enclosing an extract of one from the Governor of Havana. I am happy in the opportunity of congratulating you on the important success it announces to the arms of his Catholic Majesty, (Washington refers to the capture of the British forts at Baton Rouge and Natchez by Gálvez) which I hope is a prelude to others more decisive. These events will not only advance the immediate interests of his Majesty, and promote the common cause, but they will probably have a beneficial influence on the affairs of the southern States at the present juncture.

The want of any certain intelligence of the fleet, which sailed from New York, I should attribute to their having been disconcerted in their voyage by the tempestuous weather, which prevailed for some time after their departure. A variety of circumstances combined to prove, that the intention of the embarkation was for Southern States. All my intelligence agreed in this point. The composition of the detachment; Governor Martin and several refugees from South and North Carolina having embarked in the fleet; the current of the English accounts, by which it appears that General Clinton was expected to be in South Carolina as early as November, in which he was probably prevented by Count D'Estaing's operations in Georgia; these circumstances conspire to satisfy me, that the Carolinas were the objects. But, notwithstanding this, I think the precautions you are taking to put the Spanish dominions upon their guard are wise. It can have no ill consequence; and it is advisable to be provided against all contingencies. It would not be surprising if the British general, on hearing of the progress of the Spanish arms in the Florida (probably the siege of Mobile), should relinquish his first design, and go to the defense of their own territories.

I shall with the greatest pleasure comply with your request for giving you information of all the movements of the enemy, that come to my knowledge, which may in any manner interest the plans of your court; and I have written to General Lincoln agreeably to your intimation. Every motive will induce him to whatever may be in his power to effect the diversion desired. If the enemy prosecute the plan, which I suppose to have been originally intended, he will necessarily find his whole attention employed at home on the defensive; but if they direct their force to another quarter, I am persuaded he will make the best use of his to give them all possible annoyance and distraction.

I have the honor to be, &C.[15]

The events described above occurred while the Franco-Spanish alliance met with unquestionable success at sea. British ships were simply swept off the Channel and the Straight of Calais. Also, the Home Fleet sought hasty protection in Portsmouth when one of its 64-gun ships was captured. This allowed Rochambeau to get through Atlantic waters for the final victory at Yorktown. In a letter to Governor Morris in November 1779, Washington expressed the hope that the British "panic" would extend throughout the kingdom, with its effects, consequently, felt on the American side.[16]

Throughout this time, Don Juan de Miralles continued to coordinate the implementation of commercial interchange between the thirteen colonies and Cuba, as noted in directives from Madrid, through Havana. Yet another aspect of his mission was to continue with the filing of protests on behalf of Spanish merchant mariners captured by North American corsairs, such as *Hugh Hill* and *Philip Trask*, protests that had to be filed through the French minister, given Miralles's continued lack of official diplomatic recognition. In spite of the fact that the cooperation between Spain and the thirteen colonies was now overt, these piracies continued, demonstrating the lack of control the Continental Congress had over all the states.

The complex financing of purchases, services, and loans made by Don Juan de Miralles on behalf of the North American cause jeopardized his estate. He, his brother-in-law, Juan Eligio de la Puente, and his secretary, Francisco Rendón, had to make use of all their expertise and resources to meet as much of each obligation as possible. Yet all the debts had not been satisfied at the time of Miralles's death. One of the most important financial contributions by Miralles made possible the refurbishing of Commodore Alexander Gillon's squad so that it was able to depart Havana and return north. Both Miralles and his brother promised the collateral needed to back the loan. When the creditors feared that they would never be paid, they sued both men to collect from their estates. The Continental Congress had agreed in writing to advance $125,000 to Gillon, more than enough to satisfy the Cuban expenses.

In April 1780, when Miralles was assured that his designation as the official Spanish diplomatic representative was soon to come, he decided to travel from Philadelphia to Morristown where Washington had established his headquarters. After several days of uncomfortable traveling over snow and slush, the Spanish representative, accompanied by the French plenipotentiary, the Chevalier de la Luzerne, and Francisco Rendón, Don Juan's secretary, reached Morristown. They were greeted by Washington and two hundred troops. Horses were provided for the guests, who joined the parade into the city. They were received with a thirteen-gun salute and the applause of many of the townspeople. The guests inspected their surroundings. General Washington personally showed them the British positions in New York and Staten Island. They stayed at the official residence of the General. Because Miralles had contracted pneumonia, he was given one of the comfortable upper-story bedrooms. Although attended by the best available doctors, Miralles was unable to leave his room, even for the military parade conducted in his honor on April 24.

The French minister returned to Philadelphia on April 25, but Miralles was confined to bed, severely ill. Mrs. Washington personally attended to him. The General visited him daily to learn of his health, and sent a report to Minister Luzerne every day. Don Juan's condition seemed to improve at first. But, by the 28th of April the report on his health was pessimistic and he died that afternoon. Washington notified the Continental Congress and Minister Luzerne that very evening of the sad event.

On April 29, the funeral was led by a Catholic priest, with great pomp and luxury, as attested by Dr. James Thacher in a detailed chronicle. He mentioned the gold ornaments on the suit, the three-cornered hat, the white silk socks, the shoe and knee buckles adorned with diamonds, the profusion of diamond rings, and the magnificent gold watch garnished with diamonds and showing several rich seals. General Washington attended the ceremony, and then marched at the head of the splendid mile-long procession, accompanied by members of his staff and several members of the Continental Congress. Other Army officers and numerous respectable citizens followed. The coffin was carried by four artillery officers in full uniform. A one-gun salute was fired every minute during the funeral march, until the coffin was placed in a big wooden box, and then in a grave in the local cemetery. On the night of April 30, 1780, the password in the Morristown headquarters was "Miralles."

A permanent guard was placed at the grave site, as ordered by Washington, until the body was taken to Philadelphia. It was then sent to Havana on board one of the ships that had been assigned by Miralles to that route.

A requiem Mass for Don Juan's eternal repose was celebrated in the Catholic Chapel of Philadelphia early in May. It was attended by many of the representatives of the U.S. government, including James Madison who was to be the fourth President of the Union. General Benedict Arnold also attended the Mass. Already in the British camp, he afterwards wrote to a friend whom he was trying to convince to join him:

> What is America but a land of widows, beggars, and orphans? And should the parent nation cease her exertion to deliver you (from Congress) what security remains to you for the enjoyment of the consolations of that religion for which your fathers braved the ocean, the heathens, and the wilderness? Do you know that the eye which guides this pen lately saw your mean and profligate Congress at mass for the soul of a Roman Catholic in purgatory and participating in the rites of a church against whose anti-Christian corruptions your pious ancestors would have witnessed with their blood?[17]

George Washington was prompt in notifying the government of Cuba. In a letter to the captain general, Marshall Don Diego Navarro, dated April 30, 1780, he wrote:

> Sir,
>
> I am extremely sorry to communicate to your Excellency, the painful intelligence of the death of Don Juan de Miralles. This unfortunate event happened at my quarters the day before yesterday, and his remains were yesterday interred with all the respect due to his character and merit. He did me the honor of a visit, in company with the minister of France, and was seized on the day of his arrival with a violent billious complaint, which after nine day's continuance, put a period to his life, notwithstanding all the efforts of the most skillful physicians we were able to procure. Your Excellency will have the goodness to believe, that I took pleasure in performing every friendly office to him during his illness, and that no care or attention in our power was omitted toward his comfort or restoration. I sincerely sympathize with you in the loss of so estimable a friend, as, ever since his residence with us, I have been happy in ranking him among the number of mine. It must, however, be some consolation to his connections to know that in this country he has been universally regretted.

May I request the favor of your Excellency to present my respects to the lady and family of your deceased friend, and to assure them how much I participate in their affliction on this melancholy occasion? I have the honor to be, with the highest respect and consideration, your Excellency's, &C.[18]

On May 11, 1780, Washington wrote to the Chevalier de la Luzerne, minister of France, that the attentions and honors paid to "Monsieur Miralles" after his death were a tribute to his character and merit, and dictated by the sincere esteem that [he] always felt for him. Don Juan's widow wrote a letter to Washington, thanking him for his condolences and for the attentions to her deceased husband.[19]

Some writers have tried to present Don Juan de Miralles as a liberal and romantic figure, identified with the cause of independence of the North American colonies. This interpretation does not have documentary support. On the contrary, his behavior matched perfectly and brilliantly that of a career diplomat. His close collaboration with Washington did not preclude his being loyal to the interests of his own country. For example, the new Foreign Minister of Spain, Floridablanca, in contrast to his predecessor Grimaldi, was not at all concerned about the borders between the emerging North American nation and the Spanish territories, or even about the navigation on the Mississippi. These matters influenced Floridablanca's judgment only when his attention was called to them by the Spanish officials in Cuba and, later in Florida, on the basis of "dispatches from Miralles." The latter were quite pertinent, full of vision of the future. He was a gentleman of great stature. He and Washington held each other in high esteem. Neither one of them deceived the other, although it is reasonable to assume that they knew their countries might have conflicting interests after the war.

The outcome of the eventual peace negotiations was disappointing to Spain since, as earlier mentioned, neither France nor the United States kept its promise to withhold a settlement until Gibraltar was returned to Spain. Nevertheless, Spain continued friendly relations with both allies, until Napoleon I invaded Spain and installed his brother on the Spanish throne, and until an unsuccessful attempt by the southern States to seize Florida (instigated by Madison and Monroe). Some historians called this the First Spanish-American War. Of course, both countries were at war in 1898, during the brief Spanish-American War.

Don Francisco Rendón succeeded Don Juan, and continuing his work, particularly in expanding trade, especially the supply of wheat to Cuba. Washington trusted him, and he enjoyed success because of the Spanish involvement in the war. He and Washington worked in close cooperation and exchanged military intelligence. In April 1782, they met in Philadelphia to discuss matters related to final war operations, at which time Washington reminded him about the two donkey stallions that he expected to receive from Spain to breed mules in Mount Vernon.

Don Diego Gardoquí, the merchant and shipper from Bilbao who had been instrumental in the implementation of the financial and military assistance to the thirteen colonies, took charge in 1785, as the first plenipotentiary of Spain in the United States. Rendón did not return to Havana. He toured New England, the Mississippi Valley, travelled down the river to New Orleans, and then went directly to Spain where he was rewarded with the appointment of *Intendente de Hacienda* (Treasury representative) in Zacatecas, Mexico. He spent the rest of his life there.

A plaque at Saint Mary's Church, 244 South 4th Street, Philadelphia, refers to the presence, on the 4th of July 1779, of Don Juan de Miralles at the "First Public-Religious Commemoration of the Declaration of Independence. In attendance at the Holy Mass then sung were the Continental Congress, the President and Official Heads of the new government, the officers of the Army and Navy, and the French and Spanish Ministers." The same plaque commemorates a Mass of Thanksgiving for the British surrender of Yorktown held on November 4, 1781. The error in referring to Miralles as a "Minister" is further evidence of his exemplary performance.

The final resting place of Don Juan de Miralles's remains is the crypt of the old *Iglesia del Espíritu Santo* (Holy Spirit Church), at the corner of Cuba and Acosta Streets, Havana.

JORGE FERRAGUT:
FREEDOM FIGHTER

I am in Las Palmas, among palms, cedars, olives, pomegranates
. . . a sky like turquoise, a sea like lapis lazuli, mountains like em-
eralds, air like heaven, sun all day, and hot. . .huge balconies with
grape vines overhead, Moorish walls. . . .

Thus was Majorca described by Frederick Chopin in a November
1837 letter to his dear friend, Julián Fontana in Paris.[1] This vivid
tableau would be an equally apt description of nearby Minorca,
whose Moorish-walled capital, Ciudadela, was the birthplace of
Jorge Ferragut. Despite the idyllic surroundings, life in eighteenth
century Minorca was not always tranquil. Minorca was equally cov-
eted by the British, French, and Spanish, due to its strategic location
in the western Mediterranean and its protected port of Mahón. Admiral Andrea Doria defined the situation in a well-known couplet:

Los puertos del Mediterráneo son
Junio, Julio, Agosto y el puerto de Mahón.[2]

After 400 years of Spanish rule, the British controlled Minorca
from 1713 to 1756, when it was conquered by the French. The British regained control in 1763, by treaty ending the Seven Years' War.
After nineteen years of rule, the British were again ousted. Sixteen
years would elapse before the British had a final, four-year reign
over Minorca, from 1798 to 1802, when the island was ceded to
Spain. In the middle of this tumultuous century, a humble sailor
named Antonio Ferragut married Juana Mezquida in the cathedral
of Ciudadela. So poor was Antonio that he was unable to afford the
whole payment of 17.5 *sueldos* of Juana's dowry, and he had to pay
it in two installments instead of one.[3] Despite Antonio's low social

status, the 1750 ceremony was attended by prominent citizens of the capital. The Ferragut family was highly regarded in both Minorca and Catalonia due to their past deeds.

Their son Jorge, born September 29, 1755, was initiated into the hazards of the sailing trade very early in life. By the time Jorge was ten years old he went to sea, and

> from 1765 to 1773 was employed chiefly in the Mediterranean. While in the Russian service, he aided in the destruction of a Turkish fleet as one of the crew of a fireship [gunboat] that set fire to the fleet.[4]

The naval battle described was undoubtedly the Battle of Tachesma which took place between July 5th and 6th, 1770. It was fought in two stages under the command of two British officers in the Czarina's service. One of them, Flag Captain Samuel Grieg, directed the movements of four gunboats in a successful night action against the Turkish fleet. Ferragut is thought to have been aboard the gunboat commanded by a Russian officer, D. Ilin, that set fire to a Turkish ship-of-the-line. Jorge later left the naval service, either in Italy, or perhaps at Mahón, a regular point of debarcation used by the Russians with the consent of the British.[5]

We know that Jorge Ferragut returned briefly to Minorca in 1772. Years later, in a family Bible preserved by his sons, he recorded that he departed forever from his native land on April 2, 1772. One can only speculate on his reasons for leaving Minorca. An eagerness for adventure and the lure of the Indies probably influenced his decision. No doubt the turmoil in his homeland and native antagonism to British rule contributed to Ferragut's devotion to freedom and resentment of the British. By 1773, therefore, he had made his way to Havana. Soon he was working in various capacities on merchant ships. His actual whereabouts remain obscure. By the age of twenty, he was in command of a small trading schooner and acquainted with many Gulf ports, including Veracruz. A voyage to New Orleans, then part of Spanish Louisiana, opened new horizons to him. With his fluency in English, he learned many facts about the rebellion in the New England colonies that would soon ignite the American Revolutionary War. He observed that the local Spanish authorities tolerated the smugglers' traffic in arms and other types of aid destined for the fighting rebels.

Young Captain Ferragut had reached a turning point in his life. Relishing the prospect of fighting against the British, he decided to join forces with the gallant rebels. He first called at Port-au-Prince, Haiti, where he loaded his schooner with arms, ammunition, and naval stores. From there he departed for Charleston. The selection of Charleston as his port of destination was very sound for it lay within the sailing range of his schooner and was a city inhabited by many Frenchman and Spaniards. He arrived in 1776 to a warm welcome. The local authorities, fearing a British amphibious assault, had unsuccessfully sought assistance from Havana. The fate of the schooner, once unloaded, is unknown. However, we do know that Ferragut subsequently entered into the sea service as a lieutenant on a privateer. His previous war experience helped him in his new career. In 1778, he was appointed a first lieutenant in the Carolina Navy, where he was commissioned to supervise the building of several war galleys. He accomplished this job satisfactorily, leading one to speculate that he learned something of shipbuilding working in the British naval shipyard of Mahón.

When Savannah was under siege, Ferragut was selected to command a galley and sail there to render assistance. Sailing through the connecting channels, he arrived in time to resist the invaders. The battle was a bloody one, and ended in the defeat of Ferragut's troops. Those who survived returned to Charleston. After the fall of Savannah, the British invaded Charleston. They approached the outskirts by land and sea with forces superior to those of the rebels. General George Washington predicted that the probability of sustaining a defense was nil, if the British fleet passed the bar.[6] Military and civilian forces decided to make a stand, and did so until the end when they were forced to retreat. By then, it was too late. Ferragut, among others, became a prisoner of war.

Ferragut was imprisoned on Haddrell's Point across the Cooper River from Charleston. As soon as he regained his freedom through a prisoner exchange, he looked for a ship. This time, on his own as a privateer, he fought against the British merchant ships. In a board-

ing action, a musket ball seriously wounded his right arm. He re-
covered ashore, but was unable to return to his command post because his arm was semi-paralyzed. The disability forced him to
leave the Revolutionary navy. Yet so imbued was he with devotion
to the American cause, that he made his way far inland, until he
found and joined the forces of General Francis Marion as a volunteer.

General Marion was a legendary guerilla fighter. His irregular
army grew progressively larger as it gained combat experience. At
about the time that Jorge joined the General, he Americanized his
name to George Farragut. His first action under Marion was at the
Battle of Cowpens, in which Marion and Colonel William Washington defeated the regular British army led by Lieutenant-Colonel
Banastre Tarleton.[7] After the British rout, Colonel Washington pursued Tarleton so single-mindedly that Washington became sepa-
rated from his troops. Seeing Colonel Washington's vulnerability,
Tarleton turned back and with two British officers attacked the
hapless Washington. The Colonel's life was saved by the timely arrival of an American sergeant and his 14-year old bugler. Contrary
to the accounts of some writers, Farragut was not the courageous
soldier who rescued Colonel William Washington (sometimes himself wrongly identified as George Washington).

George Farragut was appointed commander of a voluntary artillery company by General Abner Nash. He fought with distinction
near Wilmington, North Carolina and at Beaufort Bridge. During
the march of the British General Charles Cornwallis, from Georgia
to Virginia, Farragut raised a company of volunteer cavalry and harassed the enemy's rear until they left the North Carolina border. He
was soon commissioned by the state as a cavalry captain. When the
Revolutionary War ended, Farragut received the thanks of Marion
and Nash for his efforts on the behalf of the new nation.

The new civilian

> found himself, like the greater part of his adopted countrymen,
> called to the task of building up his own fortunes, neglected dur-
> ing [the war's] continuance; and, by so doing, to help in restoring
> prosperity to the new nation.[8]

Farragut went into the wilderness of Eastern Tennessee and became a typical frontiersman, a sort of jack-of-all-trades, able to perform one day as a sharp-shooter and the next as a builder of houses. His restless activities caught the attention of William Blount, the governor of the new state of Tennessee. Blount appointed him a major in the Militia. In 1792, Farragut established his residence in Knoxville. The next year, he took part in a campaign against the Cherokee Indians, under the command of General John Sevier. Two years later, in 1795, at the age of forty, he married thirty-year old Elizabeth Shine, daughter of Captain John Shine and a native of Dobbs County in North Carolina. They had five children. The eldest, William, and George (who later changed his name to David), were reared amid the dangers of the Indian incursions. On one occasion, Elizabeth sent David into the loft while she guarded the barricaded front door armed with an axe.

At the turn of the century, Eastern Tennessee was one of the most backward areas in the United States. Farragut realized that it offered little realistic hope for bettering his family's fortunes. That opportunity arrived when his friend, William C. C. Clairborne, governor of the Mississippi Territory, moved to New Orleans in 1804. Clairborne took the post of governor of the southern part of recently-purchased Louisiana called the Territory of Orleans. Farragut and his family moved south, too.

Clairborne was very close to Thomas Jefferson who had been President of the United States since 1801. Jefferson

> differed definitely on naval questions from. . .John Adams. The one wish[d] to reduce the naval expenditures to the lowest terms, the other to appropriate most generously for officers, seamen, ships. . . .[9]

Jefferson favored a Navy for defensive purposes, and when authorized by Congress, ordered the construction of ninety small wooden gunboats between 1803 and 1806, and 188 in 1807. Clairborne was thus able to employ Farragut. His first job was in the construction of the twenty-nine gunboats required for the defense of New Orleans. Those boats had average dimensions of an eighty-foot length, a seventeen-foot width, and a six-foot depth. They carried one or two large guns of twenty-four or thirty-five pounds, and were manned by crews of between twenty-five and forty-five men. After the construction was completed, Farragut became the captain of Gunboat II, and later was appointed Sailing Master on March 2, 1807.

Joined by his wife and children, the Farraguts settled in the "Spanish" side of the territory that was claimed by the Americans. Navy Secretary Robert Smith ordered Sailing Master David Porter, father of Commodore David Porter, to the New Orleans station as a token of good will toward the commodore. There the elder Porter met and served with Farragut. In early June 1808, Porter senior suffered a sunstroke while fishing on Lake Pontchartrain. Farragut saw the event and took the elderly sailing master home where Elizabeth nursed him until his death on June 22. Shortly thereafter, Elizabeth died, a victim of yellow fever and, possibly, from exhaustion, having taken care of Porter while she herself was ill.

Commodore Porter was very grateful to the Farraguts. He offered to help them by taking one of their small sons under his care. With the consent of his father, George (who later changed his name to David) entered under the protection of Porter. Many years later, as David G. Farragut, he became the first admiral of the United States Navy. It was widely rumored that David G. Farragut was a natural son of the Commodore. The historian Charles Lewis proved, however, that the rumor is without the slightest foundation.[10]

Farragut continued his service patrolling the Mississippi River. In 1811 he was ordered to go to Pascagoula. Finding the area to his liking, he bought a plantation near Point Plaquet. During the War of 1812, he assisted in minor missions with his gunboat, although he was practically incapacitated for naval service. His right arm had been paralyzed since taking a musket ball during the Revolution and he was now afflicted with other ailments. Because Farragut was a highly esteemed veteran, he was allowed to remain on his beloved farm and enjoy the pay of a sailing master, at least for a while. Unfortunately, war expenditures forced Secretary of the Navy William Jones to dismiss Farragut from the Navy. Although he appealed the decision, he was unable to change it. He was therefore unable to fight at New Orleans and contribute to the defeat of the British there. Farragut lived two years more. He never again would see the palms and olives, the emerald mountains, the lapis lazuli sea, or the heavenly air of his native land. Instead, he was surrounded by maples and cypresses, swampy flat lands, muddy waters, and the stifling air of his own plantation in his adopted country. Did he miss Minorca? Perhaps, but every time Farragut filled his hands with American soil, he said that he felt happy to have dedicated the best years of his life to the freedom of America.

PADRE FÉLIX VARELA:
DEFENDER OF HUMAN RIGHTS

On February 25, 1988, about six hundred Floridians gathered in St. Augustine's *Plaza de la Constitución* to unveil the first public monument erected in the United States to honor the memory of Padre Félix Varela. Extracted from a local underwater quarry, the solid coquina rock was the same type used to build the San Marcos Castle. The monument faces the Cathedral of St. Augustine. As a child, Varela witnessed the beginnings of its construction. In his later years, Varela celebrated many Masses there. He also passed many hours in the plaza entertaining children with his violin and giving them informal religious instruction.

St. Augustine's mayor, Kenneth Bisson, presided over the unveiling ceremony. He noted another reason why the location of the monument was so fitting. Varela was one of the staunchest defenders of the Constitution for which the plaza was named.[1]

A plaque embedded in the coquina rock reads:

Padre Félix
VARELA
Havana • St. Augustine
11/20/1788 • 2/25/1853
Beloved Member of
St. Augustine Community
Main Ideological Founder
of the Cuban Nationality
Educator, Philosopher
Speaker and Writer
Advocate of Human and Civil
Rights in Cuba and USA
Father of the Underprivileged
Advocate of Popular Education
and Religious Freedom
Pioneer of American
Catholic Journalism
Vicar General of the Catholic
Archdiocese of New York (1837-53)
Félix Varela
Bicentennial Committee
St. Augustine 2-25-1988

Varela's Legacy

Félix Varela y Morales is considered one of the most innovative and foresighted thinkers of Cuba. He was the first to propose the abolition of slavery and complete independence for Cuba. He introduced reforms to the educational system of Cuba, and he was elected as one of the Cuban representatives to the *Cortes* (Legislature) of Spain.

He spent the last thirty years of his life in the United States where he built up a social health ministry, founding day-care centers for working mothers, orphanages, and schools for boys and girls. He ministered to the sick in hospitals and helped the underprivileged. A prolific author, publisher, and editor of journals and magazines in English, he became a civil rights advocate for Native Americans, as well as immigrant groups then entering New York, such as Italians, Poles, Hispanics, and especially, Irish. He defended the human and civil rights of Catholics and non-Catholics alike.

Early Childhood in Havana (1788-1794)

Varela was born on November 20, 1788 in Havana, Cuba, the third child of his parents. His mother, María Josefa, born in Santiago de Cuba, was the daughter of regimental commander Lieutenant-Colonel Bartolomé Morales y Ramírez who was a native of Castille. Varela's father, Lieutenant Francisco Varela y Pérez, a native of Tordesillas in Old Castille, had served as paymaster of the militia and a runner of human cargoes on slave ships from the Canary Islands.

Before the age of four, Varela lost his mother. The Morales kin took charge of him.[2] Félix's father, now a Captain, remarried and had another son, Manuel.[3] Their father died when Félix was only six, whereupon Félix was sent to St. Augustine to live with his maternal grandfather.

The St. Augustine Period (1794-1801)

Don Bartolomé Morales y Castillo, a Brevet Colonel, commanded the third battalion of the regiment of Cubans garrisoned in St. Augustine, capital of the Spanish colony of East Florida. San

Marcos Castle, with its thick coral-rock walls, became Félix's child-hood home. Don Bartolomé took pride in his precocious ward. He declined the post of governor, preferring to watch his dreams ful-filled in his descendants. Doña Rita, Félix's godmother and aunt, also cherished the young boy as her own.

The towering bastions of San Marcos Castle were named for Sts. Peter, Paul, James, and other holy men. Yet there was nothing sacred about the chains and instruments of torture in the castle vaults. Félix was troubled by the bragging of the men, describing forays against the Native Americans, slave raids, and British guerilla attacks. In the town, he witnessed another cause for sorrow: in the wide plaza facing St. Augustine's church, black humans were sold like cattle.[4]

Despite the remoteness of the colonial outpost, Félix was fortu-nate in his educational opportunities. Varela attended a free public school, run by a Cuban priest, Father Francisco Traconis. Fathers Thomas Hassett and Miguel O'Reilly, two Irish priests trained in the Irish Seminary of the University of Salamanca, also were instruc-tors. Established in 1787, this school was the first integrated free public school in what is now the continental United States. In this school, children of European, African, and Native American back-ground mingled.[5]

Father O'Reilly was eminently qualified. He was both under-standing and possessed a great intellect. In addition to Latin, theol-ogy, mathematics, and music, he was versed in English, Spanish, French, and Greek. Father O'Reilly served as Vicar of East Florida, supervised the completion of the St. Augustine church, and was chaplain of the troops and at the hospital. Despite all these duties, he still found time to satisfy the intellectual and spiritual craving of his most apt pupil, the young Varela.[6]

When Varela approached his fourteenth birthday, the time came for him to choose a military career, as had all the Morales fam-ily before him. However, Varela declared, "I wish to be a soldier of Jesus Christ. I do not wish to kill men. I wish rather to save their souls."[7]

Varela stood firm. His grandfather sent him to relatives in Havana, to enroll in the ancient seminary of San Carlos, hoping his grandson would clamor for the more adventurous life of a soldier as he grew older. Before sailing for Havana, he was saddened by the death of Doña Rita. She was buried in St. Augustine at the Tolomato Cemetery.[8]

Educational Formation (1801-1821)

Unwittingly, Don Bartolomé had sent the young Varela to a Havana that was intellectually stimulating. The military routine of the San Marcos Castle soon turned into a sordid memory. In 1802, Varela entered the San Carlos Seminary, the oldest college in Cuba. In 1804, he also enrolled at the University of Havana.[9]

In Havana, Félix's educational fortunes would continue. Where Father O'Reilly left off, Father José Agustín Caballero (1771-1835) took up. He was an eclectic philosopher, an editor of *El Diario*, and translator of the works of Condillac. Bishop Juan Espada y Fernández de Landa, Spanish-born patron of the island's most brilliant intellectual period, became Varela's mentor. Espada had gathered under his leadership a group of brilliant independent and advanced thinkers in addition to Father Caballero. Among them were the following: Father Juan Bernardo O'Gavan y Guerra (1782-1838), descendant of an Irishman who had fled from Oliver Cromwell, who taught physics, ethics, and modern philosophy; Havana's own Dr. Tomás Romay y Chacón (1769-1842), a medical doctor who engaged in pioneer studies on yellow fever; and, Colonel Manuel Tiburcio de Zequeira y Arango (1760-1846), also from Havana, a co-editor of *Papel Periódico*, and the first poet to sound the theme of Cuban patriotism.[10]

Initial Teachings

Under the aegis of Bishop Espada, Varela taught the younger students at San Carlos in Latin and Rhetoric. He also set his hand to writing. One of his earliest works, a play entitled *El Desafío* ("The Duel"), became a repertory item for later generations of students. He also continued studying in preparation for his ordination. For relaxation, he played the violin. An accomplished performer, he also inaugurated classes in music, and in 1811, helped found the Philharmonic Society of Havana, the first of its kind in Cuba.

On two occasions, Varela applied for openings at the San Carlos. Both times, older individuals were appointed. Yet, the Bishop had taken note of Varela's brilliant performance.

Early Life as a Priest

The young theologian was ordained a deacon in 1810. A year later, Don Bartolomé returned from St. Augustine, aged and sick. Félix thought the old soldier's forbearance had earned him the right to witness his grandson's consecration. And so, at Félix's request, Bishop Espada ordained Félix Varela in 1811, when he was just twenty-three years old. Finally, in 1812, Varela was selected to the vacancy created by the promotion of Father O'Gavan. Bishop Espada gave the following directive to his new teacher of philosophy, ethics, and physics: "Take the broom and sweep away all that is not useful."[11] Fathers Caballero and O'Gavan had opened the way. Now Varela was to lead the thought of Cuba boldly out of the tradition-bound past.

During the decade from 1812 to 1821, Félix Varela earned a reputation as being Cuba's most illustrious philosopher and teacher. He not only revolutionized the teaching of philosophy at the seminary, but he added news fields of study. His creativity and energy were prodigious. He lectured, wrote, and — most importantly — thought deeply and well.

Father Varela published several textbooks and treatises on philosophy in Latin. Later, he led the way by teaching and publishing in the vernacular (Spanish), as well as in English in the United States. His books were used as textbooks in seminaries and colleges all over the Americas.

He modernized the teaching of philosophy by emphasizing the student's own ability to think analytically. He was also the first to teach chemistry, biology, magnetism, and electricity in Cuba. He designed and set up laboratories complementing those subject areas by building the laboratory equipment himself. He emphasized field research, especially in biology.

In 1821, in view of the re-establishment of the Spanish Constitution of 1812, Bishop Espada asked Father Varela to teach a course on constitutional law. This became the first class on this subject in Spanish America. In that class he emphasized the human rights aspects. His course was so popular that even the windows were jammed with students.

When he assumed the chair of philosophy, there were thirty-nine students in all of the San Carlos. In 1821 some two hundred students jostled for admission to Varela's course on constitutional law. Padre Varela caused learning to become vital, pertinent, and fashionable in Havana.

The popularity of Padre Varela's "Constitutional Law," as well as his other courses in political science, moved Espada to request that Varela seek public office as one of Cuba's representatives to the Spanish *Cortes* (Legislature). At first Varela declined. Later, he was ordered to do so by the Bishop. Varela ran for office and was elected as the representative of Western Cuba. Varela went off to Spain with his violin, his wit, and his great sense of humor.

The Legislative Effort in Spain — *Las Cortes* (1821-1823)

On April 28, 1821, Padre Varela departed for Spain with Tomás Gener and Leonardo Santos Suárez, the other two Cuban representatives who would serve on the *Cortes*. Padre Varela would never return to his beloved island. They disembarked at Cádiz on June 7 and proceeded to Seville and Madrid. On October 3, 1822, the Cuban representatives were sworn into the *Cortes*.

During the term of these *Cortes*, Padre Varela presented three major legal projects:

1. Recognition of Spanish-American Independence:
   He urged Spain's acceptance and recognition of the independence of the recently liberated Spanish-American republics.

2. Granting of Autonomy to Remaining Colonies:
   Autonomy would be granted to the remaining Spanish colonies, such as Cuba, Puerto Rico, and the Philippines. This

commonwealth concept preceded the British Commonwealth by fifty years.

3. The Abolition of Slavery:
Varela proposed the total and absolute abolition of slavery in Cuba. Varela's plan struck a blow to the economic interests of some of his most influential voters. Still, he argued that morality took precedence over economic interests. Varela has been called the first Cuban Abolitionist.[12]

In 1823, French troops invaded Spain to defend the monarchy against the *Cortes.* Ferdinand VII condemned a number of legislators to death, including Varela. Under fire of the French soldiers, the Cuban representatives rowed to Gibraltar and safety. They took the first ship out of Gibraltar, the *Draper C. Thorndike.* Its destination was the United States of America.

Padre Varela in the United States (1823-1853)

The legislators arrived in New York City on December 15, 1823. Varela continued his journey to Philadelphia. There he awaited his canonical documents from Havana so that he could practice as a priest outside his diocese. Meanwhile, he gained greater fluency in English.

El Habanero

In 1824, he published a second edition of *Lecciones de Filosofía* and began publishing *El Habanero*, a literary, scientific, and cultural newspaper. *El Habanero* was one of the first Spanish newspapers to be published in the United States. *El Habanero* was smuggled into Cuba from Philadelphia through Yucatán and New Orleans.

Early in 1825, the Spanish government retaliated with a pamphlet written by a pupil of Padre Varela. This pupil was identified as Juan Agustín de Ferrety, the same man who betrayed the conspiracy of the "*Rayos y Soles de Bolívar*," a Cuban group associated with Simón Bolívar.[13]

Padre Varela had a response ready for Ferrety. *El Habanero* continued to hammer at the historic necessity of Cuban independence. Varela was trying to prepare the minds of Cubans for a peaceful change and eventual self-government.

To Francisco Vives, Governor of Cuba, Varela seemed a serious threat, one that he wanted eliminated. Vives's cronies raised the sum of 30,000 pesos to hire an assassin and pay for his passage to the United States. The agent arrived in the U.S. in March, 1825. A letter from a friend in Havana forewarned Varela of the agent's purpose. Varela's friends urged him to go into hiding, but he only smiled at their concern. He continued producing *El Habanero*, saying that a good priest has no fear of death. His friends, nevertheless, notified the mayor and the chief of police. As things developed, there was no need for action to be taken. The would-be assassin soon boarded another ship for Havana.

Twenty years later in *Verdad*, a Spanish paper published by José Antonio Saco in New York City, Padre Varela recounted how he had come face to face with the hired killer and talked him out of his evil errand. The lure of money was no match for the intense patriotism of the priest. Varela felt compassion for the wretched man who had been sent to slay him. According to Antonio Hernández Travieso, Varela's Irish Catholic immigrant parishioners also intimidated the assassin into leaving New York.[14]

On May 11, 1825, the High Court of Seville affirmed sentences confiscating all of Varela's assets. On June 27, 1825, King Ferdinand banned *El Habanero* from Spain and adjacent islands and ordered his officials to take the necessary measures to secure compliance:

> Don Félix Varela, ex-deputy of the so-called *Cortes*, now actually a refugee in the United States of America, is publishing there, a tract called *El Habanero*, in which, not content with inciting the loyal vassals of His Majesty to rebellion, he carries his audacity to the point of seeking to injure the sacred character of his lawful sovereign.[15]

Padre Varela continued his magazine almost a year after the edict against it, defying both royal wrath and threats of death. The seventh, and probably final, edition was issued from New York in the Spring of 1826. Censorship of incoming mail, however, gave the paper little chance of reaching its intended readers in Cuba.

Publications in Spanish

Padre Varela did not, however, abandon his efforts for Cuba. He continued to counsel Cuba's expatriates and to write for her young men at home. To help the predominantly rural economies of Cuba and Latin America, he translated Humphrey Davy's *Elements of Chemistry Applied to Agriculture*. To encourage the adoption of democratic institutions, he also translated an annotated version of Thomas Jefferson's *Manual of Parliamentary Procedure*. He hoped to instruct Cubans and Latin Americans on how to run the senate of a free country. In 1826, he also published the collected poems of Manuel de Zequeira y Arango, the first poet to emphasize the theme of Cuban nationalism. He continued to revise and update his popular *Lecciones de Filosofía*, issuing the third, fourth, and fifth editions in 1828, 1832, and 1841, respectively. His works became the standard textbooks in many Latin American universities.

From 1829-1831, Varela collaborated with his protegé, José Antonio Saco, on *El Mensajero Semanal* ("The Weekly Messenger"), a world news bulletin which they published from 7 Nassau Street, New York. Saco returned to Cuba in 1832 and became editor of the *Revista Bimestre Cubana*, which he made into the outstanding publication of the island. Varela contributed articles to the *Revista* on subjects as diverse as Spanish grammar and the right of women to receive an education. In 1835, Varela had already been appointed Vicar General of the Diocese of New York. He began publishing his tribute to hope, *Cartas a Elpidio* ("Letters to Elpidio") in which he continued to advise the young men of his fatherland against ignorance, prejudice, and fanaticism.

During the 1840's, Varela wrote occasionally for the New York newspaper *La Verdad*, a journal supported by Cubans for the dissemination of democratic principles and ideals. In March 1841, the *Repertorio Médico Habanero* reported on an apparatus whose specifications Varela had sent to Havana, designed "to lower the temperature, purify, and renew the air," in hospitals. The device anticipated air-conditioners developed a century later.

The New York Priest

Padre Varela's pastoral work in New York City began in 1825, when his credentials arrived from the Chancery of Havana. At the time, there were only two Catholic churches and five Catholic priests in the entire city of New York. Varela became assistant pastor of St. Peter Church. There were relatively few Catholics in New York City and, with a few notable exceptions, they occupied the lowest economic and social echelons of society.

In February 1825, the Irish Bishop of New York, John Connelly, died. The pastor of St. Peter's, Father John Power, became Vicar General of the diocese. Padre Varela established himself quickly as an invaluable aide. By now his command of English was competent enough not only for parish duties but also for participating in the beginnings of American Catholic journalism.

The two young priests had much in common. Devoted to their vocations, they were both scholarly and well-trained in theology. Each had fled a homeland victimized by political tyranny. While retaining a profound loyalty to their native islands, both priests appreciated the unprecedented freedom from harassment enjoyed by residents of the United States. They were eloquent, literate, and able to turn easily from pulpit to press. Like Padre Varela, Father Power supplemented his teaching with books of his own authorship. Both attracted followers by their sincerity, intelligence, and their personal magnetism. Their one significant difference would help them to work together. Recognition and a position of authority were important to John Power who took steps to attain the episcopacy. Padre Varela was content with accomplishment and happily left "superiority of status" to others.[16]

Varela opened day schools for both boys and girls adjacent to Christ Church, which he had acquired in 1827 with money donated by various Cubans. He taught alongside the hired teachers and taught Sunday School himself. Money for the support of Christ Church and for its poor immigrant flock came from New York benefactors and Father Varela's private resources. His half-brother, Manuel, the Morales cousins, and the Havana disciples did not forget their friend and schoolmaster. Varela's *Lecciones de Filosofía*, widely used as a textbook in Latin America, provided an income which he invested in spiritual and charitable works in New York.[17]

On September 1829, New York's Bishop, Jean Dubois, sailed for Europe to seek funds and priests for his diocese. He named Fathers Power and Varela as Vicars General. The two vicars accomplished much. Six new churches were dedicated in the diocese during the Bishop's absence, and a seventh had its cornerstone laid. The Sisters of Charity opened schools for girls in Mulberry Street, in Barclay Street, and at Albany. Father Varela's schools in Ann Street and John Street offered, besides basic education, instruction in grammar, spelling, needlework, music with use of the piano, and from five to six P.M., lessons in French and Spanish.[18]

Through a generous gift, Varela was able to build a combination nursery and orphan asylum for the children of poor widows and widowers.

A cholera epidemic struck the city in 1832, banning public meetings and closing churches and schools. Those who could afford to, sent their families to rural retreats. Both Power and Varela remained at their posts. Varela virtually lived in the hospitals. He visited the immigrant ships suspected of bringing the scourge to the city. He argued his way into quarantine to carry the consolation of the sacraments to the sick. People cried out against the Irish who now were blamed for the plague, as well as for their poverty and support of the Pope. They had, however, nothing but praise for the selfless devotion of the Catholic clergy to the victims of the epidemic.

On October 27, 1833, a huge fissure spread across the interior wall of Christ Church during Holy Communion. The church could not be saved. The parish merged with another and a new Romanesque edifice was erected on James Street. St. James was dedicated in September, 1836. Its basement became the meeting place of the Catholic Association. Yet, it was a third church under his care which became known as "Father Varela's Church." The Church of the Transfiguration was acquired by a wealthy Swiss businessman, John Delmonico. An admirer of Father Varela's, Delmonico happened to be passing by during the auction of a reformed Scotch

Presbyterian Church. On impulse, knowing that Father Varela needed a church, he made a successful bid.

Father Varela purchased the house behind this church for a pastoral residence. It served as his home for his remaining years in New York and as a reception center for new priests and Cubans in search of counsel.[19]

Varela's church accounted for many "firsts" in diocesan history. Varela saw the value of lay participation. He organized a "total abstinence" society[20] almost a decade before Ireland's father Theobald Mathew began his work with American audiences. He also organized a Ladies' Aid, a Sewing Society, a Ladies' Society of Charity, and other charitable groups.[21]

Father Varela was the embodiment of selflessness, a prototype of the venerable Bishop Miriel in Victor Hugo's *Les Misérables.* Varela's income from Cuba and the gifts from prosperous friends were instantly diverted to the needs of his church and its poor.[22]

Stand Against Bigotry

A matter of grave concern began to claim the attention of the Vicars General of New York. Anti-Catholicism, which had been in eclipse during the liberal years of the early Republic, was now reappearing with renewed force.[23] By 1830, the Anti-Catholic campaign was unified and strong.[24] Power and Varela did not let the challenge go unanswered. A series of debates were held throughout the city. The *Truth Teller* and some of the Protestant journals opened their columns to these debates. After a few months, the war of words was terminated by the anti-Catholic Reverend William Craig Brownlee. Of the principal Catholics protagonists, the intellectual Cuban was the most restrained and scholarly.[25] Avoiding inflammatory rhetoric and vindictiveness, Padre Varela cited chapter and verse and historical fact to correct his adversaries and, concurrently, to enlighten the over-credulous and the ignorant among his own people. Varela also organized a series of weekly conferences on Christian doctrine, in which all the priests of the city participated, so that Catholics might better know their faith before they attempted to defend it.[26] Typical of his calm response to anti-Catholic

crimes was the editorial he wrote following the 1844 riots in Philadelphia when several Catholic churches and a library were burned:

> [O]ut of the smoldering ruins of our churches and edifices, may
> spring up a monument which, while it records the horrors of fa-
> naticism, will stand as a warning and a caution to future genera-
> tions.[27]

Varela's English Writings

On April 2, 1825, Padre Varela began publishing the *Truth
Teller*, a quasi-diocesan weekly. Articles he authored appeared
anonymously in this periodical from time to time. He also established *The Youth's Friend* (*El Amigo de la Juventud*), a bilingual periodical which was intended to contribute to the mutual
understanding between English- and Spanish-speaking peoples.
This pioneer children's magazine in the Diocese of New York represented the first of the Cuban priest's many English-language peri-
odicals. With his assistant, Father Joseph A. Schneller, an Austrian
former Jesuit, he published the *New York Weekly Register* and the
Catholic Diary which catered particularly to Irish-Americans. Varela
involved the Irish patriot and educator, Patrick S. Casserly, in this
periodical.[28] This publication continued in print for four years,
eventually supplanting the *Truth Teller* as the outstanding Catholic
voice in New York. Subsequently, Varela started the *Catholic Observer*, of which little is known at present.[29]

In the *New York Weekly Register*, Varela defended, among others,
the Native Americans against the injustices and abuse they suffered.
The press of the time justified these cruelties on the rationale that
American Indians were not entitled to any human rights. Varela's
plea for justice was ahead of its time.[30]

In an era of blinding religious animosities, Varela was the pioneer ecumenist, able to conduct dialogue without violence,
astonishing his opponents by his knowledge, his patient exposition,
and his liberalism. Catholics during the 1830's were seething over
the deliberate, unpunished burning by a mob of such buildings as
the Ursuline convent and library at Charlestown, Massachusetts, the
arson destruction of St. Mary's Church in New York, the seminary

in Nyack, and the Sisters of Charity School on Mulberry Street. To each new attack, Father Varela urged forbearance.

Padre Félix Varela's reasoned and moderate tone may be observed in a magazine which he published during 1830 and 1831 in response to *The Protestant*. Its title, *The Protestant's Abridger and Annotator*, discloses its purposes. The author's straight-forward, moderate, friendly, hopeful tone absolves most non-Catholics from the fanaticism displayed in *The Protestant*.

In July 1838, Padre Varela published "School Books which Have Attacks on the Catholic Religion," in *Children's Catholic Magazine*.[31] With this article, the effort to eliminate bigotry in New York's public schools began.[32]

In April 1841, Varela began a monthly magazine, *The Catholic Expositor and Literary Magazine*. The Reverend Dr. Charles Constantine Pise collaborated with him on this project. Pise was the first Catholic priest to serve as chaplain to the U.S. Congress.[33] The magazine was both literary and philosophical. Varela wrote an essay on Kant, the "Origin of our Ideas," and a comparison of the five Bibles issued by the American Bible Society.

The Expositor endured for almost four years. During this time, Varela was also editing the *Young Catholic's Magazine*, a successor to the popular *Children's Catholic Magazine*. His works were disseminated widely beyond the original audience. Father Varela had become a recognized leader among American Catholics. He was quoted in many publications, including the *United States Catholic Miscellany*, a pioneer Catholic weekly out of Charleston, South Carolina.

Return to St. Augustine

During the winter of 1846, friends fearing for his life on medical grounds, removed him to Florida. He was soon back in New York, resuming the same feverish routine in disregard of his physical limitations. The next winter, however, forced him back to St. Augustine for a longer stay. By the summer of 1849, renewed energy induced him back to the Church of the Transfiguration. By winter, he was again rigid with pain, choking with every breath, unable to lie down or even recline.

Padre Varela would end his years in St. Augustine, serving as a priest there as long as he had strength to breathe. On a Christmas Day, 1852 visit to Father Varela, one of his friends grew alarmed at his failing health and poverty. He wrote to Francisco Ruiz in Havana, Varela's successor to the philosophy chair at the San Carlos Seminary. News spread quickly through Havana and a considerable sum was collected to aid the beloved priest. José María Casal and his wife arrived in St. Augustine on March 3, 1853 with the donation from Havana, too late to console or aid Father Varela. He had surrendered his soul peacefully on February 25 with the words: "*Venid a mi, Señor!*" ("Lord, come to me!")

The unassuming and unhurried citizens of St. Augustine took their time in bidding farewell to Padre Varela. The room where his body was laid was packed to overflowing. The Spanish, Irish, Minorcan, and Black mourners recalled his benevolent deeds. In a somber procession to the Tolomato Cemetery, were joined all the clergy of the area, the children from the boys' and girls' schools, and the hundreds of mourners "without distinction of age, sex, color, or condition."[34]

Padre Varela would not have had it any other way.

DAVID G. FARRAGUT:

FIRST ADMIRAL OF THE UNITED STATES

David Glasgow Farragut, first Admiral of the United States Navy, is celebrated in American history books for his naval contributions during the Civil War. Yet the Civil War achievements occupied only five years out of a varied and distinguished career that spanned almost sixty years.

David G. Farragut, born on July 5, 1801 near Knoxville, Tennessee, was the son and grandson of sailors. The distinguished career of his father, born Jorge Ferragut, is discussed in an earlier essay. Although David was taken under the protection of Commodore David Porter when he was a young boy, David remained fluent in Spanish and identified closely with his Spanish heritage. Throughout his life, he maintained close contacts with Spanish-speaking countries and their people.

He saw his first action at age eleven. The ship on which young Farragut berthed captured a great number of British vessels off the coast of Valparaíso, Chile during the War of 1812. He is said to have suppressed an attempted mutiny by his prisoners with an energy uncommon in such a young man.[1]

Following the War of 1812, he accompanied the first American minister, Mr. Poinsett, to the court of Emperor Agustín de Iturbide in Mexico.

The first time Farragut visited Spain was in 1815. The war between the United States and Algiers (over the Barbary States' piracy) had just ended when the flag ship *Independence*, to which he was assigned, landed in Cartagena, Spain. His fleet anchored in Málaga, Spain on August 13, and a brilliant reception was organized aboard the ship. He revisited Málaga in 1817 as an officer aboard the *Erie*.

On that occasion, he attended a reception given by British Consul Kirkpatrick where he met, among others, the Consul's daughter, the Countess of Montijo, who later became the mother of the future Empress of France. In 1819 he had the opportunity to visit Málaga and Cádiz again.[2]

In October 1822 he participated in the attack on the port of Veracruz, after which he dined with General Antonio Santa Anna who had captured the city the year before. At that time, the fortress of San Juan de Ulloa, which controlled the shipping traffic of that city, was still held by the viceroy of New Spain. Farragut also visited Tampico for two weeks where he enjoyed the hospitality of its inhabitants and the many parties given in his honor.

Farragut was able to visit Minorca and its city of Mahón on several occasions. Seeking Mahón as a safe harbor during bad weather, Commodore Chauncey permitted the crew, including Farragut, to go ashore three days a week from April to June 1817. Farragut again visited Minorca during the summers of 1819 and 1820, and many years later while on an official visit during the Christmas holidays of 1867.[3]

In 1842, Farragut was aboard the frigate *Delaware*, sailing along the eastern coast of South America. He visited Montevideo, Uruguay and arrived in Buenos Aires, Argentina on July 16 of that year. He remained in Argentina for four months, giving him an opportunity to form a friendship with President Juan Manuel de Rosas and his daughter Manuelita.[4]

Farragut became a popular hero in the United States because he won many laurels during the Civil War. At the beginning of the war, he was placed in command of the fleet which was to block the Southern ports. Then, in 1862, he organized a flotilla which sailed up the Mississippi River, destroying the rebel ships anchored in New Orleans. For five days they bombarded the city until it surrendered to Union General Butler. This action and the attack at Vicksburg earned him Lincoln's praises and a promotion to rear admiral. However, his greatest fame was to come after his taking of Mobile in August 1864. For this feat, he was appointed vice admiral and given a hero's welcome in New York City. At the end of the war, in 1866, Congress created the title of admiral in order to more fully honor him.

After the Civil War, the United States wanted to demonstrate its ascendancy to the countries of the Old World. Congress decided to send the fleet to visit the main capitals of Europe under the command of David G. Farragut. Because Farragut's leadership brought the North so many victories at sea during the war, he was the logical choice to lead the legation. Aboard the frigate *Franklin*, Farragut arrived in Cherbourg, France on June 18, 1867, accompanied by his wife. During this trip he dined at the Tuilleries with Emperor Napoleon III and the Empress Eugenia, daughter of his old friend. In London he was feasted by the Admiralty and was received by Queen Victoria. The Russian fleet came out to meet him at Kronstadt. The King of Denmark gave a magnificent banquet in his honor at his palace in Copenhagen, with the King of Greece as one of his guests.[5]

Spain welcomed him in Cartagena on December 5, 1867. The poet Carolina Coronado greeted him with a poem called "Admiral Farragut and His Arrival in Cartagena":

> Hail the great Farragut! His swift ship has brought him to
>   Spanish shores
> And the sea greets him with brilliant waves
> The world repeats his name echoed majestically by the
>   deep
> As gallant flags to the Tajo carry his fame.
> Where now all sing the praises of his glory
> I was the solitary bird who sang to you praises from the
>   shores.
> Even when the Northern star was darkened.
> Now that your star shines triumphantly
> My song is needed no more.
> Your stars alone are enough.[6]

El Siglo Illustrado, a Madrid newspaper, reproduced the poem, thereby contributing to the success of the visit. Farragut arrived in the capital of Spain with his wife and five officers on December 11. He stayed at the Paris Hotel where he was met by the American ambassador, Mr. Hale, and by the embassy secretary, Mr. Perry. He was also greeted by the Prime Minister of Spain and the Secretary of War, General Narváez.[7] Queen Elizabeth II of Spain and her husband met him. The Queen is reported to have said:

> Admiral Farragut, it pleases me to welcome you to Spain and I assure you that your name and glory have preceded you. I am proud to know that your ancestors came from my kingdom.[8]

Farragut also had a chance to renew his friendship with the Countess of Montijo.

On December 19, 1867 Farragut's fleet arrived in Mahón, Minorca. When he disembarked on Christmas morning, he was greeted by dignitaries from Mahón and Ciudadela. While in Mahón, he stayed at the Squella family palace. Villagers, knowing of his arrival, showered him with affection. City Hall honored him by making him an "adoptive son."[9] Farragut used this visit to delve into his family history. One of his excursions took him to the cathedral where he was able to see his father's baptismal record. His curiosity about his ancestors had been aroused earlier by a book given to him by the historian, George Tickner. The book had poems by Mosen Jaime Febrer, including one which praised his ancestor, Pedro Ferragut. Thereafter, Admiral Farragut began to use a family crest. It depicted a horseshoe, which he found had been used by many of his ancestors. "Ferragut" comes from *ferradura* or *herradura*, meaning horseshoe. To the basic design he added a fleet of ships lined up for battle, representing the course his life had taken.[10]

Farragut left Mahón on January 5, 1868 and returned to New York, arriving November 10.[11] A plaque commemorating this European visit has since been given by City Hall to the Naval Academy of Annapolis in June 1953.[12] On May 30, 1970, a monument in honor of Farragut was inaugurated. Its unveiling was attended by U.S. Ambassador Robert C. Hill and many local and state dignitaries.

In November 1868, Elizabeth II of Spain was deposed. The newspaper, *Army and Navy Journal* published an article entitled, "A Suggestion for the Spaniards" which set forth the following argument: Why don't the Spaniards set aside all the dynastic differences which separate them, and join forces around Admiral Farragut, electing him their king or emperor? The article came forth with many arguments to support their suggestion: he is of Spanish blood, he speaks the language like a native and is proud of his Hispanic ancestry, and he has vast experience in dealing with democratic institutions which democrats can accept easily, while those preferring a king can find ways to favor him, especially when they reexamine his abilities as a naval leader. The paper went on to say that the coronation of David I would be a sacrifice for Farragut, but one he would willingly accept if it were in the best interest of Spain. With him, Spain could establish a close relationship with the United States, and it would win the sympathy of liberal Europeans; republicanism could be practiced until the king himself decided the country was ready for the inauguration of a Republic.[13]

It is intriguing to speculate how the course of American and Cuban history might have been altered had Admiral Farragut become David I of Spain. His reaction to the article is not known. After almost sixty years of service to America, Farragut died in Portsmouth, New Hampshire on August 14, 1870.

FEDERICO
FERNÁNDEZ CAVADA:
LOYAL TO TWO FLAGS

Federico Fernández Cavada was a native of Cuba, born in Cienfuegos, Las Villas Province. In his early youth, nothing seemed to foretell that the frail-looking youngster was destined to distinguish himself for his bravery, intelligence, and determination. He was one of the most remarkable personages of two American nations at a time when both those nations experienced traumatic wars.

Fernández Cavada's life and achievements are very difficult to trace, due to the paucity of written information now available. One of the few sources that can be relied upon, and certainly the most important one, came in 1871 from the pen of O. Wilson Davis, a former comrade in arms. It is entitled *Sketch of Frederick Fernández Cavada, A Native of Cuba*.

Federico's father was a Cuban who married an American from Philadelphia. His father died at an early age and his mother decided to return to Philadelphia with her two young sons shortly after her husband's death.

In his book *Pioneros Cubanos en U.S.A. 1515-1898*, José Isern dedicates an entire chapter to Cavada. In it he states that Federico was at first a student in a boarding school in Wilmington, Delaware, and after spending a few years there, he completed his education in Philadelphia.[1] He no doubt received a very thorough and first-rate education because he would later distinguish himself as a writer, cartographer, diplomat, soldier, poet, and artist. From the diversity of the skills he mastered, one can appreciate the versatility, intelligence, and ability with which he was endowed.

Cavada's first great adventure took place on the Panama Isthmus. There he marched alongside Colonel Trautwine, studying the best route for a railroad that would unite the two oceans. He helped chart its course and actively participated in the construction of the railroad. During his stay in Panama, Cavada contracted malaria. The illness would affect him for the rest of his life.

Upon his return to the United States, he had to remain relatively restful in order to recuperate. He spent this period reading, writing, and sketching. His tranquillity was cut short by the secession of southern States from the Union.

Federico's background, convictions, and sentiments impelled him to join the Union cause. On July 20, 1861, he presented himself before O. Wilson Davis, the recruiting officer (and later his biographer), and joined the Twenty-third Regiment of Volunteers of Pennsylvania. Federico offered himself as a front-line officer and pledged to underwrite the costs of organizing a military company. During his first interview with Davis, he informed him that he had been educated in the United States, but that he was Cuban by birth. He spoke candidly of his poor health. Asked if he could withstand the rigors of military life, he responded: "I don't know, but I am willing to try."[2] And so, Cavada joined the Union Army with the rank of captain.

Because of his talent for sketching, Cavada was ordered to serve as an engineer when his division was assigned to the front line. One of his duties at the front was carried out from a hot air balloon. These were used "as the Eyes of the Army of the Potomac."[3] Cavada participated in numerous battles, including Antietam, Fredericksburg, North Anna, Petersburg, and Gettysburg. He served under such outstanding military officers as Generals McClellan, Pope, Burnside, Hooker, Graham, Birney, and Meade. Not only did he establish a close friendship with these men, but he also earned their respect and admiration. In his military career, he achieved the rank of lieutenant colonel of the 114th Regiment of Pennsylvania Volunteers and became a member of General Birney's staff. During the Battle of Gettysburg, one of the fiercest engagements of the Civil War, his company was nearly annihilated by the

Confederate forces. He and the Brigade's Commander, General Charles K. Graham, fell prisoner.

As a prisoner of war, Federico was sent to the Libby Concentration Camp in Richmond, Virginia. Cavada remained in prison from July 1863 until January 1864. Not even when forced to endure the most inhumane and deplorable conditions, could he remain idle and purposeless. While in prison, he wrote of the living conditions to which he and his fellow-prisoners of war were subjected. His writings were taken clandestinely from the camp by soldiers who risked their personal safety to help a comrade in arms. In 1864, as soon as he regained his freedom, his book was published in Philadelphia by King & Baird under the title *Libby Life*. Cavada's own drawings illustrated passages of the book. Cavada also assisted O. Wilson Davis in preparing his book, *Life of General Birney*, by drawing maps of the Battle of North Anna.

Years later, another tireless freedom fighter, Armando Valladares, employed his time in prison as Cavada did, by describing in horrifying detail the deprivations suffered by political prisoners. Both writers, Valladares and Cavada, recount the overcrowded conditions, the scant and nauseating food, the lack of adequate clothing, the insects and parasites that plagued them, and the primitive sanitary conditions available to them. However, Cavada does not mention physical or mental torture, nor secretive midnight firing squads, nor irrational humiliations, all of which were so familiar to Valladares.

After he was exchanged, due to his precarious health, Fernández Cavada left the army to enter the diplomatic corps. At his request, he was granted the position of United States consul attached to the important harbor of Trinidad in Cuba's Las Villas Province. Thus, Federico returned to his native country. In the mild climate where he spent the next few years, he regained his health to the extent that he wrote his friend Davis: "I am very happy to inform you that ever since I arrived my health has improved marvelously."[4]

The letter to Davis reveals much more than the state of Cavada's health; it also discloses his political convictions, his judgment, his powers of perception and prediction, and his high ethical standards:

> The public opinion here is genuinely interested in the political events taking place in the United States. . . .All seem to understand the importance of the principles at stake. The radical element in favor of the abolition of slavery, although it may seem strange, is not limited only to those who do not have slaves, even those who own a large number of them are among the followers of the new ideology. The definite extinction of slavery in the Americas seems to be the inevitable consequence of its extinction in the United States. Once that slavery is abolished in the American Union as a solution to the serious problem that is being debated there, it would be practically impossible to maintain slavery in Cuba, such a close neighbor of American freedom. . . .I seriously doubt if the deployment of the troops and its probable results are discussed in the United States with more passion and interest than it is done here. . . .Perhaps you are surprised to learn that the cause of the Union has such passionate followers here. If Cuba belongs geographically to America, why should it belong politically to Europe?[5]

From this passage, one perceives Cavada's conviction of the political similarity between the countries. He extols their interrelationship and their common destiny. He also realized that the genuine interest Cubans had in every development in the United States was not always reciprocated by the majority of Americans as to developments in Cuba. He closes his letter to Davis in the following way:

> This letter overextended itself and consequently has taken too much of your time. I tend to forget that Cuban politics and the welfare of Cuba are not as interesting to other people as they are to me.[6]

Something else is revealed of Federico in his letter to Davis — a writer's command of English and a poet's soul. Cavada included with his letter a poem dedicated to the memory of General Birney. The poem is reprinted in its entirety below.

Cavada served as United States consul in Trinidad, Cuba from the fall of 1864 to February, 1869. Because he yearned for Cuba's independence, after resigning his diplomatic post, he again took up the cause of freedom. On account of his vast military experience, he was immediately appointed commander of the forces fighting in the

District of Trinidad. Before long he was promoted to commander of all forces fighting in Las Villas Province, and finally, commander-in-chief of the Cuban Revolutionary Army. In his position as commander-in-chief, he had to transfer his general quarters and field of military operations to the Province of Camagüey. He left his brother Adolfo, who by that time had also joined the rebel army, in charge of the forces fighting in Las Villas Province. Cavada had to fight against an Army that was far larger, and better equipped and supplied, than his own. Nevertheless, he gained major victories, taking several Spanish forts by assault. He was seriously wounded during the war and spent three months in grave condition before recovering and returning to the battlefield.

On Tuesday, July 4, 1871, *La Gaceta de la Habana*, the official government publication, printed the news that General Federico Cavada and Admiral Osorio had been taken prisoner by the Spanish forces. According to the announcement, Cavada was to be taken to Puerto Príncipe, the capital of the Province of Camagüey, for a court martial.

Later, it became public knowledge that Cavada had found Osorio wounded and seriously ill. In order to save Osorio's life, Cavada attempted to take him out of Cuba so that he could receive proper medical attention. During this effort, they were discovered and apprehended by the enemy.

The American press picked up the news immediately. The *New York Herald*, in its July 4, 1871 edition, published the following:

> Habana, July 3— The Spanish Battleship *Neptuno* captured rebel General Federico Cavada while he was attempting to leave the island. He has been taken to Puerto Príncipe to stand trial. His execution seems to be certain. The *Neptuno* also took prisoner Cuban Admiral Osorio, who gained recognition when he captured the Spanish Coast Guard *Commanditore*. Osorio was taken to Nuevitas to stand trial.[7]

As soon as some of Cavada's comrades from the Union Army learned the news, they contacted the rest of his regiment. They petitioned President Grant to intercede on Cavada's behalf to prevent his execution. Other prominent citizens in the United States who had respected and admired Cavada also joined the petition. Every avenue was pursued in attempting to save his life. The United States secretary of state wired the request from President Grant to the minister of Spain in Washington. The minister of war called the captain general (governor) of Cuba, supposedly responsible for examining Cavada's records. Hundreds of appeals signed by the most prominent figures in the United States were sent to the Spanish government in Cuba within a very short span of time. Scores of honorable men did everything they could to prevent Cavada's execution. The ranks of his defenders included Generals Grant, McClellan, Pope, Burnside, Hooker, Graham, Meade, Sickles, Von Vliet, Porter, and Sheridan among others. Wires were also sent by well known public figures such as John W. Porney, Moses Taylor, James P. Lacombe, Hamilton Fish, Samuel Sloan, Edward S. Sanford, John Hoey, and A.J. Drexel. Their efforts proved futile: Federico Fernández Cavada had been summarily executed by a firing squad on July 1, 1871.

A few days later, eyewitnesses to the execution disclosed the details of the capture and death of Cavada. While trying to escape from the island by boat, the men were unable to avoid pursuit from the battleship *Vigía.* Cavada and his friends returned to land where they were pursued by Spanish sailors and soldiers. Most of the members of the rebel group were able to escape. Cavada refused to leave the gravely-wounded Osorio behind. They were both then captured by the Spaniards. They were first taken to Nuevitas and from there, Cavada was taken to Puerto Príncipe to be executed.

After washing himself and changing into clean clothes, Cavada requested pen and paper. He wrote a letter to each of the top rebel commanders while waiting for his death to come. He walked resolutely to the firing squad, smoking a Cuban cigar. A few seconds before the soldiers opened fire, he tossed his hat into the air and exclaimed: "Goodbye Cuba, forever!"

BIRNEY'S GRAVE

The solemn sounds were hushed;
The martial music and tolling bell,
The plaintive beating of the muffled drums,
And the echoed volleys of the funeral guns;
And from the new made grave, where slept
The hero of many battles, all were gone — All save
  one, for as the twilight came
Shrouding the silent grave-yard in the pall
Of falling night, there lingered still
An humble soldier leaning on his crutch.
Oh, who shall say what stirring thoughts they were
That stayed him at his chieftain's grave!
The thrilling memories of the battle field,
The rattling musketry, and the cannon's sound
The deadly struggle and the desperate charge,
And the proud form of him who slept
The everlasting slumber in the new made grave,
Dashing through the blinding battle smoke,
The manly voice that urged him in the fight,
The flashing eye and waving sword,
And the noble face that when the day
Was won; these all in the dim twilight
Were bending over him.
This humble, war-bruised veteran was the last,
The noblest mourner at the grave that day;
And the silent prayer he offered
Went up to plead at Heaven's golden gate
For him who was the soldier's friend
A long way he had come — a long way — Limping on his
  crutches through the idle crowd
Which thronged to gaze upon the funeral pageant—
A long way, to breathe his sincere prayer
O'er the noble dead, and shed upon the grave
This touching tribute of a soldier's heart.[8]

MARIANO GUADALUPE VALLEJO

California's early history often evokes images of romance, grandeur, and excitement. Memorable are the stories told of the Hispanic period with its missions and soul-saving *padres*, dashing figures like the legendary Zorro, elegant *haciendas* and wealthy *rancheros*. Few, however, have studied the life of one of the most fascinating and powerful *Californios* of this period, Mariano Guadalupe Vallejo.

As a military, political, and social leader, Mariano Guadalupe Vallejo (1808-1890) sought always to serve his community. He was a military *comandante*, a member of the legislature, and an agricultural experimentor. He was "a man who was far ahead of his day in thought, education, humanitarian measures and progressive ideas."[1] What is, perhaps, most interesting about Vallejo was his ability to give his personal allegiance and service to the three different governments which controlled California during his lifetime: Mexico, independent Hispanic California, and the United States.

Vallejo was born in Monterrey, California to a wealthy and distinguished family of Spanish descent. One of his direct ancestors, Admiral Alonzo Vallejo, was with Columbus on a voyage to Spain.[2] Vallejo received a well-rounded education as a young man and knew Spanish, French, Latin, and some English, bookkeeping, arithmetic, literature, social studies, and more.[3]

As a young man from an influential family, Vallejo seemed destined for one of three careers, and in fact once remarked:

At seventeen, three careers lay open to me. . . .I could enlist in the army and eventually become an officer, raise cattle on the side, or I could enter politics and raise cattle on the side, or I could denounce either the military and political fields and enter upon the profession of cattle-raising alone.[4]

Remarkably, he accomplished all three, first entering the military. By the time he was graduated from Monterrey military academy in 1823, Mexico had declared its independence from Spain.

He served as a cadet in the army for four years and then became *alférez* (head) of the Monterrey base. Later he was appointed *comandante* of the San Francisco *presidio*.[5] By the time he was twenty-two, the Mexican governor of California appointed him military commander-in-chief. Serving in this capacity, Vallejo put down Indian disturbances, explored the San Francisco Bay area, and directed colonization efforts in Northern California to establish a buffer zone with the Russian settlement.[6]

In addition to his military career, Vallejo entered politics and was elected to the *Diputación* (legislature) in 1830. Vallejo joined the rebels in a short-lived revolt (1831-32) against the Mexican authorities. He, and other prominent *Californios*, had differences with the appointed governor. They believed that the governor did not exert enough force in Northern California to help the citizens nor to keep out the Russians.[7]

Vallejo was deeply involved in a successful plot to remove the governor. Although he was an officer and his actions could be considered treasonous, he justified his behavior on the ground that he was also a member of the legislature and needed to act in the best interests of California. Eventually, a newly-appointed governor granted amnesty to those who had been involved in the *coup*.[8]

After good relations had been restored between the leaders and the governor, Vallejo was directed to establish new colonies in the northern frontier area. Successful colonies were founded at Petaluma and Santa Rosa, although the settlers experienced many hardships.[9] In 1834-35, he colonized the fertile Sonoma area, giving it a name from an Indian word meaning, "Valley of the Moon." He later lived there with his family.[10]

By this time, Vallejo had courted and married Francesca Benecia Felipa Carrillo, the daughter of a prominent local family of Spanish ancestry.[11] They had sixteen children, each named after a figure in whatever book Vallejo was reading at the time of their birth, *e.g.*, Plato, Napoleon, and Eugenia.[12] The family lived in *Lachryma Montis*, a huge home on one of their three ranches. Mexican authorities had granted Vallejo immense tracts of land; he became the largest landowner in California and ruled over his holdings as a virtual lord.[13]

Vallejo's power was increased further during another revolt (in 1836) against an unpopular Mexican governor. Although Vallejo's exact role in the fabrication of the plot is unclear, he took no action against his own nephew, Juan Bautista Alvarado, when Alvarado declared California an independent country.[14] The *Diputación*, which was in session at the time, elected Alvarado governor and Vallejo commander-in-chief of the military. Vallejo was said to have remarked: "They [the *Diputación*]. . .refused to listen to my excuses and fairly commanded me to accept. There was nothing left. . .but to render such services to my country, a new one though it be."[15]

Preoccupied with the problems of Texas, Mexico was too busy to intervene. California was governed for almost six years by Alvarado, age twenty-seven, and Vallejo, age twenty-nine, at the beginning of their stewardship.[16] Mexico regained California in 1842, but the unrest and instability continued. Along with the long-standing problems of Indian unrest, poorly-trained and equipped soldiers, and the fear of outside intervention, a new problem emerged. California had to cope with the growing numbers of foreigners who were settling there.[17]

The government leaders were greatly alarmed by the influx of Americans and other non-Mexicans into California. The fertile land and the potential for trade attracted many settlers. Some Americans openly agitated for direct control by the United States, especially those who were alarmed about possible British advances in the area after the Russians left.[18]

After the United States declared war against Mexico in May 1846, unrest spread among Americans living in California. Although he was well known as an advocate of United States annexation as a means of restoring peace and stability, Vallejo was badly mistreated by a group of Americans in the Bear Flag Revolt of June 14, 1846.

Approximately twenty to thirty-five Americans living in the Sonoma area decided to declare California an independent republic. They burst into Vallejo's estate. While most remained outdoors to watch, a small group entered his home to force him to sign a proclamation declaring their grievances against the Mexican government. Although disconcerted by the disruption and destruction of some of his property, Vallejo played the generous host and allowed the men use of his wine cellar, especially the brandy. After imbibing for several hours, the only sober one left, William Udem, prepared a proclamation with Vallejo's help. As a result, Vallejo and several of his friends were arrested and imprisoned at Sutter's Fort for several weeks under terrible conditions.

Meanwhile, William Todd, nephew of Mrs. Lincoln, created a flag to commemorate the occasion and symbolize the new republic.[20] This flag was made from a sheet of Mexican homespun, his wife's red flannel undergarments, and either brown paint or brown berry juice. It depicted a bear and had a star and some stripes. Even though some said the bear looked more like a pig, it was raised in the Sonoma plaza while the proclamation was read and the Bear Flag Republic was declared.[21] The flag was later removed when officials of the United States government entered in July and formally took over California.[22]

Although bitter over the actions of the Bear Flaggers, Vallejo was still convinced the United States could provide the best government. He urged the *Californios* to accept its control peacefully. His pleas were disregarded. Widespread warfare continued.[23] Upper California became a United States possession, and the conflict ended only by the Treaty of Guadalupe Hidalgo (February 2, 1848) which concluded the Mexican-American War.[24]

Once annexation was certain, the American governor called for a constitutional convention and an election of delegates to it. Vallejo was one of the seven *Hispano-Californios* who were chosen, and his knowledge of the American system was a great asset to the convention.[25] Once the government was established, he served in the first state senate.[26]

Although his political career continued to be successful under U.S. control, Vallejo encountered difficulties related to his land holdings. The American government, in an attempt to settle questions related to land ownership, passed legislation to resolve ownership disputes. Squatters had settled in many areas, and the government would not, or could not, evict them. Thus, Vallejo lost thousands of his acres.[27] Still, he refused to denounce the actions of his new government, and instead supported American control, declaring: "The inhabitants of California have no reason to complain of the change of government, for if the rich have lost thousands of horses and cattle, the poor have been bettered in condition. . . ."[28]

With his personal fortune declining rapidly, Vallejo travelled to Washington (1863-1865) to try to settle the land disputes. Although only partially successful, he enjoyed the trip and met many important people, such as Grant, Sheridan, and even President Lincoln. When the assassination of the President occurred, he returned to his Sonoma home.[29]

Once back in California, Vallejo pursued many interests relating to improving the quality of life in the region. He experimented with his vineyards to improve the quality of wine, and won many prizes for his efforts.[30] He offered 155 acres of land to the state for a new capital to be established in the city of Vallejo, but Sacramento was chosen instead.[31]

Equally interested in preserving the history of his beloved state, he wrote a *Historia de California*, covering the period up to 1850, but a fire destroyed most of the manuscript. In 1873, he gave hundreds of his documents, now named the "Vallejo Documents," to Hubert Howe Bancroft who was writing a historical work. Bancroft described Vallejo's work as "not only the most extensive but the most fascinating of its class; and while. . .a strange mixture of fact and fancy. . .it is a most useful aid to understanding California history."[32]

In his late sixties, Vallejo continued his political activities by running for presidential elector (1876), but lost in a close vote. A few years later, he visited Mexico. His last trip was to Monterrey, his birthplace, to celebrate the anniversary of the United States flag being raised there.[33] He continued to live at *Lachryma Montis*. Even though he now held only 280 acres of land and was no longer the richest man in California, he was comfortable. It was there that he died on January 18, 1890. His wife and eight of his nine surviving children were present, and he was buried nearby.[34]

Both the State of California and the United States governments have honored him. California made his home and seventeen surrounding acres a park.[35] His portrait has been hung in the State capitol building at Sacramento.[36] The United States named a Polaris submarine the *USS Mariano G. Vallejo* in his honor. It was christened and launched on October 23, 1965.[37]

Thus, the request written on his tombstone has been fulfilled:

Remember me! when frozen cold,
My heart forever sleeps;
and over my abandoned grave
The tomb-flower softly creeps.
Never more to see thee; But my soul
of fire immortal cannot perish!
and through the night's mysterious calm
Borne on the sighs of zephyrs —
cherish and hear the voice dear that
Say to thee — Remember me![38]

Vallejo is remembered for his many contributions to the people of California and its governments. He was not only the last *comandante* of the Spanish period, but was also a prominent *Hispano-Americano* during the beginning of United States control. In summarizing the life and career of Mariano Guadalupe Vallejo in California, it is worthwhile to note that:

Three times was this man called upon to instantly readjust himself to a new regime, the laws and administration of a new country, and three times did he nobly respond. . . .Each time he served under a different flag he was highly praised as the man rendering the greatest service of any member of the State's population.[39]

JOSÉ MARTÍ

A towering political and intellectual figure in the history of Spanish America, José Martí was a poet, statesman, essayist, philosopher, and a gifted orator. His dedication to Cuban sovereignty and to Latin American unity made his name synonymous with liberty throughout the hemisphere. Martí's contribution to the United States goes beyond the enduring and universal nature of his philosophy. He was also a keen observer and prolific commentator on United States society.

Born in a humble section of Old Havana on January 28, 1853, Martí was the eldest son of a Spanish couple who had recently immigrated to the island. A precocious child, by the age of sixteen, Martí had already published several poems and had founded the newspaper *Patria Libre*, (*The Free Fatherland*). At age seventeen, Martí was sentenced to six years of hard labor for being sympathetic to the 1868 revolutionary uprising against Spanish domination. After a few months he was released and deported to Spain. There, in a series of political essays, he publicly denounced the horrors of political imprisonment in Cuba.

After having graduated from Law School at the University of Saragoza in 1874, he moved to Mexico where he began his literary career in earnest. He wrote volumes of poetry and essays, one play, *Amor con amor se paga* (*Love Can Only Be Repaid by Love*), and he translated Victor Hugo's novel, *Mes Fils* (*Our Children*). While in Mexico, Martí continued to speak and write condemning the Spanish colonial oppression of his homeland, publishing regularly in the journal *Revista Universal* (*Universal Review*). Around that time, Martí married Carmen Zayas Bazán, daughter of a wealthy Cuban family who owned sugar cane plantations.

His unyielding devotion to democratic principles soon placed him at odds with the dictatorial regime which emerged in Mexico. He left Mexico for Guatemala. After a brief stay, he abandoned that country, rather than to remain silent in the face of the abuses of power committed by that country's strongman.

After a brief period of residence in France, Martí was allowed to return to Cuba in 1878 as part of a general amnesty. Due to his continued political activities, however, he was once again exiled from Cuba to Spain. From there he travelled to New York City and proceeded to Venezuela where he founded the journal *Revista Venezolana* (*Venezuelan Review*), which brought the country's intellectual elite to its pages. The political views expressed in the journal soon provoked Venezuela's dictator, Antonio Guzmán Blanco, and so Martí returned to New York where he was to remain, except for brief travels, from 1881 to 1895.

While in New York, Martí continued his literary production and also wrote many articles, both for the New York press and for the most influential newspapers of Latin America. Over the years Martí also served as consul and special delegate in the United States for various Latin American countries.

From New York, as part of his journalistic endeavors, Martí analyzed American society with great clarity and accuracy, covering for over fourteen years every electoral, cultural, and economic event. It is through Martí that Latin American readers really became acquainted with the United States society for the first time, just as years earlier the Europeans first learned about the United States from the writings of Alexis de Tocqueville.

With uncompromising honesty, Martí would compare the two Americas, criticizing and praising the failures and achievements of both cultures. He admired the North American experiment in self-government, its devotion to liberty and tolerance, as well as its egalitarian quality. Martí was also positively impressed by American individualism, industriousness, and its enterprising spirit. He was critical of American materialism, prejudice, and ethnocentrism, all of which he censured. He believed that as a result of its insatiable appetite for material success and its vanity for what it had achieved, the United States was falling into a pattern of dangerous and reprehensible attitudes.

Martí repeatedly warned of the grave consequences that could result from the American expansionist tendencies prevalent at the turn of the century. This attitude was made more dangerous by the fact that Latin America was lagging behind in the institutional, economic, and technological fields *vis-á-vis* the United States. He attributed this fact mostly to Latin America's lack of comparable success in its democratic experiment.

The United States was in the midst of an expansionist fever; the western frontiers had been conquered, the Industrial Revolution was at a fever pitch, and sea power was being promoted as a key to greatness in the nation. The need for overseas markets was coupled with the firm belief that the American people were destined to create an overseas empire that would expand American institutions to the "less" gifted and civilized people of the world. Logically, the first to be affected by such expansion most likely would be the Latin Americans, the closest neighbors of the United States.

Martí knew that this attitude ran counter to the interests, needs, and desires of the Latin American people, and that it could spark major conflicts and needless bloodshed among the people of the two Americas. He believed that such a philosophy ran counter to the deeply held principles basic to American democracy, such as a people's right to self-determination and cultural integrity. He also believed that, eventually, the exultation of power and military grandeur would rend the moral fabric that sustained democracy in the United States.

Martí reiterated this message on countless occasions, in his columns in the New York and Latin American press, in speeches across the nation, and in private conversations with influential Americans of his day. He would also argue that United States' ignorance of Latin America was the greatest danger to the Americas; that once knowing Latin America, the United States would learn to respect it. While Latin America was struggling to find that system of laws and institutions which best suited its body-politic and the character of its people, Latin Americans did have a rich and multifaceted culture, including a history of monumental accomplishments and epic deeds. He argued that the two Americas needed to learn about each other and from each other for the sake of their people, their freedom, and democracy.

During his long term of residence in New York, Martí also became a tireless spokesman against the Spanish colonial system in Cuba. He formed the Cuban Revolutionary Party in order to organize a new war against Spain. The first war, known as the Ten Years' War (1868-1878) ended in failure. Martí established a newspaper called *Patria* (*Fatherland*) to serve as a medium of expression for the revolutionary cause. He travelled widely in the States to lecture to Cuban exiles and whomever else cared to listen to his oratory.

After years of effort, Martí finally was able to organize and unite the numerous Cuban factions and their most prominent leaders. On February 24, 1895, the anti-Spanish forces received instructions for the uprising. Always a fighter with the pen and spoken word, Martí was also one of the first to join the battle. His decision to engage in combat ran counter to the wishes of his compatriots. They knew that his philosophical and oratorical contributions were invaluable to Cuba's struggle for freedom. Yet, Martí refused to remain a mere observer. On May 19, 1895, only days after landing in Cuba, Martí gave his life to the cause of freedom for his homeland. José Martí's legacy would have been impressive enough were he only known as the apostle of Cuban independence and as a mentor and guide to the Latin American culture and political conscience. He was more, however. His legacy spanned the literary field, where he is considered one of the greatest writers of the Hispanic world. In his poetry, as in his essays, we find universal and enduring truths.

As a Hispanic literary writer, Martí culminated the romantic movement's efforts toward an aesthetically elaborate prose. Most important, he is also the precursor of the modernist movement in poetry. His best known poems are his *Versos Sencillos* (*Simple Verses*) written in 1891. They address the concepts of friendship, justice, sincerity, and freedom, and have been a source of inspiration to Latin American writers, artists, and musicians for generations. His most important book of poems, *Ismaelillo* (1892), was written for his son. Out of his special devotion to children he created the magazine *La Edad de Oro* (*The Golden Age*), which served as a source of entertainment and learning for children throughout the American continent. He also wrote novels and plays. However, Martí's greatest contribution to Hispanic-American literature were his essays, due to the innovation he brought to Spanish prose. It is through his essays that Martí, the thinker, the social observer, and the moralist, left an intellectual legacy which is as relevant today as it was one hundred years ago.

The most distinguishing characteristic of Martí's thoughts and philosophy of life were its ethical foundations. Both as an artist and a political theorist, Martí always identified the good with the truth. To him, aesthetics, or the philosophy of beauty, was but an aspect of ethics, or the philosophy of morals. As an artist, he could not conceive of literature as a purely aesthetic end in itself; rather, he would emphasize literature's practical virtues, its ability to express the sincere emotions of mankind and its capacity to create an individual and collective moral conscience. His concept of literature explains his reserved admiration for Oscar Wilde and his veneration and love for Walt Whitman, whom the Latin Americans learned to appreciate through Martí's writings.

Politically, José Martí thought it was possible to reconcile individual and collective needs. Freedom was incomplete if either one was subjected to the other. He believed that the task of government is to put an end to the injustices of society by acting as an equilibrating force. Government should promote social concern, invest in the education of the poor (believing education to be the birthright of every person), and assist the poor in gaining independence through land grants and agricultural support mechanisms. To Martí, free nations could only be based on the close collaboration of all social classes, and not in the struggle of one class against the other:

> It is the duty of humankind to raise up humankind. . . .One is guilty of all abjection that one does not help to relieve. . . .Only those who spread treachery, fire and death out of hatred for the prosperity of others, are undeserving of pity.[1]

Martí's appreciation of society, politics, and government was solidly grounded in his most basic concept of mankind. Essentially, he felt that "mankind formed two factions: those who love and build, and those who hate and destroy [and that] everything that divides mankind, everything that categorizes, separates, or corrals them is a sin against humanity."[2] Thus, with regard to races, he would deplore those:

> feeble thinkers, thinkers by lamplight. . .who invent and rekindle book learnt races that impartial travelers and loving observers look for in vain in the order of nature, where the universal identity of mankind is evident in its victorious love and its turbulent appetites. . .for the same soul equal and eternal emanates from bodies different in shape and color.[3]

Martí would also refuse to judge people based solely on their particular social class. To him, "double-breasted frockcoats and humble shirts fit apostles and bandits alike." His conviction was that while "every human being has within itself an ideal being, . . .the seed of the despot is in every person."[4]

Martí knew the frailty of human beings in resisting the temptations of power. Thus, while he challenged his contemporaries to eradicate the abuses of unjust people, he also warned against those

> who in order to climb up in the world pretend to be frantic defenders of the forsaken so as to have shoulders on which to stand.[5]

Regarding absolute social doctrines, he would argue that

> he who under the pretext of guiding the young teaches them absolute doctrines and preaches to them the barbarous gospel of hate instead of the sweet gospel of love, is a treacherous assassin, ingrate to God and enemy of humankind.[6]

With all his devotion to justice and freedom, his dedication to the humble of the earth, and his adherence to the gospel of love, politics became for Martí "the art of raising unjust humanity towards justice. . .of favoring and harmonizing the various interests with virtue and the general welfare as its goal."[7]

All of these ideas and beliefs, in essence, were Martí's legacy to the people of the Americas. His exemplary life and uplifting message of love and freedom will continue to inspire people of goodwill for generations to come.

DR. CARLOS J. FINLAY:
DISCOVERER OF THE MOSQUITO
TRANSMISSION OF YELLOW FEVER

In the United States, Dr. Walter Reed is still generally credited with originating the theory of yellow fever transmission by mosquitoes. Although he deserves merit for confirming the mosquito theory, its actual originator was a modest Cuban physician whose name is rarely mentioned in this country, Dr. Carlos Juan Finlay.

Dr. Finlay was born in Camagüey, Cuba on December 3, 1833, a date now celebrated in the United States as the "Day of American Medicine." At an early age he was sent abroad to study. He later travelled in the United States and studied medicine at Jefferson Medical College in Philadelphia. He returned to Cuba after his graduation and began to practice general medicine and ophthalmology.

Finlay became interested in finding the cause of yellow fever as a result of his work with its victims. He began to observe these patients and note the incidence of this dreadful disease. At first, he was "lured by the climatic theories"[1] and he investigated the possibilities for several years. On concluding his research in 1872, he detailed his observations and "presented [them] to the Havana Academy of Sciences."[2]

His opinion changed, however, in 1879 when the first American Yellow Fever Commission went to Cuba. The Spanish governor-general assigned Finlay to work with the Commission as a consultant. In the course of his work with the Commission's president, Dr. Stanford E. Chaille, Finlay realized that his earlier theory was incorrect. The Commission did not reach a definite conclusion, but its partial finding subsequently adopted by Finlay was the following:

"The poison of yellow fever spreads, multiplies, and is endowed with the function of reproduction which is limited to living organisms."[3] This statement discredited earlier theories that the quality of the air produced the disease in certain individuals, or that it was produced by putrid substances from dead sea organisms that were injected into stinging insects, as Dr. Louis Daniel Beauperthuy had suggested in 1853. The latter wrote that yellow fever, cholera, and other tropical diseases had this common origin, and he blamed a variety of mosquito that is not the actual agent, as later Finlay proved. The report of the Commission intensified to critical levels the controversy between those who supported the contagion theory and those who did not. Finlay carefully studied both opinions and their supportive evidence. Through dialectic reasoning, he reconciled both in a third conclusion which he stated as follows:

> A great number of tests supporting each of these conflicting opinions must be accepted as perfectly true, which necessarily leads to this other consequence, namely that a third, independent condition has to be accepted to explain these two categories of fact.[4]

Again, Finlay began to investigate, but with a living organism in mind as the missing link that would explain the contagion, discarding previous concerns about the bedding and articles of clothing, or inoculation from sources other than a sick person. This time he noticed that yellow fever did not exist in places of high elevation, for "as regards altitude, the highest limit at which it (had) been observed (seemed) to be 4,000 feet above sea level."[5] He also noticed that the rise in the number of cases of yellow fever was directly proportional to the increase of the invasion of a certain mosquito. After analyzing his observations and performing several experiments, Finlay finally concluded that the culprit was a mosquito which he named "*Culex*" (later known as *Stegomya Fasciata*, and now known as *Aedes Aegypti*). He studied the insect to the point of establishing its diurnal character, as well as the reasons why it could stand the rays of the sun which would kill other species, its breeding, and even its transportation of the infection in its proboscis.

Finlay's theory of mosquito transmission was rejected by several world health commissions when he first presented his findings at the International Sanitary Conference held in Washington in February 1881. There he stated that the spread of the disease required the concurrence of three conditions: the previous existence of a sick individual in a particular stage of the infection; a subject suitable to become ill, and the presence of an independent agent to carry the infection from the former to the latter. He deliberately omitted mention of the mosquito until he could perform a complete experiment. He carried out this experiment successfully in Havana, assisted by his friend and co-worker, Dr. Claudio Delgado. Six months after the Washington conference, Dr. Finlay presented the results of his research, *i.e.*, his complete theory, including the identification of the agent *Culex* or *Stegomya Fasciata*, before the Havana Academy of Sciences, in a detailed and documented paper on August 14, 1881. No one paid attention. He went before the Academy again, on August 23, 1885. This time he drew some attention, but there was no subsequent action.

The Second American Commission for the investigation of yellow fever arrived in Cuba in April 1888. Its president did not believe Finlay's theory, and consequently the work of the Commission ended in failure.

As soon as the Cuban-Spanish-American War was over, the United States sent a third commission. This group reached the erroneous conclusion that the disease was produced by the Sanarelli bacillus, according to the theory formulated by the Italian physician of that name. However, the corresponding report did not satisfy the authorities, and they left Dr. Arístides Agramonte in charge of further investigations. This scientist disproved the Sanarelli theory, and a new failure was recorded. Amazingly, the United States' scientists neither attacked nor even commented upon Finlay's theory. They simply ignored it. In contrast, Finlay's research was the subject of intense discussion in France and Spain.

Eventually, a fourth commission was appointed by the U.S. government. It included Drs. Walter Reed, James Carroll, Arístides Agramonte, and Jesse Lazear, with Reed presiding. This time, according to Dr. Reed's words, the Fourth Commission would carefully study the intestinal bacteria of sick and healthy individuals in the area. At least Finlay's theory would be considered as an alternative. Again, the American scientists failed in their work with the Sanarelli-bacillus frame of reference.

Dr. Reed was ready to go back to the United States, leaving the other members of the Commission to investigate the mosquito theory. He had no faith in it because he thought "it had no scientific foundation." A chance occurrence, however, changed the course of events. It is described below, in a translation from the Spanish article by Dr. Gilberto Cepero:

July 31, 1900 was another warm Cuban day for Dr. John Ross, young naval physician who had been appointed Director of *Las Animas* Hospital, Havana, by the U.S. Intervention Government, after the Cuban-Spanish-American War of 1898. As usual, he greeted his Cuban colleague, Dr. Carlos Juan Finlay who was visiting his patients at eight o'clock in the morning. The young American was especially devoted to the illustrious old man. After the usual "good morning," Dr. Ross asked Dr. Finlay "Did you learn that the Commission has discarded the Sanarelli bacillus?"... After a pause, Dr. Finlay responded, "You know that my opinion is that the germ is invisible, either because it's too small or because it doesn't absorb coloring substances. We are wasting precious time. To finish yellow fever all we have to do is to isolate the sick from the *Stegomya* mosquito." In so saying, he reached into the pocket of his jacket for the laboratory test tubes that were always protruding and eliciting so many scornful comments. Looking at the blue eyes of the scientist, and smiling ironically, Dr. Ross challenged Finlay by saying, "Then, how can you explain the fact that non-immune personnel in this hospital have not been infected working among so many yellow fever patients and so many mosquitoes?" The venerable face was illuminated as he answered Dr. Ross, "Have this Administration Building fumigated, and tomorrow I will help you prove that the *Stegomya Fasciata* (now known as *Aedes Aegypti*) is not present in this place."

The next day, numerous doctors and staff personnel waited with great expectation. When Finlay arrived, the seals were broken, and all doors and windows were opened. Among the thousands of mosquitoes lying dead on the floor and furniture, not a single one displayed the typical legs striped in black and white. The Finlay mosquito did not exist in *Las Animas* Hospital.[6]

Compelled to spread the news of this certain evidence, Dr. Ross left at once for the palace of the captain general. He wanted to report directly to the governor. In a memorable letter, written some months later, he described his explosive impatience as the carriage proceeded slowly through the old Havana streets. He felt that one of the most dramatic events in the history of medicine was then transpiring, and the figure of Finlay acquired gigantic proportions in his mind.

While he was enthusiastically advising the physician and General Leonard Wood, young Enrique Loynaz, the governor's aide, interrupted both men to introduce Dr. Walter Reed. Having finished his bacteriological investigation, Dr. Reed had also come to report to the governor before leaving for the United States. Wood asked Ross to repeat what had happened at the hospital that very morning. As soon as the naval doctor finished, the general sprung to his feet and addressed Dr. Reed sharply:

> You know that we have been criticized in Washington with very good reason. More American soldiers are dying than those lost in the war against Spain. I order you to visit Dr. Finlay and get informed of his research, and also that the commission investigate this matter. We have to end yellow fever.[7]

Reed's answer was, "General, that idea has no scientific foundation. Besides, we have spent all funds." Immediately, Wood authorized the treasurer, Mr. Oscar Gans, to transfer ten thousand pesos from a surplus of the Fire Department.[8]

Thus, according to the account rendered by U.S. Navy Doctor John Ross, the U.S. Army Dr. Walter Reed was ready to leave without even considering Dr. Finlay's scientific work. In marked contrast, the dedication and humanity of the modest Cuban scientist was demonstrated in his unselfishness. He gave Dr. Reed every piece of data and every statistic he had patiently gathered during his nineteen years of research. He also gave him a container, saying, "Here, these are the eggs of the yellow fever transmitting mosquito." As the members of the theretofore frustrated Commission left his house, carrying off all the scientific evidence that he had given them without hesitation, Dr. Finlay told his friend Dr. Díaz Albertini:

At last they will confirm the mosquito theory. How much Science will benefit! I have waited nineteen years for this moment, but at last we will defeat the pain and death caused by the terrible yellow disease, and progress won't stop before this implacable enemy.[9]

Finlay's theory was fully confirmed. "Confirmed," that is, not "proven," because it had already been proven with Jesuit friars and Spanish soldiers whom he had inoculated with their consent. The Fourth American Commission confirmed his theory with cavalry soldier William D. Dean, and with two of its members. One of them, Dr. Carrel, allowed himself to be bitten by the *Stegomya* to prove that Finlay's theory was false. He capitulated when he developed unequivocal symptoms of the sickness. The other, Dr. Lazear, agreed to study the theory and also fell victim to a voluntary infection. He kept records of the process as long as he could, but he died, a martyr to science, on September 23, 1900, ten days after having been bitten. His diary contained much invaluable data, including details of the brilliant investigation design and scientific procedure.

When General Wood read the report of the Fourth Commission, chaired by Dr. Reed, he was disappointed that the research and success of the Cuban doctor was not credited in it. To partially compensate for the oversight, he organized a banquet to honor Finlay on December 22, 1900. It was presided over by the governor himself. The three members of the Commission still present were invited. (Reed was vacationing in Pennsylvania.) That was the semi-official recognition given to the discoverer of the transmitting agent of yellow fever. General Wood also gave Finlay the credit he deserved in his report to the U.S. chief of the Sanitary Office.

After confirmation of the theory, a sanitary campaign was carried out. It consisted essentially of the measures that had been recommended by Dr. Finlay. The campaign concentrated on eradicating the *Culex* mosquito, renamed *Aedes Aegypti*, in order to stop the spread of yellow fever. Carried out by Colonel W.C. Gorgas, it was successful in places such as Cuba and the Panama Canal Zone. Dr. Gorgas, a member of the Fourth Commission and the chief sanitary officer in Havana, had been asked, even begged, by

Finlay for almost two years to apply the simple principles he believed necessary: fight the mosquito and isolate the sick. Gorgas refused, having no faith in Finlay. Moreover, he considered him to be a maniac. Nevertheless, when Gorgas was finally ordered to implement the actions recommended by Finlay, the terrible yellow death was eliminated from Cuba forever, and in only seven months. This success led Dr. Gorgas to refer to the theory as "Finlay's theory," and to regard the work of Dr. Reed and his Commission as merely experimenting with it on humans.

Dr. Gorgas repeated his eradication campaign in Panama, where the French had failed in their attempt to construct a canal. Yellow fever had claimed 52,000 of the 85,000 French canal workers. The application of Finlay's ideas enabled the completion of that gigantic work of modern engineering. Dr. Francisco Domínguez Roldán, medical historian devoted to vindicating the memory of Dr. Carlos Juan Finlay, did not exaggerate in claiming:

> With Finlay, the French would have been able to build the Panama Canal. Without Finlay, the Americans would not have finished that huge project with the ease and sanitation that have reduced the loss of life to an insignificant percentage.[10]

From the 4th to the 7th of February, 1901, the Third Pan American Medical Convention was held in Havana. Of particular interest was the discussion of the already confirmed theory. Finlay attended, as did the members of the Commission, Drs. Reed, Carroll, and Agramonte. Dr. Wyman, surgeon general of the Occupation Army, summarized the work of his forces in eliminating the epidemic from Cuba. He completely ignored Finlay's theory. Dr. Finlay was the chairman of the General Medicine Section. He read a paper about the propagation of yellow fever and the progress made in this area during the nineteenth century. As he rose from his seat and walked to the podium, the members of the Congress gave him a warm ovation.

Then it was Dr. Reed's turn, and it was his assignment to disclose the report of the Fourth Commission, of which he was the chairman. Again, not a word was said concerning Finlay. The voices of the Mexican representatives, Drs. Carlos M. García and Manuel

Macías, as well as that of the Cuban Dr. José López del Valle, put into proper perspective Dr. Finlay and his work on yellow fever since 1881.

The Cuban Academy of Sciences in Havana repeatedly recognized Dr. Finlay. On December 3, 1901, his birthday, the Academy met to honor the scientist. His portrait was unveiled in the ceremonial hall. The minister of France decorated him with the Legion of Honor Cross, and Governor Wood appointed him honorary chairman of the National Sanitary Commission. This appointment included a pension for life. The large, select audience gave him a prolonged and heartfelt ovation. As was typical, this great man disregarded himself and used to opportunity to pay homage to his co-worker:

> This work proceeded with the effective cooperation of my noble friend, Dr. Claudio Delgado who, from the beginning, received my theory with enthusiasm. I say it here and I have said it in various instances. . . . Perhaps it would have remained fruitless and even perished if I had not been encouraged by this unforgettable companion whom I make a participant of the deep satisfaction that I experience today.[11]

The International Congress of the History of Medicine in Madrid, Spain (which included representatives of the United States) unanimously approved the motion of the Cuban delegation to recognize Finlay's theory about the transmitting agent of yellow fever. The Chairman, Dr. Gregorio Marañón added, "whose priority and total credit for the transcendent findings belongs to him, and only to him."[12]

Several monuments were erected to Finlay's memory in Cuba, and his name was given to more than one hospital and street. In Miami, Florida a bust and a plaque give credit to Finlay's work. On Collins Avenue, Miami Beach, Florida there is another bust of the scientist. In Paris, France, the old Rue des Usines had its name changed to his. His likeness is to be found with those of Fleming, Koch, and Madame Curie at the Sorbonne University in Paris. In Cuba, the Finlay Institute is devoted to medical research, and the

National Order of Merit "Carlos J. Finlay" was created to honor medical achievement.

The entire New World paid homage to Finlay in Dallas, Texas in 1933 when the "Day of American Medicine" was inaugurated. His birthday, December 3, was chosen to honor all leaders of medicine in the Western Hemisphere. Nevertheless, there was an attempt to challenge Finlay's achievement in Rome during the Fourteenth Congress of the History of Medicine. The delegation of Venezuela intended to read a paper about the works of the French physician Dr. Beauperthuy. After the presentation of evidence against their position, and the reiterated proof of the unquestionable merit of Dr. Finlay, the Venezuelan delegation forfeited. On the contrary, this delegation reminded the other members that it was a representative of Venezuela who first recognized the achievement of Finlay during the Sixth Pan American Conference in Havana in 1928. Again, the 1954 Congress of the History of Medicine unanimously conferred the exclusive honor to Dr. Finlay for the discovery of the transmitting agent of yellow fever, and for the application of his doctrine in the form of adequate measures to clean the tropics of the dreaded disease. Again, the unanimous approval included the U.S. delegation.

In 1935, Dr. Francisco Domínguez Roldán published in French the most complete documented work about the unquestionable attainments of Dr. Carlos J. Finlay. The book discredits the claims of all other scientists, and earned for its author the Vernois Award of the Paris Academy of Medicine. The book was translated into Spanish, but not into English.

The most persistent defender of Dr. Finlay has been César Rodríguez Expósito, a medical historian who was highly instrumental in obtaining the approval and ratification of the statement:

> The Fourteenth International Congress of the History of Medicine, which sat in Rome, Italy, once more ratifies that only Carlos J. Finlay, of Cuba, and solely to him, the discovery of the yellow fever transmitting agent, and, to the application of his doctrine, the improvement of the tropics.[13]

A bust of Dr. Walter Reed was placed in the Washington National Gallery in 1921, with a plaque stating that he discovered and proved in 1901 that mosquitoes were the instrument that transmitted yellow fever. One year after Dr. Domínguez Roldán's book was published, the bust was removed from the Gallery and placed in Walter Reed Hospital, with only his name appearing on the plaque. This tacit recognition was never made officially explicit in textbooks in the United States.

The above-mentioned Congress of Medicine in 1954 also recommended the dissemination of a declaration to vindicate the achievement of Finlay, and to correct erroneous textbooks. The approval was unanimous and included the vote of the delegation of the United States.

Certainly Dr. Reed and his commission deserve the credit for confirming the validity of the mosquito theory to the world. However, they should not be credited with originating this theory. This honor belongs solely to Dr. Carlos Juan Finlay, without whose valuable work yellow fever might have flourished for many more years, causing countless more deaths.

Dr. Carlos Juan Finlay died in Havana, Cuba on August 20, 1915.

The Spanish-Cuban-American War of 1898

For four centuries Cuba was a colony of Spain. By the end of the eighteenth century, its inhabitants began to evidence a sense of national identity. From then on, the desire to separate from their parent country grew ever stronger. In the ten years between 1868 and 1878, a state of war existed between Cuba and Spain. It ended with the defeat of the Cuban independence cause.

Organized by Cuban patriots and led by José Martí, a new war broke out on February 24, 1895. As before, the insurgents depended on arms and ammunition captured in combat or purchased in the United States with donations from Cuban exiles and other sympathizers. The U.S. government interfered with the flow of weapons, on the grounds that it violated U.S. neutrality. Many attempts to arm the Cuban patriots failed, when Spanish agents tipped off the U.S. authorities, or when shipments were captured at sea by U.S. or Spanish forces. Still, many military supplies and men did reach the Cuban liberating army.

Valiant determination, not easy success, marked the early months of the conflict. The Cuban second-in-command, General Antonio Maceo, succeeded in moving a column from one end of the long, narrow island to the other, in a historical and remarkable military march of about 800 miles. A strong, disciplined and very well-equipped Spanish army of nearly 160,000 men fought them almost constantly and placed almost insurmountable obstacles in their way.

Maceo was killed in action near Havana. José Martí had already been killed in action in Oriente. But these grievous losses did not stop the Cubans. General Máximo Gómez commanded the army, and his new second-in-command was General Calixto García, a man of great prestige, well known in the United States and in Spain as a veteran in the fight for Cuban independence. He operated in the Oriente region, the largest of the provinces and the one with the highest mountains. Máximo Gómez was fighting west of Oriente, in the extensive region of Camagüey. Both reported to the civil authority of a Republican-style governing council that resided in the Cubitas mountains of Camagüey. This Council was represented in the United States by a revolutionary junta located in New York. The junta was an active and effective exile group which worked unceasingly for the cause of Cuban independence, and to maintain the logistic support of its fighting forces. They were responsible for the strong U.S. opinion in favor of Cuban freedom.

The liberating army devastated the sugar cane plantations and destroyed enough sugar mills to reduce the main source of revenue of the colonial government to a fraction of its pre-war level. In despair, the Spanish captain general forced the rural population to relocate to cities and towns in order to deprive the insurgents of their food supply. The result was the spread of starvation and plague that killed primarily peasants or "*reconcentrados,*" by thousands every day. The photographs taken of these unfortunate people bear a horrifying similarity to those of World War II concentration camp victims. Still, the Cuban soldiers would not quit. Of the estimated 225,000 men sent by Spain to fight the rebels, nearly 135,000 had been casualties of the constant fighting and of the tropical diseases that decimated them, particularly during the rainy season. About 65,000 of them were holding the line at the end of 1897. They had lost control of about three-quarters of the countryside, particularly in the Oriente and Camagüey regions. They kept most of the ports, as well as practically all big cities, because they retained mastery over the sea which was, of course, necessary to bring supplies from Spain. The Spanish treasury was in severe trouble. The colony was no longer a source of revenue, but a bottomless pit into which national finances were sinking.

This was the situation in the winter of 1897-98, when the United States sent the *Maine* to Havana. One of the newest battleships in the fast-growing U.S. Navy, it was sent in support of the U.S. citizens who might be endangered by the bitter political struggle. The ship sank in the harbor after a horrible explosion, and the U.S. Government blamed Spain for it. Both countries assigned investigating commissions and their reports were contradictory.

The American press, particularly the Hearst papers, took advantage of the situation to inflame public opinion. War was inevitable despite the fact that Spain had abandoned the policy of "reconcentration" and had assigned relief funds to help the victims. In the United States, a heated debate raged between those who believed that Cuba should be unconditionally independent, and those who sought an opportunity for expansion of territory and international influence. President McKinley's position was not clear. His diplomacy aimed at intervening without recognizing the right of independence or acknowledging the Cuban insurgent government.

The Cuban revolutionary leaders guaranteed full cooperation with U.S. military forces against Spain. They did not demand that the Washington administration guarantee a reciprocal recognition of their Republic. McKinley hesitated to grant official recognition to the governing council of the Cuban patriots. He may have reasoned that such recognition was premature. He certainly believed that recognition would limit the available courses of action that the United States could pursue to whatever were the preferences of the insurgents. In his message to Congress on April 11, 1898, he made the following statement:

> To commit this country now to the recognition of any particular government in Cuba may subject us to embarrassing conditions of international obligations towards the organization so recognized. In case of intervention our conduct would be subjected to the approval or disapproval of that government. . . .We would be required to submit to its (the Cuban government's) direction and to assume to it the mere relation of a friendly ally."[1]

In summary, McKinley wanted free hands. The recognition of independence meant treating the Cubans as equals, as France and Spain had treated the thirteen colonies 120 years before. Furthermore, recognition would create an obstacle to annexation. Nevertheless, the Cuban patriots stood by their promise to fight Spain alongside the Americans, evidencing their faith in the people of the United States.

With few exceptions, discussions of the Spanish-Cuban-American War in American books leave the reader with the impression that the Cubans were either marginally involved or of little use in the struggle. John F. Kendrick, an historian and veteran of the war, referred to this injustice on the following terms:

> "Not one American in 10,000 realizes how important the Cuban army was in our Spanish war. . . .Our histories simply state that we did it all. . . .Isn't honor overdue where honor was earned?"[2]

The War Department of the United States decided to accept the Cuban assistance, evidenced by their famous "Message to García," carried by Lieutenant Andrew S. Rowan. It was a verbal message because the United States as yet had not declared war against Spain. A legend grew, depicting the dangerous mission as the deed of a single hero who spoke no Spanish and was not at all familiar with the territory occupied by the Cuban army, but who succeeded against insurmountable obstacles. Not even Lieutenant Rowan's memoirs give a fair account of the assistance rendered by Cubans who made his success possible.

Rowan went to Jamaica, a British colony about 80 miles south of the Oriente Province of Cuba, with intentions to land in that very region. This was the largest of the island's provinces, then almost completely controlled by the insurgents under General Calixto García, second-in-command to General Máximo Gómez. General Gómez was the Commander of the Cuban Liberating Army, with headquarters in Camagüey province, also extensively occupied by the Cubans.

Rowan had no ability to continue, until he got in contact with the delegate of the Cuban Revolutionary Junta in Jamaica. This delegate took him to Major Gervasio Savio, a Cuban officer who regularly carried mail and passengers between Cuba and Jamaica, and who agreed to transport Rowan, if so instructed by the delegate of the Cuban Revolutionary Government in New York. Secretary of

War Alger made the request. This resulted in the expected authorization, if the U.S. officer paid for his passage, as proof of the existence of the Cuban government. The War Department paid the Cuban government, and Savio carried Rowan in his small boat. They arrived at Ensenada de Mora, in the southwest tip of Oriente. The usual detachment of Cuban troops was waiting. Savio and Rowan had communicated in English, but from this point, Rowan had to resort to his very limited vocabulary in Spanish to communicate with the soldiers. He explained that he wanted to see General García and that he had a message for him. The soldiers guided him across the Sierra Maestre towards the encampment of General Salvador Hernández Rios. The party moved through narrow trails in the woods, wading across rivers, up a narrow path to the top of a mountain. As they reached another path, descending the northern slopes of the Sierra, they met a Cuban cavalry patrol commanded by Lieutenant Eugenio Fernández Barrot, aide of General Hernández Rios. This officer spoke English. Rowan was able to explain his objective to him. Fernández escorted the U.S. Army officer to General García's headquarters. On the way, they received the news that García had taken Bayamo City on May 1, 1898. There Rowan identified himself with a letter of introduction from the Revolutionary Junta in Jamaica and then delivered his verbal message to the Cuban general in person. The purpose was to coordinate military operations to be carried out by the armies of the United States and Cuba, and to learn from García what his logistical needs were so that assistance could be given.

García sent Rowan back to the United States on May 2, accompanied by a Cuban military mission under General Enrique Collazo, assisted by Colonel Carlos Hernández and Lieutenant Colonel Dr. Gonzalo García Vieta. They carried military information, maps, memoranda, and a message to the Secretary of War, dated from Bayamo, May 1, 1898. Written in English by García, the note read:

To the Sec. of Ward [sic] U.S.A.—

Dear Sir:

> I confer into General E. Collazo my entire confidence full powers
> to slate [sic] in view to you giving particulars of importance ver-
> bally, of great value for further intelligence between that Depart-
> ment and this Army.[3]

After an uneventful return, Rowan reported to his superiors and
omitted practically any mention of Cuban assistance. Collazo and
his associates personally informed Secretary Alger and General
Miles in Washington about García's military plan, asked for its approval, and requested the pertinent supplies. García reported that he
had 3,000 men armed with Remingtons and captured Spanish
Mausers, but they were extremely short of ammunition. The rest of
the troops were not well-armed. The plan asked for arms and ammunition for 15,000 men. These supplies were to be off-loaded on
the north coast of Oriente, at a point to be agreed upon. They
would be used to launch an attack against the port of Gibara with
U.S. naval support, and then against the inland city of Holguín. The
latter was under Spanish control, under Lt. General Salcedo and his
10,000 men. The fall of Holguín would mean total Cuban control
of Oriente. General Rios was moving to seize Manzanillo on the
southwest coast of the province, while General Rabí was already
surrounding Palma Soriano and Santiago. Generals Menocal and
Capote were doing the same to the ports of the north coast, including Gibara. García himself would attack Holguín as soon as American supplies arrived. Once these objectives were taken, García
would go west with 8,000 to 10,000 men to continue operating as
the U.S. command deemed necessary.

García's plan coincided with the one originally conceived by
General Miles, in the sense that the last and decisive battles would
be fought in western Cuba. The plan was also outlined in a letter
from García to his superior, General Máximo Gómez, in which he
also reported on his interview with Rowan. As a consequence of the
plan, García displaced considerable force towards the west.

The U.S. command then changed plans, without coordinating
with Gómez. The change was based on the fact that the Spanish flotilla under Rear Admiral Pascual Cervera entered Santiago Harbor
on May 19, 1898. This resulted in a decision to displace the main ef-

fort to that area. Because the sizeable forces under Gómez were far away, in position for the decisive battles conceived in the original plan, they couldn't be near Santiago to reinforce García. He received his first supplies (7,600 Springfield rifles, half a million bullets, 150,000 rations and other equipment including mules and horses) on May 26, through the Cuban-controlled port of Banes. On June 6, Colonel Carlos Hernández, one of the officers sent to the United States with Rowan, arrived at the same port with a message from General Miles, informing García of his intentions to disembark thousands of men to attack Santiago de Cuba by land and sea.

García answered the same day, offering his full cooperation once again. He would protect the landing with the necessary forces. He also informed Miles of the presence of six Spanish warships in Santiago, and described the defenses of the city, as well as the deployment of about 12,000 Spanish soldiers between Santiago and Guantánamo, with another 3,000 in reserve. He reported his constant pressure on Holguín to prevent reinforcement of Santiago from that Spanish stronghold. He immediately began to comply with his part of the U.S. command plan, and relieved the fears and frustrations of some Cubans by sending a proclamation to all commands in the Eastern Department stating that American soldiers were landing in Cuba to help liberate the island, and that it would be shameful if Cubans didn't cooperate to defend their country in the field of battle.

According to García's strategy, the Cuban liberating army would attempt to prevent the reinforcement of Santiago as follows: The 4th Cuban Division under General Luque de Feria was positioned to pin down the Spanish army in Holguín; a division from Camagüey under General Lope Recio, was placed in Victoria de Las Tunas, blocking the way of any Spanish reinforcements that might enter Oriente from Camagüey. The 1st Cuban Division under General Pedro A. Pérez stopped Spanish General Pareja and his 6,000 men in Guantánamo. A small division commanded by General Salvador Hernández Rios, overwhelmingly outnumbered by the Spanish forces under Brigadier Luis Excario, was given the responsibility of preventing this Spanish army from leaving Manzanillo towards Santiago, or at least harassing it en route. García left his camp facing Holguín and, in a forced march of five days, went through the highest mountains of Cuba to reach the outskirts of Santiago. He arrived on the south shore at El Aserradero on June 19, 1898. Before García's arrival, Admiral William F. Sampson, commander of the U.S. fleet out of Santiago, sent Lieutenant Victor Blue to the headquarters of General Jesus Rabí, the Cuban commander of that area. Rabí showed Lt. Blue all the Spanish batteries around Santiago.

The result of this advice, was that the fleet began bombarding those defenses on June 16, 1898. The Admiral was able to report to the Secretary of the Navy that "the batteries were silenced completely," and that the Cubans were of "great assistance at Guantánamo. . . ."[4] He referred, of course, to the capture of Guantánamo harbor by U.S. Marines and Cuban soldiers. One of the reports on this operation stated:

> The insurgents now with the marines number only 80, but they show splendid bearing, are clever scouts and invaluable in skirmish work, and seem to have an utter contempt for Spanish marksmanship. These little black men, when ordered forward into the struggle, go unconcernedly towards the Spanish lines, absolutely without fear of the foe. In fact the Cubans have joined the marines in scouting for a mile around the American camp and it is believed that their cooperation accounts for the failure of the enemy to make an attack last night. The insurgents know the ground so well that it is impossible for the Spanish bushwhackers to get close enough to do any damage.[5]

For the first time a Cuban flag was raised atop and saluted on board an American warship on June 16, 1898, when General Pedro Pérez paid an official visit to the *Marblehead*. A salute of honor was fired, and he was received by an honor guard.

On June 20 of the same year, General García was invited by Admiral Sampson to confer on the cruiser *New York*. He made a highly favorable impression and inspired great confidence in Sampson, a man who was not prone to trust other persons easily. He was perceived as a man "of the most frank and attractive manner and of a very military appearance," in the words of historian H. Tither-

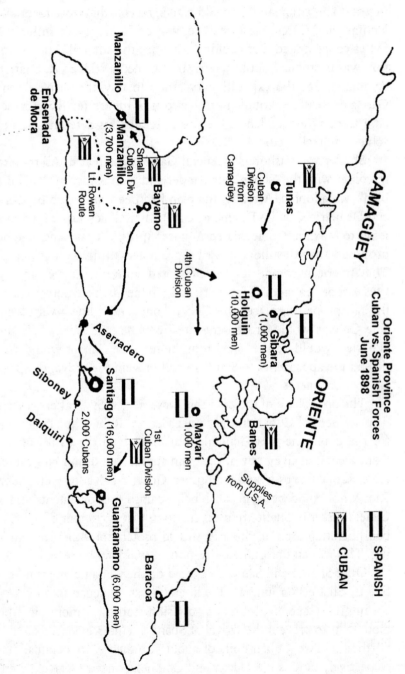

ington. The commanders could not agree on the most favorable landing site. García preferred the west of Santiago where he had forces concentrated, but couldn't convince the admiral. The operation was postponed until the arrival of General William R. Shafter, commander of the expeditionary army. In leaving the *New York*, García expressed gratitude for the efforts of the United States to secure Cuban independence. He also reiterated his determination to achieve a quick victory.

Shafter went ashore to General García's camp at El Aserradero to confer with the Cuban commander and with Sampson. "García's plan" was adopted. Actually, the plan had been conceived by General Demetrio Castillo Duany, as García himself acknowledged in a letter to Máximo Gómez dated August 18, 1898. That same day, he proposed that Castillo Duany be promoted to division general.[6] The American command was presented with alternative landing sites east of Santiago, at Daiquirí, and Siboney (where García's family had property), places the Cuban commander knew very well. The Cubans would protect the site from the land side, while the U.S. fleet would do the same from the sea. The Cubans would also defend the approaches to Santiago and prevent the arrival of Spanish reinforcements.

The only phase of the plan that was rejected by Shafter was the displacement of Cuban troops under General Rabí. The plan called for the deployment of General Rabí's forces on the banks of the Contramaestre River, one of the main approaches from Manzanillo. Here Rabí's troops would strengthen General Salvador Hernández Rios who would be trying to block Spanish reinforcements under General Escario. Shafter refused, insisting that every unit of the Cuban liberating army in the area should protect the American landing. This was an unfortunate decision, as will later be seen.

Once Shafter and Sampson agreed on the Cuban plan (as modified by Shafter) on June 20, the liberating army began to move accordingly. General Cebreco's division took positions in the mountains to prevent the arrival of Spanish reinforcements from the northwest. Two Cuban units of about 500 men each, commanded respectively by Castillo Duany and Colonel González Clavell, were transported to Sigua, east of Santiago, by the U.S. Navy, and took Daiquirí in a rapid assault, with the help of other small Cuban units already in the area. They immediately proceeded to defend the beachhead. In the mean time, more Cuban troops arrived on U.S. ships. One Cuban casualty was due to an unfortunate error. A Lieutenant Remigio Castañeda enthusiastically waved a captured Spanish flag. The U.S. Navy saw it and opened deadly fire, killing the young officer. Realizing the cause of the bombardment, Castillo rapidly waved a Cuban flag and the guns ceased at once.[7]

Simultaneous with the establishment of the Daiquirí beachhead, a diversionary operation was carried out by the allies. The U.S. fleet bombarded the coast near Cabañas, while General Rabí launched a fake attack to strengthen the maneuver. On June 25, General García was transported from Aserradero and was landed at Siboney with Generals Rabí, Lora, and Portuondo, together with 3,000 troops. The real Cuban concentration occurred at Daiquirí and Siboney, forming a protective ring between the Spaniards and the U.S. expeditionary force. An Associated Press dispatch to "The State," June 14, 1898, from a correspondent with the expedition read as follows:

> The Cuban insurgents bore their share in the enterprise honorably and well. Five thousand of them, in mountain fastness and dark thickets of ravines, lay all last night on their guns, watching every road and mountain path leading from Santiago de Cuba to Guantánamo. A thousand of them were within sight of Daiquirí, making the approach of the Spaniards under cover of darkness an impossibility.[8]

While U.S. troops were landing in heavy surf, their destination beaches were covered by 1,500 Cuban troops. At the same time, other Cuban troops attacked the Spaniards inland, preventing their moving to attack the landing site. The Cuban protection was so effective that the expedition landed with no opposition. General Arsenio Linares, Spanish defender of Santiago, wrote in the *Heraldo de Madrid*, September 9, 1898: "Without the help of the Cubans, the Yankees never could have disembarked. The assistance of the *insurrectos* was extremely powerful. A proof of this is that the North

Americans disembarked only where the insurrection was strongest."[9]

Once the landing had taken place and consolidated, Cuban troops built fortifications and emplacements, and dug trenches around Santiago approaches. This was an invaluable service, but García became infuriated when he learned that Shafter intended for these to be their only duties — to carry supplies and dig trenches for the Americans. García protested that they should be given more worthy assignments. The attitude of the American command mirrored the anti-Cuban bias of the U.S. press before the war. Reporters anticipated very little assistance from the Cuban Army. The myth of Lieutenant Rowan and his "Message to García," had colored public opinion.

The media bias stopped temporarily during the battle of Guantánamo and the landing at Daiquirí, but it resumed shortly afterwards. García's opposition to Shafter's policy of using Cubans only for logistic support work was misinterpreted as a refusal by the Cubans to both work and fight. Americans began digging trenches. The Associated Press reported that Cubans were killing Spanish prisoners. When asked by the War Department, Shafter answered, "Dispatch as to killing prisoners by Cubans absolutely false. No prisoners have been turned over to them, and they have shown no disposition to treat badly any Spaniards who have fallen into their hands."[10]

The fact is that the Cubans never refused to dig trenches and build roads, but they were in very poor physical condition. They had been living off the land, mostly on fruits and vegetables, and were simply not strong enough to sustain such labor for prolonged periods of time. Many, indeed, were suffering from malaria. When American troops charged quickly ahead in battle, soldiers dropped their heavy rolls containing food. The Cuban army was accused of stealing them. No doubt some were stolen by Cuban soldiers, but the majority were taken by some of the 20,000 inhabitants of Santiago who had to flee their homes with nothing to eat, under threat of artillery fire from the combatants.

Charles Johnson Post, an American soldier in the field, bitterly wrote later about "the war correspondents who sneered at the Cubans and ridiculed their rifles, and their fighting. The correspondents knew nothing of it."[11] (It might be pertinent to note that the Cuban liberating army had its original flag since 1850, the same that has always symbolized the Republic of Cuba, its own original national anthem since 1868, still current today, as well as a legal organization and other attributes, such as original bugle calls and a beautiful march.)

Shafter ordered Brigadier General H.W. Lawton to take a defensive position on the Siboney-Santiago road. Ahead of him, Shafter was using Cuban troops under General Castillo Duany and Colonel González Clavell to keep pressure against the 1,500 Spanish troops entrenched in Las Guásimas. This task was performed all day with a minimum of casualties. Shafter's orders were to keep up the fire without advancing. Major General Joseph Wheeler was at the rear with the U.S. cavalry, dismounted, because of a lack of horses. Wheeler decided to move ahead of both Lawton and the Cubans during the night. One of his brigades, including The Rough Riders, escaped Lawton's attention and reached the very vanguard. Led by General S.B.M. Young, who insisted in occupying Las Guásimas road together with the Cubans, joined them in firing on the Spaniards. Colonel González Clavell was unable to discourage Young from moving ahead, but agreed to give him information and a few guards for the march, without joining him in what he considered an ill-advised action. Young marched against the Spaniards at dawn. The body of a dead Cuban soldier on the roadway alerted them to the proximity of the enemy. The Spaniards were driven back to Las Guásimas on June 24, after inflicting many casualties. The Dodge Commission which investigated the conduct of the war, found that the Spanish command had already decided to abandon the position because of the heavy losses inflicted by the Cubans the previous day. At any rate, this skirmish was the first engagement of U.S. troops in the war, and their losses exceeded those of the Spaniards in an action of no military significance. Later Young blamed the Cubans for not having joined him. The fact is that he disobeyed his superiors, and ignored the sound advice of Colonel González Clavell.

The American command ordered the advance on Santiago on June 30. The next day, the outer perimeter was attacked from the east. There stood San Juan Hill, on the left flank of the route to the fortified village of El Caney. General Adna R. Chaffee attacked the heights of San Juan, while ordering 1,200 Cubans to open the road to El Caney. His appraisal was that these troops were "very useful" to him. Another Cuban contingent was placed to block Spanish reinforcements from the north. Shafter's plan included a fast occupation of El Caney by Lawton's division and a brigade of regulars totalling about 7,000 men, plus 1,200 Cubans from González Clavell's division. Once these forces engaged, the remaining 8,000 men would move down the road to San Juan Hill, guided by an observation balloon while going through the woods. Shafter and Lawton estimated that El Caney would be captured in two hours because its garrison consisted of only 1,200 men. However, despite unquestionable bravery by many American soldiers, chaos and confusion were also present among them. The splitting of forces between both defensive positions of the Spaniards was due to an American underestimation of the enemy, this despite Cuban warnings. The observation balloon above the advance guard gave away the American positions, already in jeopardy because of the smoke of their black powder rifles and artillery. The Spaniards had not a single piece of artillery at El Caney, but their rifle fire was quite effective. It caused numerous casualties among Cubans and Americans, particularly the former who were positioned near the U.S. artillery.

Lawton asked General García for reinforcements, and a platoon of Cuban infantry entered the village with the Americans, to drive the enemy out of the fortified houses. This operation took eleven hours, instead of two, due to the stiff resistance of 520 Spaniards (not 1,200) under General Vara del Rey. The general was mortally wounded and evacuated on a stretcher while the action was still in progress. His farewell to his men was to raise his sword and shout: "FIRE, AND LONG LIVE SPAIN!" At that moment another bullet ended his life. With no artillery support, this enemy unit fought

6,654 American and Cuban troops who were attacking with four pieces of artillery. The surviving Spaniards had to be routed in house-by-house fighting. Only the Spanish Colonel Puñet and sixty survivors entered Santiago that night, carrying the dead body of their commander.

The resulting delay disrupted the original plan at San Juan Hill. Generals Kent and Wheeler waited there for Lawton to finish El Caney and countermarch to attack simultaneously from the right. Their units were deployed on the left flank, supported by a battery of guns. Badly behind schedule, Kent and Wheeler had to attack by themselves. Again, the two Spanish companies (500 men) defending the heights with the help of two artillery pieces, opened such fire that Colonel Wycoff fell dead, followed by two other officers.

Some confusion in the assault occurred when the first battalion of New York 71st Volunteers could not sustain the fire and retreated in disorder over the U.S. rear guard. According to General J. Ford Kent in his account, "The Heroic Charge on San Juan," the American officers made a line behind them, and made them resume the charge reinforced by two fresh battalions. At that time, Cuban Colonel Carlos González Clavell had already advanced with his seasoned troops and re-established the abandoned firing line. This action earned him a field commendation by Colonel Leonard Wood. About 1,000 casualties were counted before the final assault. The brave General Wheeler was sick, but he left his bed to resume command from a stretcher. Again, the defending Spaniards fought to the end, and they had to be overcome by a massive and frantic charge of American and Cuban troops.

The battle cost the lives of ninety per cent of the Spanish defenders, eight per cent of the attacking Americans, and more than twenty-two per cent of their participating Cuban allies. By this time, the Americans were beginning to understand what the ill-armed liberating army had been up against. That same day, July 1, 1898, Spanish Navy Captain Joaquín Bustamante tried to recover the hill with a contingent of seamen from Cervera's ships, but he was repulsed and mortally wounded by the new defenders who were overwhelmingly superior in number.

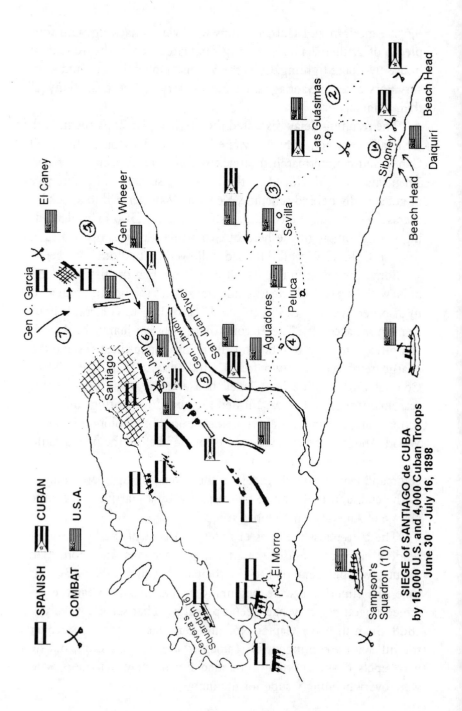

SIEGE of SANTIAGO de CUBA
by 15,000 U.S. and 4,000 Cuban Troops
June 30 -- July 16, 1898

From El Caney and San Juan, the U.S. Army advanced up to the perimeter of Santiago, while Calixto García advanced overnight to position his men on the American right flank. The next day, García took the villages of Cubitas and Boniato, on the northern approaches.

Alarmed by the heavy casualties, Shafter urgently requested García (thus far in reserve because of Shafter's earlier orders) to try to stop General Pando who was expected with a reinforcement of about 5,000 Spanish soldiers. But it was not Pando advancing from Holguín; the liberating army had him and his 10,000 men effectively pinned down. It was General Escario, marching rapidly from Manzanillo with 3,500 troops. This was precisely what General García had tried to prevent when he asked Shafter to let him order General Rabí and his 2,000 experienced Cuban soldiers to leave Siboney and deploy on the northwestern approaches on June 27. Shafter now demanded from García exactly what he had earlier refused. At the same time, Shafter asked Sampson to try to force his way into the port because American troops had suffered so many casualties. Sampson refused. Then Shafter communicated to the secretary of war that he had found strongly organized defenses and his line was too weak. He also said that he was considering a retreat to a new position between San Juan River and Siboney. General García reacted very negatively to these plans. The plans were later rejected by Washington.

The situation changed radically when Admiral Cervera was ordered to leave Santiago on July 3, to fight the splendid U.S. Navy squadron under Sampson. His six ships came out one-by-one, because there was no other way, initially presenting only their forward batteries to the whole broadside of the waiting American line, already accurately ranged on the narrow passage. Not a single ship survived, and the casualties were quite heavy. The U.S. Navy suffered only one casualty. Cervera was taken prisoner ashore by Cuban General Cebreco's forces, and turned over to the U.S. Naval forces under receipt. The Admiral requested this, on the basis that he "had surrendered to the U.S. Navy." This disaster weakened the will of the besieged Spanish army to fight.

The allies continued closing in on the city. That same day, Calixto García occupied San Vicente and Dos Bocas. The enemy evacuated El Cobre and several strongholds in the perimeter on July 4, and started sending envoys to parley with the U.S. command. Negotiations continued until the ninth. The Spanish even requested to be allowed to leave the city. García advised that such a movement would be most inadvisable. Nevertheless, Shafter consulted with the American government which denied the Spanish request.

On July 9, news arrived of the Spanish intention to move across Santiago from Holguín. Calixto García reinforced that front with General Lope Recio, who was in Las Tunas.

At 3 P.M. on July 10, 1898, the whole line of besieging Americans and Cubans opened fire, with the support of naval guns. There was another armistice on the 11th.

On July 13, a Cuban regiment commanded by Colonel Luis Martí attacked a Spanish column moving from Mayarí to Holguín to further reinforce the latter's garrison against the mobilizing Cuban forces. Martí captured two Krupp guns and a stockpile of ammunition before the Spaniards drew back to their original positions. This ended the Spanish attempts to retrieve Santiago. That same day, General Miles, head of the U.S. Army, expressed to Calixto García his deep appreciation for the cooperation of the Cuban troops.

On July 16, 1898, the surrender of Santiago was signed under a kapok tree between San Juan and Fort Canosa. From then on, this tree has been called the "Peace Tree." The Cuban command was not present. Shafter notified García of the surrender after it had taken place. He asked García to give instructions that no Cuban troops would enter Santiago, because no such entry by either Americans or Cubans would occur for some time. Notwithstanding those instructions, he did enter the city on the 17th, followed by his own band and troops, and took possession of Santiago without inviting the Cuban commander.

The surrendering General Linares would later say that without the Cuban assistance, the Americans would have never landed. Ex-Captain General Weyler declared that without Calixto García's help, the Americans would not have been able to land, successfully attack Santiago, and force it to surrender. Shafter, alone, seemed unwilling to assign credit where it was due.

The U.S. Army occupied the city, left the Spanish civil government in charge of the usual administrative chores, and forbade the entrance of the Cuban liberating army. Shafter extended his exclusion to Admiral Sampson. He told General Demetrio Castillo Duany, the originator of the whole plan for a Cuban-American campaign, that Cuba was an American land, conquered by the United States of America. This news spread like a gunpowder fire. Only the immense prestige of General Calixto García controlled the indignation of the liberation army. García wrote an historical letter to General Shafter:

"A rumor, too absurd to be believed, General, describes the reason of your measures and of the orders forbidding my army to enter Santiago for fear of massacres and revenge against the Spaniards. Allow me, sir, to protest against even the shadow of such as idea. We are not savages ignoring the rules of civilized warfare. We are a poor, ragged army as ragged and poor as was the army of your forefathers in their noble war for independence, but like the heroes of Saratoga and Yorktown, we respect our cause too deeply to disgrace it with barbarism and cowardice."[12]

In his report to the Secretary of War, General Miles wrote:

"It will be observed that General García regarded my requests as his orders, and promptly took steps to execute the plan of operations. He sent 3,000 men to check any movement of the 12,000 Spaniards stationed at Holguín. A portion of this latter force started to the relief of the garrison at Santiago, but was successfully checked and turned back by the Cuban forces under General Feria. General García also sent 2,000 men under Pérez, to oppose the 6,000 Spaniards at Guantánamo, and they were successful in their object. He also sent 1,000 men, under General Rios, against 6,000 men at Manzanillo. Of this garrison, 3,500 started to reinforce the garrison at Santiago, and were engaged in no less than 30 combats with the Cubans on their way before reaching Santiago, and would have been stopped had General García's request of June 27 been granted" (by Shafter, of course).[13]

The United States occupied Cuba until May 20, 1902, when the country was turned over to a freely-elected government.

Chronology of Events

Involving Hispanics in the United States and Neighboring Countries

1400's

1492   The first voyage of Christopher Columbus (1451-1505) begins a wave of European exploration of the Americas. On October 12, the *Niña*, *Pinta*, and *Santa María* arrive at an island in the Bahamas that the natives call Guanahaní. Columbus claims the island for Spain, naming it San Salvador. He continues to explore the Bahamas and finds several other islands, Santa María de la Concepción (today, Rum Key), Long Island, Crooked Island, and Fortune Island. On October 27, Columbus arrives at a large island that natives call Cuba and he names it Juana. He sails along the coast of the Cuban provinces of Camagüey and Oriente. He then sails to another island which he names La Española (Hispaniola). On Christmas Day, the *Santa María* hits a reef and sinks. With the remains of the flagship Columbus builds the first fort in the Americas, called Navidad or Natividad.

1493   During Christopher Columbus's second voyage, he encounters the Lesser Antilles and names several islands: Dominica, Santa María Galante (today, Mariegalante), Todos los Santos (today, Les Saintes), Santa María de Guadalupe (today, Guadeloupe), Santa María de Monserrate (today, Montserrat), Santa María la Antigua, and San Martín. On November 14, 1493 Columbus's men engage in combat with Caribs on the island that is now St. Croix. Columbus names the island Santa Cruz, and the surrounding islands, *Once Mil Vírgenes*, thus the current name, Virgin Islands. Three of these Virgin Islands (St. Thomas, St. John, and St. Croix) are U.S. possessions. On November 19, Columbus encounters Puerto Rico. He calls it San Juan Bautista; the Indians call their island Borinquen. Upon arrival in Hispaniola, Columbus founds Isabel, the first settlement in the Americas. He later sails to Cuba and Jamaica.

Pope Alexander VI divides the "New World" between Spain and Portugal, granting Spain the larger portion.

1498   On Columbus's third voyage, he makes landfall on July 31, 1498, on an island that he names Trinidad in honor of the Holy Trinity. Sailing from Trinidad, Columbus explores the Orinoco River delta and becomes the first European to see Venezuela and the Guyana coast. On August 15, he names an island Margarita, its present name, and on August 31, he reaches Hispaniola. Columbus encounters difficulties governing Hispaniola. Eventually, a royal commissioner, Francisco de Bobadilla, arrests Columbus and his brother, and sends them both back to Spain in chains.

1500's

1500   Portuguese explorer Gaspar Corte-Real makes his second trip to Greenland. Harsh winter weather forces him off course. He also explores Hamilton Inlet in Labrador. According to one legend, Corte-Real inadvertently gives Canada its name by remarking, "*Ca, nada*" ("Here, nothing") after a failed attempt to find a northwest passage to Asia. One of Corte-Real's ships, with the explorer on board, is lost at sea while attempting to return to Portugal.

        Italian Amerigo Vespucci and Spaniard Alonso de Ojeda (and in a separate expedition, Vicente Yañez Pinzón) explore the coast of Brazil. Each is credited with the early sighting of the Amazon River.

1502   Columbus begins his fourth and final voyage to the New World. He sails around the Lesser Antilles and the coast of Honduras, Costa Rica, and Panama. He is later marooned in Jamaica, rescued, and brought to Hispaniola.

1507   German cartographer Martin Waldeesmüller publishes a map in which the name "America" appears for the first time. The New World is, thus, named after Italian navigator Amerigo Vespucci.

1508   Spanish explorer Sebastián de Ocampo proves that Cuba is an island by circumnavigating it.

        Gold mining begins in Puerto Rico and the first settlement on that island, Caparra, is founded.

1511   Spanish colonists and forces under Diego de Velázquez de Cuellar conquer Cuba.

        The first enslaved Africans arrive in the Caribbean (Hispaniola). Nicolás de Ovando, Spanish governor of Hispaniola, has royal authorization to bring enslaved Africans to the island.

        Dominican priest Antonio de Montesinos argues in a sermon that Hispaniola Indians are humans who have souls and should not, therefore, be forced into slavery. He tells the Spaniards on Hispaniola who are cruel to the Indians that they will be damned.

1513   Juan Ponce de León explores the east and west coasts of what is now Florida. He discovers the Gulf Current. He names the Tortugas islands.

1517   Francisco Hernández de Córdoba leads an expedition into Florida, and is the first European to sight and explore Yucatán.

1518   Juan de Grijalva explores the coast of the Yucatán and Mexico.

1519   Hernán Cortés sails from Cuba to the coast of Mexico. He lands near modern-day Veracruz and marches against the Aztecs. By 1521, that empire falls to him. Cortés brings Arabian horses from Spain to North America.

        Alonso Alvarez de Piñeda explores the west coast of Florida and the Gulf of Mexico. He is the first European to reach the Mississippi River.

1526   Lucas Vázquez de Ayllón becomes *adelantado* of *La Florida*. He founds the first European city in present-day United States, San Miguel de Gualdape. Ayllón's expedition leaves from Hispaniola with five ships, eighty-nine horses, and about 600 people. Among those in the expedition were three Dominican missionaries, enslaved Africans, and women. The colony of San Miguel de Gualdape, on the coast of Georgia is abandoned after six months.

1528-1536

Pánfilo de Narváez lands in Tampa Bay, Florida and moves his soldiers north to present-day Tallahassee. Attacked by Indians, Narváez builds ships on Florida's Gulf coast and sails toward Mexico. He dies at sea. Alvar Núñez Cabeza de Vaca, the treasurer of the expedition, and eighty others are shipwrecked on the Gulf coast of Texas.

Eventually, Cabeza de Vaca, the African Estebanico, and two others reach Mexico City. Cabeza de Vaca's report to the Mexican viceroy Antonio de Mendoza confirms three important facts: 1) several native tribes speak of the Seven Cities of Cibola; 2) there are vast herds of bison; and 3) turquoise is available in the lands they have traveled. Upon his return to Spain, Cabeza de Vaca wrote a book entitled *La Relación*, recounting his adventures in Florida and the southwest United States. His was the first book written by a European about the United States.

1539   Estebanico the African explores Arizona and New Mexico together with Father Marcos de Niza. Estebanico is killed by the Indians.

Hernando de Soto is named governor of Cuba and *La Florida.* He sails from Spain to Havana and leaves his wife Isabel de Bobadilla as governor of Cuba. She becomes the first woman to govern a territory in the Western Hemisphere. De Soto lands in Tampa Bay and explores ten southern states. He reaches the Mississippi River in 1541. A year later, he dies of a "fever." The survivors of the expedition sail down the Mississippi River and reach New Spain (Mexico). Among his soldiers were Cuban-born *mestizos*. His expedition spreads disease throughout the southern United States, causing the death of thousands of Indians.

1540   Hernando de Alarcón is sent to support Francisco Vázquez de Coronado by sea. He sails from Acapulco and sails into the Gulf of California, sighting the Colorado River as it empties into the Gulf of California.

García López de Cárdenas is the first European to see the Grand Canyon in Arizona.

1540-1542

Francisco Vázquez de Coronado explores the Southwest in search of the Seven Cities of Cibola, encountering the Hopi, Apache, Pawnee, Zuñi, and Wichita tribes.

1545   Bartolomé de las Casas begins his tenure as bishop of Chiapas, Mexico. He is met with some hostility from the Spanish colonies, because he seeks equitable treatment for the native peoples.

1559   Tristán de Luna y Arellano becomes governor of *La Florida.* He brings 500 soldiers, 1,000 settlers, and 240 horses to Ochuse, near present-day Pensacola. De Luna also tries unsuccessfully to set up a colony at Santa Elena, in present-day South Carolina. He explores territory that is now Georgia. The expedition fails and he returns to New Spain (Mexico).

1562   French Protestant immigrants (Huguenots) attempt to establish a settlement in the southeastern United States. Later they set up a fort in present-day Jacksonville, Florida. Their presence prompts King Philip II of Spain to increase colonization of this area.

1565   Pedro Menéndez de Avilés becomes governor of *La Florida* and defeats the French forces that had established Fort Caroline in present-day Jacksonville, Florida. He founds Saint Augustine on September 8, 1565 as the first permanent European settlement in the United States. He founds the first mission in the United States, Nombre de Dios. Menéndez governs *La Florida*, which extends from the present-day state of Florida to Canada, for almost ten years. During this time he founds six other settlements and missions, San Mateo (Fort Caroline), Santa Lucía (Saint Lucie County, Florida), Tequesta (now, Miami), San Antón (Charlotte Harbor area), Tocobaga (Tampa Bay area), and Santa Elena (Parris Island, South Carolina). Menéndez brings farmers, settlers, women, children, enslaved Africans, and missionaries. The first European child, Martín Argüelles, was born in Saint Augustine. Menéndez is also appointed governor of Cuba.

1573   Jesuits attempt to establish a mission in the Chesapeake Bay area, called Axacán, but Indians slaughter the priests.

1586   Sir Francís Drake destroys Saint Augustine.

1598   Governor Juan de Oñate and more than one hundred Spanish colonists establish the colony of San Gabriel del Yunque, known today as San Juan Indian Pueblo in New Mexico.

1600's

1600   Juan de Oñate, the first governor of New Mexico moves settlers from San Juan de los Caballeros, founded two years earlier, to San Gabriel on the Rio Grande. Oñate serves in New Mexico until 1607.

        Pedro de Vergara goes to Mexico City, bringing seven Franciscan missionaries and seventy settlers, as well as supplies to San Gabriel in New Mexico.

1606   Juan Cabezas Altamirano, Bishop of Santiago de Cuba, visits *La Florida*. Several thousand Indians, including twenty-eight chiefs of the Timucuan, Guales, and Apalachee Indian tribes are converted to Christianity.

1610   The city of Santa Fe is founded by Pedro de Peralta, governor of New Mexico. Santa Fe is the third permanent European city established in what is now the United States, and it is the oldest state capital in the United States. Peralta serves until 1614.

1611   A Spanish ship sails up the James River in Virginia. The men are captured by the British and held for five years.

1612   Father Francisco Pareja writes two books while serving in *La Florida*, *Grammar and Pronunciation in Timucuan and Castillian Languages* and *Confessional Guide in Timucuan and Castillian Languages*. The books are published in Mexico City.

1616   The missions of Santa Isabel, San Pedro de Athuluteca, San Diego de Santuache, and San Felipe de Alaba are established in Georgia to convert Guale Indians.

1618   Fifty missions are established in *La Florida* and 16,000 Indians are baptized.

1620   The chapel of Nuestra Señora de la Leche y del Buen Parto is dedicated at the Nombre de Dios mission near St. Augustine. The chapel is the first shrine established in the first mission in the United States.

1622   The *Santa María de Atocha* and the *Santa Margarita* sink near Key West, Florida. (In the 1980's, Mel Fisher finds the *Atocha* and salvages over $400 million in coins, jewels, and artifacts.)

1629   Indians in Texas tell missionaries that a beautiful lady wearing a blue dress is instructing them in the Catholic faith. Many believe that it is Sister María de Agueda, a nun with extraordinary powers who is living in Spain.

1630   There are 60,000 Christian Indians living in twenty-five missions and ninety villages attended by fifty Franciscan missionaries in New Mexico.

1633   Construction begins on the *Camino Real* (Royal Road) between St. Augustine on the Atlantic Coast of Florida and St. Mark on Florida's Gulf of Mexico coast. The road is completed at the end of the century and a chain of missions is established along the road.

1640   Sor Juana Inés de la Cruz is born in the viceroyalty of New Spain (Mexico). At the age of sixteen, she becomes a nun. She writes many plays and poems. Her poems of love are described by Menéndez y Pelayo as the "gentlest and the most delicate that have come from the pen of a woman." She dies in 1695.

1654   A group of twenty-three Sephardic Jews, coming from Brazil, arrive in New Amsterdam (New York City). They descended from Jews living in Spain before 1492. They found the first synagogue in the U.S., in New Amsterdam.

1655   There are 26,000 Christian Indians living in forty-four missions in *La Florida*. The chain of missions extends west from St. Augustine to present-day Tallahassee, and north from St. Augustine to Santa Elena, South Carolina.

1668   Pirate John Davis sacks St. Augustine, Florida and burns the town.

1672   Construction begins on Castillo de San Marcos in St. Augustine, the largest masonry fort constructed in the continental United States. The engineer who directs the project is Cuban-born Ignacio Daza. Spaniards, Native Americans, and slaves build the Castillo. It successfully withstands two attacks by British soldiers from the Carolinas and Georgia. The entire population of St. Augustine moves into the Castillo during these attacks to seek protection.

1674   Bishop of Cuba Gabriel Vara y Calderón visits Florida for almost a year. He confirms over 13,000 natives and ordains seven priests.

1676   The Apaches lead a rebellion against Spanish forces in New Mexico, but they are defeated.

1680   Popé, a Pueblo Indian religious leader, leads a successful revolt against Spanish settlers in New Mexico. About 2,000 Spanish and *mestizo* settlers flee to El Paso, and 800 are killed by Pueblo Indians. Popé dies in 1688.

1687   Jesuit priest Eusebio Francisco Kino arrives in New Mexico. Over the next several years, Father Kino sets up a chain of missions in Arizona, among them San

Xavier del Bac, south of Tucson. Father Kino discovers that California is a peninsula, and not an island as it was believed, when he travels along the Gila and Colorado Rivers all the way to the Gulf of California in 1702. Kino maps thousands of miles in the Southwest before his death in 1711.

1689 Captain Alonso de León is sent to Texas by the viceroy of New Spain to search for and destroy French settlements. In 1682, French explorer La Salle sails down the Mississippi River from Canada. Two years later he lands on the East Texas coast with settlers. He builds Fort St. Louis on the Garcitas Creek near the coast. La Salle is killed by French rebels and the fort is destroyed. Captain de León finds the ruins of the French fort.

1690 Captain Alonso de León returns to East Texas and over the next three years builds several missions, among them San Francisco de los Tejas. In 1693, when no French soldiers have appeared in East Texas, the Spanish government decides to abandon the missions.

1691 Domingo Terán de los Ríos is appointed as the first Spanish governor of Texas. He serves for one year. Thirty-three Spanish governors rule Texas from 1691-1822. When Mexico becomes independent from Spain, nineteen Mexicans serve as governor in Texas until Texas gains its independence from Mexico in 1836.

1692 Diego Vargas, governor of New Mexico, restores Spanish rule in the territory. Leading an army of two hundred soldiers, he persuades each of the seventy-seven pueblo settlements to accept Spanish control without firing a shot. Vargas serves until 1697. Fifty-nine governors serve Spanish New Mexico from 1598 to 1822. New Mexico becomes part of independent Mexico, and fifteen Mexican governors govern New Mexico until 1848.

1693 The first of four Cuban-born governors of *La Florida* is appointed. Laureano Torres de Ayala (1645-1722) was born in Havana, Cuba. He serves as governor of *La Florida* from 1693-1699. During his term, he completes the construction of the Castillo de San Marcos in St. Augustine and builds a fort in the Spanish mission of San Luis in present-day Tallahassee. Later he serves as governor of Cuba from 1708-1711 and from 1713-1716.

The King of Spain frees from the British colonists in North America all escaped slaves who live in *La Florida*.

1698 The viceroy of Mexico sends Andrés de Arriola of Veracruz with three ships and 200 men to Florida. Arriola lands in the Bay of Pensacola and constructs Fort San Carlos, beginning the settlement of Pensacola.

1700's

1702 Colonel James Moore attacks St. Augustine with twelve ships. In the following year, Moore and the Indian allies of the British, destroy the Florida missions. Thousands of Florida Indians are taken prisoners and sold as slaves in Charleston, South Carolina. In 1707, Moore destroys Pensacola.

1716 Juan de Ayala y Escobar is appointed interim governor of *La Florida*, the second Cuban-born governor of that colony, serving until 1718. He lives in St. Augustine most of his life, serving in the army. He is also a merchant and frequently assists the colony by bringing food and other badly needed supplies.

Captain Diego Ramón and French trader Louis St. Denis are sent by the viceroy of New Spain to found missions and *presidios* (forts) in Texas.

Friar Antonio de San Buenaventura Olivares and Martín de Alarcón, governor of Texas, build the mission of San Antonio de Valero. This mission becomes famous one day under the name the Alamo. The city that grows around the mission is San Antonio.

1719   A small group of French soldiers invade East Texas.

1721   A new governor, the Marquis of San Miguel de Aguayo, is sent with 500 soldiers into East Texas. He builds ten additional missions and four *presidios* in East Texas. Governor Aguayo sets his capital at Los Adaes, located across the border from French Louisiana. He serves until 1722.

1737   Manuel José de Jústiz is appointed interim governor of *La Florida*. The third Cuban-born governor, he serves for one year.

1738   Governor Manuel de Montiano of *La Florida* establishes the first free Black town in the present-day United States. A former enslaved Mandingo, Francisco Menéndez, becomes the leader of the thirty-seven Black families in the town called Gracia Real de Santa Teresa de Mose (Ft. Mose). The town, which had a fort, was located about two miles north of St. Augustine. Menéndez becomes a captain of the Black militia and serves from 1726 to 1763. When Florida becomes British in 1763, the Blacks at Ft. Mose, Spaniards, and surviving Indians of the St. Augustine area move to Cuba.

1740   The Governor of Georgia, James Oglethorpe, launches an unsuccessful attack on St. Augustine. Havana sends assistance to the beleaguered city.

1747   José de Escandón surveys Texas. The following year he leads 755 soldiers and about 2,500 settlers into Texas. Over the ensuing seven years, Escandón distributes large parcels of land called *ranchos* to settlers. This marks the beginning of the cattle industry in Texas.

1752   Captain Juan Bautista de Anza founds Tubac with fifty soldiers and four hundred settlers.

1758   Comanche Indians destroy the San Saba mission in Texas. The following year, Comanches build their own fort in Texas and defeat Spanish soldiers.

When Spain joins France in the war against Great Britain, France secretly gives the Louisiana Territory to Spain. Great Britain defeats both countries in the Seven Years' War (1756-1763) in Europe and its North American counterpart, the French and Indian War. Spain cedes Florida to England in exchange for Havana, which earlier had been captured by the British.

Spanish rule in the Louisiana Territory lasts until 1803 in New Orleans and 1804 in St. Louis. From 1800 on, Spain is acting as a caretaker for France because it is forced to turn the territory back to Napoleon, emperor of France. Napoleon sells Louisiana to the United States. From 1766 to 1803, ten governors rule over Spanish Louisiana, a territory that encompasses thirteen states in whole or part, extending from the Gulf of Mexico to Canada and from the Mississippi River to the Rocky Mountains.

1765   Charles III of Spain sends José de Gálvez as *visitador general* to New Spain to re-organize the government of the colony and strengthen the northern frontier. Under his direction, California is settled.

Later, José de Gálvez becomes Spain's minister of the Indies in charge of the Spanish American colonies. Under his direction, Spain and its colonies in the New World give military and financial aid to the thirteen colonies during the American Revolution.

1768   A few French officials lead a rebellion against the first Spanish governor of Louisiana, Antonio de Ulloa, who arrived in New Orleans in 1766. Ulloa leaves Louisiana.

1769   José de Gálvez sends Gaspar de Portolá, named first governor of California, and Franciscan friar Junípero Serra to settle California. Portolá sets up the first *presidio* (or fort), and Father Serra the first mission, in San Diego. From 1769 to 1822, nine Spanish governors rule in California. Fourteen Mexican governors serve from 1822 to 1848, during the period that California was governed as part of Mexico.

General Alexander O'Reilly is named governor of Louisiana and arrives in New Orleans with twenty-four ships and 2,600 soldiers. Five French leaders of the revolt are executed and Spanish rule is restored. When General O'Reilly leaves the territory the following year, peace and prosperity have been achieved.

1771   Antonio María Bucareli is named viceroy of New Spain by Charles III. His rule lasts until 1779 and is marked by great progress.

1774   Juan Pérez, Bruno de Heceta, and Juan Francisco de la Bodega begin their numerous expeditions by sea, exploring the lands of present-day Oregon, Washington, and Alaska.

Juan Bautista de Anza leads an expedition from Arizona to California. He goes as far as Monterrey. In 1776, Anza leads another expedition into California. About 240 settlers, among them many *mestizos* from Mexico, join him. He establishes the mission and *presidio* of San Francisco.

1776   Two friars, Silvestre Vélez de Escalante and Francisco Atanasio Domínguez, and map-maker Bernardo Miera travel 2,000 miles through the present-day New Mexico, Colorado, and Utah.

1777   Bernardo de Gálvez becomes interim governor, and then governor, of Louisiana. He serves in this capacity until 1785. The thirteen American colonies are fighting for independence from Great Britain during his first years in office. Gálvez sends money, gunpowder, rifles, and other supplies to the armies of American generals George Rogers Clark in the Ohio Valley and George Washington in Virginia. When Spain declares war against Great Britain in 1779, Gálvez raises an army in New Orleans and captures five British forts in the Mississippi Valley. He takes Mobile and Pensacola in the British colony of West Florida. Spanish forces defeat a British and Indian allied army at St. Louis, and later invade Michigan, where they capture British Fort St. Joseph. At Pensacola, General Gálvez commands an army of over 7,000 soldiers. His army includes white and Black soldiers from Spain, Cuba, Puerto Rico, Mexico, Hispaniola, and Venezuela. His second-in-command at the Siege of Pensacola is Cuban-born General Juan Manuel de Cagigal. General Cagigal captures the Bahamas and later becomes governor of Cuba. Francisco de Miranda, the Venezuelan who later became "the precursor of the Wars for Independence in South America," was the aide to General Cagigal during the Battle of Pensacola. Bernardo de Gálvez is made a count by Charles III of Spain and is appointed governor of Cuba and then viceroy of New Spain. He dies in Mexico City in 1786 while serving as viceroy. Spain and her colonies provide crucial assistance to the patriots during the American Revolution.

1778   Havana businessman Juan de Miralles arrives in Philadelphia where he serves as an agent (unofficial ambassador) and observer for Spain in the thirteen colonies. Strongly supporting the colonists' fight for independence, he urges Spain to enter the war against Great Britain. Miralles befriends many of the American leaders and lends his personal fortune to assist their cause. Partly as a result of his efforts, Spain, Cuba, and Mexico send substantial financial aid to the colonies. While visiting George Washington, Miralles becomes gravely ill. Mrs. Washington personally attends to him in his final days. General Washington presides over Miralles's funeral.

1783   As a result of General Gálvez's victories over the British and his conquest of British West Florida, Spain regains Florida from England in the Peace of Paris. Spanish rule in Florida continues until 1821.

1784   Father Serra dies after having established nine missions in California. A total of twenty missions are established during the period of Spanish rule in California, and another mission during Mexican rule.

1787   The first public integrated school in the United States is founded in St. Augustine, Florida. The first teacher of this school is Father Francisco Traconis, a native of Santiago de Cuba.

1789   The Count of Revillagigedo, the Younger, is appointed viceroy of New Spain by Charles IV. His rule extends to 1794. He makes many administrative reforms, improves the finances, agriculture, industry, mining, education, and the arts. He consolidates Spanish power in California. He was one of four (of 170 total) viceroys to have been born in America. His father had been governor of Cuba and viceroy of New Spain.

Alejandro Malaspina sails from Spain with two ships on a scientific expedition. After sailing along the coast of South America and Mexico, they arrive in Alaska in 1790. He reaches a glacier, now named Malaspina Glacier. Malaspina claims Alaska for Spain.

1790   The viceroy of New Spain sends Esteban Martínez to build a fort on Nootka Bay, Alaska. Martínez heads an expedition with two ships and 195 soldiers. He builds a fort called Bastion de San Miguel de Nutka (St. Michael's Bastion of Nootka).

1791   Toussaint L'Ouverture leads a Black revolt in Haiti. He had been born a slave in 1743. For ten years, his army fights the French, British, and Spaniards. By 1801, he rules over Haiti and parts of the Dominican Republic. Napoleon Bonaparte's brother-in-law, General LeClerc, tricks him and sends him to a French prison where he dies in 1803. Haiti's independence is won in 1804, the first independent republic in the Americas.

1794   Spain cedes to England Nootka Bay and Quadra Island (now Vancouver).

1799   Sebastián Calvo de la Puerta y O'Farrill, Marquis of Casa Calvo, becomes interim governor of Louisiana. He had been born in Havana in 1754. He had served with General O'Reilly in New Orleans in 1769 and participated in the attacks against Mobile and Pensacola in 1780-1781. He also participated in the capture of the Bahamas. He serves for two years as interim governor of Louisiana. Returning to Spain, King Joseph Bonaparte promotes him to lieutenant general. After Bonaparte's fall, he moves to Paris where he dies in 1820.

1800's

1812   Jorge Ferragut and his son, David Farragut, serve in the War of 1812 in the United States Navy.

1814   The frigate USS *Essex* is captured by British ships in Valparaíso, Chile. Thirteen year old David Farragut becomes a prisoner of war.

1815   General Andrew Jackson defeats the British at the Battle of New Orleans during the War of 1812. His troops include a battalion of men born in the Canary Islands and other Hispanics from New Orleans.

The San Diego Mission in California has 50,000 acres of land, 1,250 horses, 10,000 cattle, and 20,000 sheep.

1816   José Coppinger is appointed governor of *La Florida*. Coppinger was born in Havana and is the fourth Cuban-born governor of *La Florida*. He serves until 1821, when Florida is acquired by the United States as a result of the Adams-Onís Treaty of 1819. On July 7, 1821, Colonel Coppinger lowers the Spanish flag for the last time in St. Augustine, ending a period of 288 years of Spanish rule in Florida, interrupted only by one twenty-year period of British rule from 1763 to 1783.

1821   Spain cedes Florida to the United States.

1822   Joseph Hernández becomes the first Hispanic and the first Florida-territory delegate to the United States Congress. Two years later, he is elected president of the Florida territory legislature. During the Second Seminole War, Hernández is promoted to brigadier general. He runs unsuccessfully for the U.S. Senate in 1845, then moves to Cuba, where he dies several years later.

Mexico wins its independence from Spain. Texas, New Mexico, Colorado, Utah, Wyoming, and California are now Mexican states. During the Spanish period in North America, 205 missions and 70 forts are built.

1830   There are 20,000 Mexicans living in Chicago.

1833   The 21 missions in California hold in trust for 20,000 Christian Indians 396,000 cattle, 62,000 horses, 321,000 hogs, and 200,000 sheep and goats. They produce an annual harvest of 1,230,000 bushels of grain.

Mexico passes the Secularization Act and all 21 California missions are taken over by the government. This ends the mission period, during which time thousands of Native Americans were converted to Christianity, taught to read and write, and learned crafts.

1836   Lorenzo de Zavala signs the Texas Declaration of Independence and is elected vice president of the Republic of Texas. Zavala was born in Mexico in 1788. He is one of the authors of the liberal Mexican Constitution of 1824. He served as Mexican governor, senator, minister of the treasury, and ambassador. He moved to Texas in 1835 and opposes Santa Anna's policies.

Captain Juan Seguín fights at the Alamo, along with nine Hispanic Texans, against General Santa Anna's troops. He is sent from the Alamo to get help before the final assault. He continues to fight for Texas independence. By the end of the war, he attains the rank of lieutenant colonel. He is forced, however, to leave his native land under pressure from Anglo-Americans. Several years later, he is allowed to return to Texas.

1848   The Treaty of Guadalupe Hidalgo is signed, ending the United States-Mexican War (1846-1848). Mexico loses California, Nevada, Utah, and parts of New Mexico, Arizona, Wyoming, and Colorado. The treaty protects property rights and guarantees the rights of citizenship of the Mexicans who are now living in the annexed lands. Over the ensuing years, however, the Mexicans lose their land and are treated as "second class" citizens until the 1960's.

1850   There are 100,000 Hispanics among the 23 million residents of the United States.

1851   Five hundred Cubans (including some American soldiers) invade Cuba to free her from Spain. Narciso López leads the expedition. He is captured and executed. Joaquín de Agüero also rises in revolt in Puerto Príncipe (Camagüey). He and three other patriots are executed.

1853   Father Félix Varela (1788-1853) dies in St. Augustine. During his thirty years of exile in the United States, the Cuban-born priest builds churches, schools, and orphanages in New York City and serves as vicar general of the archdiocese. Father Varela's writings illuminate Christian principles and influence many Cubans who share his desire for Cuban independence from Spain.

1859   Luis Muñoz Rivera is born in Puerto Rico. He becomes a leader for the island's independence. He does obtain autonomy from Spain for Puerto Rico and serves shortly as its Prime Minister. The U.S. Army occupation ends the brief period of autonomy. Muñoz Rivera later serves as resident commissioner of Puerto Rico in the U.S. Congress. He is the father of Luis Muñoz Marín.

1860   Spanish Basque immigrants settle in Nevada and begin a sheep industry there.

1861   The Civil War begins in the United States. Approximately 10,000 Hispanics fight for the Union and for the Confederacy. The most famous Hispanic in the Civil War is David Farragut. He blockades the South and sails the Union fleet up the Mississippi River. He captures New Orleans and assists the Army in taking Port Hudson and Vicksburg. In August 1864, he defeats the Confederate Navy at Mobile Bay. Farragut becomes the first person to be awarded the rank of Admiral by the U.S. Congress in 1866.

José Francisco Chaves fights for the North and reaches the rank of lieutenant colonel. He participates in the Battle of Glorieta Pass in March 1862 and assists the Union in recapturing Albuquerque and Santa Fe.

Santos Benavides, who serves as mayor of Laredo, Texas, becomes a colonel in the Confederate Army. His unit is called the Benavides Regiment.

Cuban-born soldiers serve on both sides of the conflict. Havana-born Loretta Janet Velázquez fights in the Confederate army disguised as a man. She participates in the Battles of Bull Run, Ball's Bluff, and Fort Donelson. Velázquez is discovered and discharged from the Army. She then becomes a successful spy for the South.

Another Cuban-born soldier, Federico Fernández Cavada, fights for the Union in the Battles of Antietam, Fredericksburg, and Gettysburg. He is captured at Gettysburg and sent to Libby prison in Richmond. Upon his release, he writes a book about his experiences as a prisoner of war. Fernández Cavada later participates in Cuba's Ten Years' War (1868-1878). He attains the rank of general in command of Las Villas province. He is captured and shot by the Spaniards.

1867   Admiral David G. Farragut visits the cities of Mahon and Ciudadela in the island of Menorca, birthplace of his father, Jorge. He visits the cathedral in Ciudadela and looks up his father's baptismal record. Later he visits the Queen of Spain in Madrid. Farragut, who spoke fluent Spanish, visited Spain several times.

1870   Admiral David G. Farragut dies.

1872   General George Meade dies. He had been born and reared in Cádiz, Spain and served during the Civil War.

1873   The *Virginius*, a ship flying the American flag, is captured in international waters by a Spanish warship. The prisoners are taken to Santiago de Cuba. The head of the expedition, Bernabé de Varona, his aide, Oscar de Varona, and other Cuban soldiers as well as eight American volunteers are executed. A British captain sails his ship into Santiago's harbor and demands that the executions be stopped. The Spaniards agree and many expeditionaries are saved.

Ricardo Flores Magón is born in Mexico. He moves to Los Angeles, California and begins the newspaper *La Regeneración*, which follows an anarchist ideology. He is later jailed and dies in prison.

1877   Donaciano Vigil is born in New Mexico. He later becomes territorial governor and serves as assemblyman in the state legislature.

1879   The "Guerra Chiquita" (Little War) begins in August, 1879, led by Generals Calixto García, José Maceo and Guillermo Moncada. The war effort is supported by Francisco Carrillo and Emilio Núñez. The war ends in less than a year.

1880   José Martí arrives in New York City where he would live for the next fifteen years. Martí writes poems, novels, and articles for many newspapers throughout Latin America. He helps interpret U.S. life and culture for Latin American audiences. He also becomes the leader of the Cuban Revolutionary Party which brings the War of Independence to Cuba in 1895. He dies fighting in Dos Ríos, Oriente, Cuba on May 19, 1895.

1881   Dr. Carlos J. Finlay (1833-1915) discovers the transmission of yellow fever by the mosquito.

1886   Vicente Martínez Ybor moves his tobacco factory and business from Key West to Tampa, Florida. The City of Tampa is founded.

1888   Lucrecia Bori, born in Valencia, Spain, begins fifteen years of performing at the Metropolitan Opera House, New York.

1889   The first conference of the American States takes place in Washington, D.C. with delegates from eighteen countries. This conference lays the groundwork for the Organization of American States (OAS), created in 1949.

1890   Mariano Vallejo dies. He was one of the earliest Californios having served in the State Senate and as a delegate to the Constitutional Convention of the State of California.

1892   José Martí founds the *"Partido Revolucionario Cubano"* (Cuban Revolutionary Party) on April 10, 1892 in New York City.

1895   The War of Independence begins in Cuba on February 24, 1895. At a meeting in La Mejorana, Oriente on May 5, 1895, the Cuban Revolutionaries ("*mambises*") acknowledge José Martí as supreme chief of the Revolution, Máximo Gómez as "generalísimo" of the liberation army, Antonio Maceo as general of the Oriente province, assisted by his brother José Maceo and Bartolomé Masó.

1897   Miguel A. Otero becomes governor of the territory of New Mexico. He serves until 1906.

1898   The U.S. battleship *Maine* explodes in Havana Harbor on February 15, 1895. The U.S. declares war against Spain on April 25, 1895. Over 17,000 soldiers invade Oriente province, and with the help of Cuban General Calixto García, defeat Spanish forces. As a result of the Spanish-American War, the U.S. acquires Puerto Rico, The Philippines, and Guam. The U.S. government establishes a military government in Cuba which controls the island until 1902.

1899   General Leonard Wood replaces General John R. Brook as Governor of Cuba in December, 1899. Under General Wood, yellow fever is eradicated. He gives Enrique José Varona the task of reorganizing the educational system of Cuba. Thousands of schools are built and a modern curriculum is implemented.

1900's

1900   Congress passes the Foraker Act allowing a Puerto Rican representative to give speeches in the U.S. House of Representatives, but not to vote.

1901   Walt Disney is born in Almería, Spain under the name José Luis Girao. His parents will later come to the United States. After his parents' death, Elias Disney adopts José Luis, whose name is then changed to Walt Disney.

1902   Narciso Gener Gonzales (1858-1902) is assassinated by a dishonest politician whom he had denounced in his newspaper, *The State*. Gonzales's father, Ambrosio Gonzales, had been born in Cuba and had fought for South Carolina as a lieutenant colonel during the Civil War. *The State* had condemned the lynching of Blacks, child labor, and the denial of women's right to vote.

1903   The U.S. supports Panama's secession from Colombia and signs a treaty with Panama to build a trans-isthmian canal.

1904   José Francisco Chaves (1833-1904), born in Padillas, Mexico (now New Mexico) is assassinated in 1904. He served as president of the New Mexico Territorial Council for eight sessions. Chaves fought in the Civil War in the Union Army and attained the rank of lieutenant colonel. He served in the U.S. Congress from 1865-1867 and from 1869-1871. He became State superintendent of instruction in 1904, serving in this capacity until his death.

1910   Porfirio Salinas, Jr. is born in Bastrop, Texas. He becomes a prominent painter. In the 1960's, five Salinas paintings hung in the White House during the Lyndon Johnson presidency.

1911   Porfirio Díaz is overthrown in Mexico. He had been president from 1876 to 1911. Ten years of revolution follows, with thousands killed and over a million Mexicans fleeing to the United States.

        Luis Alvarez is born in San Francisco, California. He becomes a scientist and receives the Nobel Prize in Physics in 1968.

1913   Ladislas Lázaro (1872-1927) from Louisiana is elected to U.S. Congress and serves until his death in 1927.

1914   The United States completes the construction of the Panama Canal.

        La Liga Protectora (The Protection League) is created in Arizona to fight discrimination against Hispanics.

1915   Anthony Quinn is born in Chihuahua, Mexico. He becomes a movie star and makes more than 100 films, winning two Oscars as "Best Supporting Actor."

1916   Ezequiel Cabeza de Baca is elected governor of New Mexico. He had been a newspaper editor. Cabeza de Baca dies a month after he begins serving as governor. A new election is held and Octaviano A. Larrazolo is elected governor. Larrazolo was born in Chihuahua, Mexico in 1859. In 1928 he becomes the first Hispanic elected to the United States Senate.

        Pancho Villa attacks the city of Columbus, New Mexico. General John Pershing and the United States Army pursue Villa's forces into Mexico.

1917   The Jones Act is enacted, making Puerto Rico a United States territory. The law permits Puerto Ricans to elect their own senate and grants Puerto Ricans United States citizenship. One hundred twenty thousand Puerto Ricans enlist in the United States Army.

1921   Alicia de la Caridad Martínez del Hoyo is born in Havana, Cuba. Later she takes her husband's last name and becomes the world-famous ballerina Alicia Alonso. Alicia Alonso and her husband, Fernando Alonso, studied in the United States in 1937 and have performed numerous times in the United States.

1923   The League of United Latin American Citizens (LULAC) is founded in Corpus Christi, Texas.

1930   The Havana Casino Orchestra, directed by Don Aspiagu, performs on Broadway. During the 1930's and 1940's many compositions by the world-famous Ernesto Lecuona are performed in the United States, including "Andalucía," "Siempre en mi Corazón" (the theme song of the movie "Always in My Heart"), and "The Breeze and I." Xavier Cugat recorded Lecuona's "Para Vigo me voy" in 1945. Cuban Miguelito Valdés's conga song "Babalú" became very popular, as did Mexican Agustín Lara's "Granada." Tito Puente, Tito Rodríguez, and Dámaso Pérez Prado popularize the mambo. Argentine, Brazilian, Cuban, and Mexican rhythms become popular in the movies, theater, and radio.

1931   Rita Moreno is born in Humacao, Puerto Rico. In 1961 she wins an Oscar as "Best Supporting Actress" for her role in "West Side Story." In 1975 Moreno wins a Tony Award for her role in "The Ritz." Two years later she wins an Emmy Award for her appearance on "The Muppet Show."

1936   Dennis Chávez (1888-1962) is elected to the United States Senate. He serves in that position until his death in 1962.

1938   Cuban American Miguel González is appointed manager for the St. Louis Cardinals baseball team.

1940   Raquel Tejada is born in Chicago of a Bolivian father and a British mother. She would later become a famous movie star under the name Raquel Welch.

        Raúl Juliá is born in San Juan, Puerto Rico. He becomes an actor and stars in such films as "Kiss of the Spider Woman" and "The Addams Family." On Broadway, he starred in the musical, "Man of La Mancha."

1941   The United States enters World War II. Over 400,000 Hispanics serve in the U.S. armed forces during this conflict. Twelve Hispanics are awarded the Congressional Medal of Honor for their courageous service in World War II.

1942   The *bracero* program begins and thousands of Mexican farm workers come to work in the United States.

1943   On June 7, 1943, thousands of sailors and soldiers attack Mexican Americans in Los Angeles. The riot is known as "Zoot Suit," a style of suit popular among Mexican American youths.

        Antonio Manuel Fernández (1902-1956) from New Mexico is elected to the U.S. Congress and serves until his death in 1956.

1946   President Harry Truman names Jesús T. Piñero as governor of Puerto Rico. Piñero becomes the first native Puerto Rican in this position.

        The G.I. Forum is organized to assist Hispanic war veterans.

1948   Mexican American Richard "Pancho" González wins the United States Tennis Association's men's singles championship.

1949   The Organization of American States (OAS) is founded.

1950   Communist North Korea attacks South Korea. The United States and sixteen other U.N. member countries defend South Korea. Thousands of Hispanics serve in the armed forces. The 65th Infantry Regiment made up of Puerto Ricans takes part in nine major campaigns in Korea. Nine Hispanics are awarded the Congressional Medal of Honor and Colonel Manuel J. Fernández of Florida becomes an ACE by shooting down many MIG fighter planes.

        Puerto Rican actor José Ferrer wins an Oscar for Best Actor for his performance in the film "Cyrano de Bergerac."

1952   Puerto Rico becomes a Commonwealth of the United States as a free and associated state.

1955   Cuban American Fernando Bujones is born in Miami, Florida. He becomes a principal dancer in the American Ballet Theater in 1974.

1957   Communist soldiers begin to fight the government of South Vietnam. The United States gradually becomes involved in the conflict. Thousands of Hispanics fight in Vietnam. Several win the Congressional Medal of Honor. A total of thirty-seven Hispanics have received this award since the Civil War.

       Chilean poet and consul in California, Gabriela Mistral, dies in the United States after a ten-year residency. She was the first Hispanic woman to win the Nobel Prize for Literature.

1958   Spanish writer and winner of the Nobel Prize for Literature, Juan Ramón Jiménez, dies in Puerto Rico. He lived in the United States for twenty years.

       Cuban composer, Julián Orbón is awarded a Guggenheim Fellowship and the following year, his "Danzas Sinfónicas" are interpreted by Balanchine.

1959   Fidel Castro overthrows the government of Fulgencio Batista in Cuba on January 1, 1959.

       Dr. Severo Ochoa is awarded the Nobel Prize in Medicine and Physiology for his discovery of RNA (ribonucleic acid) in New York. Dr. Ochoa was born in Spain and became a U.S. citizen in 1956.

1960   Manuel Antonio de Varona becomes General Coordinator of the anti-Communist Cuban Democratic Revolutionary Front. A Cuban government-in-exile organization, it worked with the Central Intelligence Agency in planning the invasion of Cuba at the Bay of Pigs. Dr. de Varona, one of the founders of the "Directorio Estudiantil" of 1930, fought Batista throughout the 1930's. In 1940 he was elected to the Cuban House of Representatives and, four years later, to the Cuban Senate. In 1948, he became prime minister of Cuba and in 1950 became president of the Senate. In 1980, de Varona organizes and becomes president of the "Junta Patriótica Cubana" to continue to fight the Communist government of Cuba. He dies in 1992 at the age of 83.

1961   Henry González is elected to the U.S. Congress. In 1958 Gonzalez became the first Mexican American to be elected to the Texas Senate in 110 years. He chairs the House of Representatives Banking Committee.

       President John F. Kennedy begins the Alliance for Progress program to aid Latin America.

       The United States sponsors an invasion of Cuba at the Bay of Pigs on April 17, 1961. Fifteen hundred anti-Communist Cubans are trained by members of the U.S. Central Intelligence Agency in Guatemala. The invasion fails; communism is consolidated in Cuba and 1,200 "Brigade 2506" soldiers are captured at the Bay of Pigs. After twenty months in prison, the U.S. government pays $62,500,000 to Castro's government for the release of the prisoners. They return to Miami. Over 200 Bay of Pigs veterans serve as officers in the United States armed forces. Many participate in the Dominican Invasion of 1965 and the Vietnam War. Several attain the rank of colonel. Erneido Oliva becomes brigadier general of the National Guard of Maryland.

       Aspira is founded in New York.

1962   César Chávez organizes the National Farm Workers Association. Three years later he calls for a strike against the grape growers of California, and in 1967, Chávez asks for a national boycott of grapes.

Mexican American Edward Roybal from California is elected to the U.S. Congress. Previously, he had served twelve years on the Los Angeles City Council. In 1992 he retires from the House of Representatives.

Brazilian Sergio Méndes plays a bossa nova concert at Carnegie Hall. Since the 1970's, a new style known as "salsa" becomes popular. The best interpreters of this rhythm are Celia Cruz, known as the Salsa Queen, Cuban Gloria Estefan and the Miami Sound Machine, Panamanian Rubén Blades, and Puerto Rican Willie Colón. Spaniard Julio Iglesias, Cuban Olga Guillot, Cuban Robert Torres and Venezuelan José Luis "El Puma" Rodríguez sing popular romantic songs.

1964   Mexican American Eligio "Kika" de la Garza from Texas is elected to the U.S. Congress.

1965   Mexican American Raúl H. Castro is named U.S. Ambassador to El Salvador.

Mexican American Joseph Montoya is elected to the U.S. Senate from New Mexico, serving until 1977.

The Freedom Airlift begins, bringing 4,000 Cubans each month for several years.

Mexican American Luis Valdez begins "El Teatro Campesino" (The Farm Workers Theater) in Delano, California. In 1978, he writes "Zoot Suit" which deals with the Los Angeles riots of 1943. In 1987, Valdez directs the movie "La Bamba," the story of singer Richie Valens, the professional name of Ricardo Valenzuela.

1966   Rodolfo "Corky" González founds "La Cruzada Para la Justicia" (The Crusade for Justice) in order to encourage Chicanos to participate in politics and to improve their lives. He later writes a famous poem, "I Am Joaquín."

Dominican designer, Oscar de la Renta, changes the name of the company he partly owns to his own name and becomes world famous for his colorful designs and perfumes.

1967   Sixty percent of Puerto Rican voters cast their ballots in favor of continuing the island's Commonwealth status, rejecting statehood.

Reyes López Tijerina and members of his Federal Alliance of Free People take over the county court in Tierra Amarilla, New Mexico.

U.S. President Lyndon Johnson and Mexican President Gustavo Díaz Ordaz sign an agreement whereby the United States gives the "El Chamizal" area to Mexico. This area was left on the north side of the Rio Grande when it changed its course in 1850 near El Paso, Texas.

Puerto Rican poet and novelist Piri Thomas writes an autobiographical novel *Down These Mean Streets* about life in East Harlem, New York City.

1968   Puerto Rican singer José Feliciano becomes famous for his version of "Light My Fire," winning two Grammy awards for the song.

Mexican American Lee Treviño wins the United States Open Golf Championship.

Mexican American singer Vicki Carr, born in El Paso, Texas, receives the 1968 "Outstanding Entertainer of the Year" Award of the Mexican American Council of California.

Mexican American singer and civil rights activist Joan Baez co-authors with her husband, David, an autobiography entitled *Daybreak.*

Mexican-born singer, Carlos Santana forms the Santana Blues Band in San Francisco.

The National Council of La Raza is founded to assist Hispanics to advance in all areas.

The Mexican American Legal Defense and Education Fund (MALDEF) is organized in San Francisco to give legal assistance to Hispanics.

San Antonio celebrates its 200th anniversary with Hemisfair '68.

Luis Alvarez wins the Nobel Prize in Physics for his discovery of subatomic particles that exist for fractions of a second.

Luis A. Ferré, an advocate of statehood, is elected governor of Puerto Rico.

Puerto Rican actress and dancer, Chita Rivero, stars with Shirley MacLaine in the film "Sweet Charity." In 1984, she wins the Tony Award for her performance in "The Rink."

1969   Mexican American Joe Kapp is voted the second "Most Valuable Player of the National Football League." Kapp had been a quarterback for the New England Patriots and the Minnesota Vikings.

Cuban American Preston Gómez is named manager of the San Diego Padres, serving until 1972. He later manages Houston (1974-1975) and the Chicago Cubs in 1980.

1970   Chicano novelist Richard Vasquez publishes *Chicano*, a novel about life in East Los Angeles.

Hispanic Women found "La Comisión Femenil Mexicana" (Mexican Women's Commission) in order to advocate women's rights.

Hermán Badillo becomes the first Puerto Rican elected to the U.S. House of Representatives.

Patricio Flores is named auxiliary bishop of San Antonio, Texas.

1971   President Richard Nixon names Mexican American Ramona A. Bañuelos as the first Hispanic treasurer of the United States.

Mexican American Jim Plunkett becomes quarterback of the New England Patriots and 1971 "American Football Conference Rookie of the Year."

Pablo Sedillo is named Director of the Division for the Spanish Speaking of the National Conference of Catholic Bishops.

1972   The Puerto Rican Legal Defense and Education Fund is organized in New York.

Puerto Rican baseball star Roberto Clemente dies in a plane crash while bringing relief supplies to victims of a major earthquake in Nicaragua.

1973   Lieutenant Colonel Mercedes Cubría retires from the U.S. Army after participating in World War II, Korea, and serving during the Cold War as an intelligence officer. Lt. Col. Cubría is the first Cuban-born woman to attain the rank of lieutenant colonel and the first to be inducted into the U.S. Army Intelligence Hall of Fame.

Maurice Ferré is elected as the first Puerto Rican mayor of Miami. He serves until 1985.

1974   Roberto Sánchez is named archbishop of Santa Fe, New Mexico. He is the first Mexican American archbishop in the United States.

Mexican American Nancy López wins the U.S. Golf Association Junior Girls' Title.

Tony Orlando, a Puerto Rican singer, debuts in a television program, the "Tony Orlando and Dawn" show.

Puerto Rican Freddie Prinze stars in a new television series, called "Chico and the Man." Two years later he commits suicide.

1975   Mexican American Jerry Apodaca is elected Governor of New Mexico.

Raúl Castro is elected Governor of Arizona.

Under the leadership of Congressman Edward Roybal of Los Angeles, the National Association of Latin Elected and Appointed Officials (NALEO) is established in Washington, D.C. for the purpose of promoting Hispanic representation in all levels of government.

1976   The National Association for Bilingual Education (NABE) is organized to promote bilingual education.

U.S. President Jimmy Carter and Panamanian President Omar Torrijos sign a treaty under which the U.S. will relinquish sovereignty over the Panal Canal Zone in the year 2000.

The Congressional Hispanic Caucus is formed in Washington, D.C. to advance the agenda of Hispanic members of Congress.

1977   Mexican American Evelyn Cisneros joins the San Francisco Ballet and becomes a principal dancer.

1978   Robert García, New York's first Puerto Rican state senator, is elected to the U.S. Congress.

Ricardo Montalbán, born in Mexico City, begins the popular television series, "Fantasy Island" which runs to 1985. Montalban has made dozens of films.

1979   Mexican American Hector Barreto founds the United States Hispanic Chamber of Commerce.

Mexican American Esteban Edward Torres becomes Hispanic affairs advisor to President Carter. He is later elected to the U.S. Congress.

Mexican American Raúl Yzaguirre, President of the National Council of La Raza, receives the Rockefeller Public Service Award. He previously served as United States Ambassador to UNESCO in Paris. He heads the largest federation of Hispanic organizations in the United States.

1980   Mexican American Gloria Moreno-Wycoff is elected president of "La Comisión Feminil Mexicana Nacional" (National Mexican Women's Commission).

Fernando Valenzuela, born in Sonora, Mexico in 1960, joins the Los Angeles Dodgers.

1981   Henry Cisneros becomes the first Mexican American Mayor of San Antonio in modern times.

Cuban American Roberto Goizueta becomes Chief Executive Officer of the Coca-Cola Corporation.

Cuban American college professor, Dr. José Sorzano, is appointed as a diplomat to the United Nations. He is later hired as a Latin American specialist of the National Security Council and serves until 1988.

1982   Mexican American Gloria Molina becomes the first woman to be elected to the California State Assembly. In 1987 she is the first to be elected to the Los Angeles City Council. In 1991 she wins election to the Los Angeles County Board of Supervisors. In 1992, Bill Clinton names her to his election campaign staff.

Armando Valladares is released from Cuban prison after 22 years. He publishes a book entitled *Against All Hope* in 1986, describing the horrors of the Communist prison system. He later serves as the United States delegate to the U.N. Human Rights Commission. Cuba is condemned by this international organization as a systematic violator of basic human rights.

Puerto Rican Rita Di Martino, director of International Public Affairs for AT&T in New York City, is appointed by President Reagan as U.S. ambassador to the UNICEF executive board.

Matthew G. Martínez from California is elected to the U.S. Congress.

1983   Mexican American Toney Anaya is elected governor of New Mexico.

Mexican American Federico Peña is elected mayor of Denver, Colorado.

Linda Chávez is appointed director of the United States Commission on Civil Rights. She is later criticized by many Hispanic organizations for supporting the English First/Official English movement.

Katherine Dávalos Ortega becomes the second Mexican American woman appointed treasurer of the United States.

Solomon Ortiz from Texas is elected to the U.S. Congress.

William B. Richardson from New Mexico is elected to the U.S. Congress.

1984   Famous Puerto Rican concert pianist, Jesús Sanromá, dies in San Juan.

Cuban American college professor, Dr. Alberto Martínez, is named ambassador to Guatemala and serves until 1988.

1985   Xavier Suarez becomes the first Cuban Mayor of the City of Miami, Florida.

Albert Garza Bustamante from Texas is elected to the U.S. Congress.

1986   Bob Martínez becomes Florida's first Hispanic governor since statehood. He previously served as mayor of Tampa.

Costa Rican-born Dr. Franklin Chang-Díaz flies in the space shuttle *Columbia* and speaks Spanish from outer space.

Congress approves the Immigration and Reform Control Law which provides amnesty for undocumented individuals who arrived before January 1, 1982.

Cuban American Otto Juan Reich is named ambassador to Venezuela.

Cuban American Dr. Modesto Maidique is appointed president of Florida International University. He is the first Cuban American named to head a major state university.

1987   Mexican American singer Linda Ronstadt wins a Grammy Award for "Canciones de mi Padre."

Mexican American Edward James Olmos stars in the film "Stand and Deliver," the story about an outstanding Bolivian American math teacher in an East Los Angeles senior high school, Jaime Escalante. Olmos also had a supporting role in the popular television series "Miami Vice."

Former Costa Rican President Oscar Arias wins the Nobel Peace Prize for his efforts to bring peace in Nicaragua.

1988   Cuban American Cookie Rojas is appointed manager of a California Angels baseball team.

Cuban American José Canseco becomes the first player in 112 years of baseball to hit forty homers and steal forty bases in the same season.

President Reagan appoints Mexican American Dr. Lauro Cavazos as secretary of education. Dr. Cavazos becomes the first Hispanic appointed to the Cabinet.

1989   Catalina Vázquez de Villalpando is named as the third Mexican American woman treasurer of the United States.

Dr. Joseph Fernandez, of Puerto Rican ancestry, is appointed Chancellor of the New York City Public Schools, the nation's largest system. Previously he served as superintendent of the Dade County Public Schools in Florida, the fourth largest school district in the United States.

The U.S. invades Panama and arrests dictator Manuel Noriega on charges of engaging in the drug trade into the U.S.

President George Bush re-appoints Lauro Cavazos as secretary of education. Mexican American Manuel Luján becomes secretary of the Interior and Puerto Rican Antonia Novello becomes surgeon general of the United States.

1990   Twenty-one current U.S. bishops are of Hispanic origin, among them Cuban-born Agustín Román of Miami, Florida.

Mexican Octavio Paz is awarded the Nobel Prize for Literature.

Cuban American Octavio J. Visiedo is appointed superintendent of the Dade County (Florida) Public Schools. He becomes the first Cuban American to head a major urban school district in the United States.

1991   Approximately 25,000 Hispanics participate in the United States armed forces during the Gulf War.

1992   Guatemalan Indian Rigoberta Menchú is awarded the Nobel Prize for Peace.

Cuban American Tony Pérez is appointed manager of the Cincinnati Reds baseball team. He is the fourth Cuban manager in major league baseball history. Pérez came to the United States from Cuba when he was seventeen years old. He played for the Reds as first baseman, appearing in five World Series and helping his team to win the World Championship in 1975 and 1976. He accumulated 1,028 home runs in his career.

Cuban American Jorge Mas Canosa, head of the Cuban American National Foundation, works with Congress and the White House to pass the Cuban Democracy Act. Previously Mas Canosa and the Foundation assisted in passing through Congress bills that created Radio Martí and TV Martí.

Raúl Yzaguirre, President of the National Council of La Raza, is elected chairman of the Independent Sector, as association of foundations, non-profit advocacy groups, and other organizations.

President George Bush signs the North American Free Trade Agreement (NAFTA) with Mexican President Carlos Salinas de Gortari. The Agreement also includes Canada. According to a Bank of Mexico study, Mexico imported products from the United States in the amount of $25,032,000,000 representing 86% of total imports in 1991.

Seventeen Hispanics are elected (or re-elected) to the U.S. House of Representatives. Hispanic representation increases to 17 from 11. Three women, three Puerto Ricans, and three Cuban Americans are among the newly elected/re-elected to Congress. The Bronx, New York is represented by José Serrano. Nydia Velázquez, former director of the Puerto Rican Affairs Office of the State of New York, becomes the first Puerto Rican woman elected to Congress.

Mexican Americans re-elected are Bill Richardson from New Mexico, Kika de la Garza and Solomon Ortiz from Texas.

Among the Hispanics elected for the first time are the following: Cuban Americans Lincoln Díaz-Balart from Florida and Robert Menéndez from New Jersey; Puerto Rican Luis Gutiérrez from Illinois; Mexican Americans Henry Bonilla and Frank Tejeda from Texas; Mexican Americans Lucille Roybal-Allard (daughter of Congressman Edward Roybal) and Xavier Becerra from California. Three are Republicans (Lincoln Díaz-Balart, Ileana Ros-Lehtinen, and Henry Bonilla) and fourteen are Democrats. Albert G. Bustamante, a Texas Democrat, was defeated.

President-elect Bill Clinton names Mexican American Henry Cisneros as secretary of Housing and Urban Development. Cisneros, age 45, served as mayor of San Antonio from 1981-1989. He joined the Clinton campaign in August, 1992. He now becomes the first Hispanic appointed to the Clinton Cabinet.

The U.S. Census Bureau projects that the present Hispanic population of 24 million people representing 9% of the U.S. population would increase to 81 million and 21% by the year 2050. Blacks would become 62 million and 16% by 2050. Asian/Pacific Islanders would increase to 41 million and 11% in 2050. Non-Hispanic whites would be 202 million and decrease to 53% of the total U.S. population.

NOTE: This chronology contains excerpts from Peopling of America: A Timeline of Events that Help Shape Our Nation by the Americans All Program. We are grateful for receiving permission to use this material.

ENDNOTES

PREFACE
1. Davis (1986), p. 10.

CHAPTER 2
1. Bourne (1922), p. 5. See Biedma.
2. *Ibid.*, p. 38.

CHAPTER 3
1. "Panuco" (1974).
2. McDermott (1974), p. 6.
3. "El Descubrimiento Siglo XVI" (1983).
4. Magill (1975), p. 3.
5. Bleiberg (1979).
6. Heusinger (1936), p. 1.
7. Wexler (1979), p. 1.

CHAPTER 4
1. Hanke (1987), p. 20.
2. *Ibid.*, p. 21.
3. Simpson (1950), p. 20.
4. *Ibid.*
5. Llorente (1984), p. 129.
6. Zorita (1963), p. 11.
7. Galmes (1982), p. 36.
8. *Ibid.*, p. 38.
9. Llorente (1984), p. 126.
10. Galmes (1982), p. 38.
11. *Ibid.*, p. 40.
12. *Ibid.*, p. 42.
13. *Ibid.*, p. 43.
14. *Ibid.*, p. 44.
15. Llorente (1984), p. 44.
16. Battillon (1976), p. 51.
17. Hanke (1987), p. 26.
18. *Ibid.*, p. 27.
19. Zorita (1963), p. 27.
20. Simpson (1950), p. 24.
21. Tebeau (1971), p. 44.

CHAPTER 5
1. The Vikings may have attempted settlement in what is today Cape Cod. There is insufficient evidence as yet to substantiate their success.
2. This colony was thought to have been located further north, in South Carolina near Winyah Bay. More recent research findings by historian Paul Hoffman indicate that the site of San Miguel de Gualdape was near St. Catherine's Island, Georgia. Judge (1988), p. 339.
3. Quattlebaum (1956), p. 18.
4. Lowery (1959), p. 153.
5. D'Anghiera (1912), p. 155.
6. Johnson (1964), p. 451.
7. Quattlebaum (1956), p. 7.
8. The tragedies befalling the native Indian peoples throughout the period of New World conquest are revisited in this act. Unaccustomed to Spanish food and numbed with melancholy over their situation, the Indians are reported to have searched among the rubbish heaped along the ditches of Puerto Plata for decaying bodies of dogs and asses with which to satisfy their hunger, rather than eat the food offered them by the Spaniards. D'Anghiera (1912), II, p. 257.
9. Lowery (quoting Oviedo) (1951), p. 154.
10. *Ibid.*, p. 161.
11. *Ibid.*, p. 162.
12. Quattlebaum (1956), 16.
13. *Ibid.*
14. The goodwill of the natives was shown in presenting the captain and his crew with gold, silver, and pearls. Quexos also brought back with him one or two Indians from each place visited to be trained as interpreters.
15. D'Anghiera (1912), p. 269.
16. Quattlebaum (1956), p. 19.
17. *Ibid.*, p. 23.
18. Lowery (1959), p. 166.
19. Sauer (1975), p. 71.
20. Lowery (quoting Oviedo) (1959), p. 24.
21. Lowery (quoting Shea) (1959), p. 105.
22. Quattlebaum (1956), p. 26.
23. Lowery (quoting Oviedo) (1959), p. 168.
24. *Ibid.*, p. 165.

CHAPTER 6

1. Bailey (1940), p. 1.
2. Hackett (1953), p. 1084.
3. Bannon (1970), p. 41.
4. Hackett (1953), p. 1084.
5. *Ibid.*, p. 1085.
6. Beck (1962), p. 61.
7. Workers of the Writers' Program (1940), p. 188.
8. Beck (1962), p. 63.
9. Workers of the Writers' Program (1940), p. 188.
10. Horgan (1963), p. 211.
11. Bannon (1970), p. 41.
12. Simmons (1968), pp. 199-200.
13. Beck (1962), p. 68.
14. Workers of the Writers' Program (1940), p. 425.
15. Beck (1962), p. 68.
16. *Ibid.*, p. 65.
17. *Ibid.*, pp. 63-64.
18. *Ibid.*, p. 68.
19. *Ibid.*
20. Bailey (1940), p. 2.
21. Workers of the Writers' Program (1940), p. 67.
22. Bailey (1940), p. 2.
23. *Ibid.*, p. 3.
24. *Ibid.*, pp. 4-5.
25. Hackett (1953), p. 203.
26. *Ibid.*, p. 208.
27. *Ibid.*, p. 209.
28. *Ibid.*, p. 210.
29. *Ibid.*, p. 20.
30. Bailey (1940), p. 7.
31. *Ibid.*, p. 8.
32. *Ibid.*, pp. 11-13.
33. *Ibid.*, p. 13.
34. *Ibid.*, p. 40.
35. *Ibid.*, p. 15.
36. *Ibid.*, pp. 19-21.
37. *Ibid.*, p. 27.
38. Cumming (1974), p. 46.
39. Bailey (1940), p. 264.
40. *Ibid.*

CHAPTER 8

1. Sparke (1976), p. 7.
2. Fairbanks (1975), p. 24.
3. Dewherst (1968), p. 82.
4. Fairbanks (1975), p. 26.
5. *Ibid.*, p. 27.
6. Dewherst (1968), p. 85.
7. Fairbanks (1975), p. 29.
8. *Ibid.*, p. 30.
9. *Ibid.*, p. 32.
10. Dewherst (1968), p. 89.
11. Fairbanks (1975), p. 33.
12. Bowman (1983), p. 42.

CHAPTER 10

1. Lockey (1937), p. 147.
2. Waterbury (1983), p. 130.
3. Curley (1940), p. 77.
4. Isern (1971), p. 39.
5. Curley (1940), p. 267.

CHAPTER 11

1. Gross (1981), p. 7.
2. *Encyclopedia Judaica* (1972), p. 1174.
3. Birmingham (1971), p. 71.
4. *Ibid.*, p. 11.
5. Gross (1981), pp. 4, 5.
6. Birmingham (1971), p. 16.
7. *Ibid.*, pp. 94-96.
8. *Ibid.*, pp. 71-72.
9. Gross (1981), p. 6.
10. Birmingham (1971), pp. 138-139.
11. Gross (1981), p. 19.
12. Birmingham (1971), pp. 43-45.
13. *Ibid.*, p. 146.
14. *Ibid.*, p. 153.
15. *Ibid.*
16. Gross (1981), p. 3.
17. *Ibid.*, p. 4.
18. Birmingham (1971), pp. 301-302.
19. Gross (1981), p. 3.
20. *Ibid.*, p. 14.
21. Birmingham (1971), p. 182.
22. *Ibid.*, p, 162.
23. Gross (1981), p. 4.
24. Birmingham (1971), p. 179.
25. *Ibid.*, p. 179-180.
26. Aizenberg (1979-1982), p. 129.
27. Dobrinsky (1986), xix.
28. Beton (1981), p. 21.
29. *The New Encyclopedia Britannica* (1987), p. 476.
30. Beton (1981), p. 22.
31. Birmingham (1971), pp. 45-46.
32. *Ibid.*, p. 24.

33. Gaon (1979-1982), pp. 9-16.

CHAPTER 12

1. Martínez (1987), p. 10 and Reparaz (1986), p. 235.
2. Archivo Histórico Nacional. Legajo 4072. Sept. 7, 1776.
3. Fernández (1985), p. 4.
4. Reparaz (1986), pp. 247-252.
5. Bonsal (1945), p. 120.
6. Portell Vilá (1978), p. 68.
7. Sariego del Castillo (1975), pp. 18-21.
8. Archivo Histórico Nacional. Legajo 3898. Oct. 28, 1794.
9. Portell Vilá (1978), p. 68.
10. Martínez (1987), pp. 20-21.
11. Fernández (1985), p. 14.
12. Fernández-Flores (1981), pp. 281-289.
13. Reparaz (1986), p. 18.
14. Caughey (1934), pp. 153-154.
15. Ibid., p. 169.
16. Martínez (1987), p. 17.
17. Caughey (1934), pp. 174-175.
18. Rush (1986), p. 5.
19. Ibid., p. 2.

CHAPTER 13

1. Portell Vilá (1947), pp. 5-6; Portell Vilá (1978), p. 23; and Fernández (1980), p. 14.
2. Portell Vilá (1978), p. 59.
3. Ibid., p. 73.
4. Ibid.
5. Ibid., p. 74.
6. Ibid., p. 75.
7. Sparks (1838), Vol. VI.
8. Ibid.
9. Ibid.
10. Isern (1971).
11. Isern (1971), p. 47 and Portell Vilá (1978), pp. 79-80.
12. Sparks (1838), p. 366.
13. Reparaz (1986).
14. Ibid.
15. Van Doren (1941).
16. Portell Vilá (1978), p. 83.
17. Van Doren (1941).
18. Sparks (1838), Vol. VII, pp. 27-28.
19. Ibid., pp. 30-31.
20. Fernández (1980), p. 15.

CHAPTER 14

1. Chopin (1973), p. 185.
2. Tunstall (1928), p. 90.
3. Fernández-Flores (1981), p. 283.
4. González López (1976), p. 16.
5. Anderson (1952), p. 290.
6. McCowen (1972), p. 5.
7. Ward, Vol. 2 (1952), pp. 755-763.
8. Mahan (1892; 1974), p. 2.
9. Paullin (1968), p. 119.
10. Long (1970), p. 42.

CHAPTER 15

1. The Plaza is named in honor of the liberal Spanish Constitution of 1812.
2. Félix became the focus of an admiring circle of females — his elder sisters, María de Jesus and Cristina, and his maiden aunts, María and Rita Morales.
3. Manuel would become a prominent tobacco merchant of Havana.
4. McCadden (1984), p. 3.
5. The St. Augustine School was not only the first integrated school, but also the first to accept slaves as students.
6. McCadden (1984), p. 5.
7. N.Y. *Freeman's Journal and Catholic Register*, March 19, 1853.
8. Father O'Reilly was later buried there. His tombstone and Varela's pantheon are still standing today.
9. The San Carlos represented the union of two separate Jesuit institutions dating from 1669 and 1724 respectively, due to the expulsion of the Jesuits in 1767. The University of Havana was established in 1728 and was administered by the Dominicans. The San Carlos housed the "avant garde" thoughts of the day. The University of Havana remained strictly Aristotelian. Both institutions were methodogically authoritarian: all instruction was in Latin and learning was accomplished by memorization and rote recitation of theses.
10. Presno (1937), p. 15.
11. Rodríguez (1878), p. 13.

12. The honor was given him by José Antonio Saco, the author of a multi-volume monumental classic work on *The History of Slavery.*
13. Hernández-Travieso (1949), pp. 295, 332.
14. *Ibid.,* p. 329.
15. Varela y Morales (1974), p. 178.
16. McCadden (1984), p. 75.
17. *Ibid.,* p. 78.
18. Herbermann (1900), pp. 320-321.
19. See Shea, *The Catholic Churches of New York City,* pp. 389-401 and 686-696 for the story of Varela's three churches.
20. 1st Annual Report, *N.Y. Weekly Reg.,* May 24, 1834.
21. N.Y. *Freeman's Journal and Catholic Register,* March 20, 1841.
22. McCadden (1984), p. 106.
23. *Ibid.,* p. 83.
24. Fanatics looted St. Mary's Church in Sheriff Street, bound up the precious bell, and set the structure afire. It was a total loss. However, the determination of New York's Catholics led to the dedication of the new building on June 9, 1833, with many high ranking Protestants in attendance.
25. McCadden (1984), p. 86.
26. Hernández Travieso (1949), p. 380.
27. *Cath. Expos.,* June 6, 1844: 240, "Editorial Observations."
28. Foik (1930), p. 121.
29. *Ibid.,* p. 61.
30. Hernández Travieso (1984), p. 430.
31. Griffin (1904), pp. 164-165.
32. McCadden (1984), p. 106.
33. *Ibid.,* p. 110.
34. Rodríguez (1878), p. 234.

CHAPTER 16

1. Piedrabuena (1965), p. 8.
2. Lewis (1941), pp. 114, 127.
3. *Ibid.,* pp. 123, 135 and Piedrabuena (1965), p. 12.
4. Lewis (1941), p. 228.
5. Piedrabuena (1965), p. 12.
6. "El Siglo Illustrado" (1867) and Montgomery (1869), p. 201.

7. Pineda (1950), p. 69.
8. U.S. Naval Institute (1943), p. 347.
9. Piedrabuena (1965), p. 12.
10. U.S. Naval Institute (1943), p. 347.
11. Piedrabuena (1965), p. 15.
12. Documents of the Naval Museum at Annapolis.
13. U.S. Naval Institute (1943), p. 367 and Welles (1911), p. 501.

CHAPTER 17

1. Isern (1971), p. 79.
2. *Ibid.*
3. Davis (1871), p. 13.
4. Isern (1971), p. 89.
5. *Ibid.*
6. *Ibid.,* p. 90.
7. *Ibid.,* p. 95.
8. Fernández Cavada (1864), p. 27.

CHAPTER 18

1. Garrison (1935), p. 70.
2. *Ibid.,* p. 64.
3. Hubbard (1941), p. 35.
4. *Ibid.*
5. *Ibid.,* pp. 73-79.
6. Batman (1985), p. 227.
7. Hubbard (1941), pp. 94-96.
8. *Ibid.,* pp. 103-104.
9. Chapman (1939), p. 464.
10. Hubbard (1941), pp. 110-111.
11. *Ibid.,* pp. 92-93.
12. Garrison (1935), p. 69.
13. Hubbard (1941), pp. 112-113.
14. Chapman (1939), p. 474.
15. Hubbard (1941), pp. 141-142.
16. *Ibid.,* pp. 145-147.
17. *Ibid.,* pp. 187-195.
18. *Ibid.*
19. *Ibid.,* pp. 226-332.
20. Lavender (1972), p. 133.
21. *Ibid.*
22. Hubbard (1941), pp. 231-236.
23. *Ibid.,* pp. 236-240.
24. *Ibid.,* pp. 274-275.
25. Norton (1913), p. 237 and McKittrick (1944), pp. 314-325.
26. Hubbard (1941), p. 308.
27. McKittrick (1944), pp. 314-325.
28. *Ibid.,* p. 336.
29. *Ibid.,* pp. 326-329.

30. *Ibid.,* p. 336.
31. Hubbard (1941), pp. 339-347.
32. McKittrick (1944), pp. 342-350.
33. *Ibid.,* pp. 346-350.
34. *Ibid.,* p. 352.
35. Garrison (1935), p. 70.
36. McKittrick (1944), pp. 353-354.
37. U.S. Dept. of Defense (1980).
38. Hubbard (1941), p. 370.
39. *Ibid.,* p. 41.

CHAPTER 19

1. Ripoll (1980), p. 69.
2. *Ibid.,* p. 113.
3. *Ibid.*
4. *Ibid.,* p. 71.
5. *Ibid.,* p. 47.
6. *Ibid.,* p. 39.
7. *Ibid.*

CHAPTER 20

1. Finlay (1940), p. 54.
2. *Ibid.*
3. *Ibid.,* p. 56.
4. Rodríguez Expósito (1971), p. 27.
5. Finlay (1940), p. 70.
6. Cepero (1977), p. 56.
7. *Ibid.*
8. Rivas (1983), pp. 22-23.
9. *Ibid.,* p. 23.
10. *Ibid.,* p. 24.
11. *Ibid.,* p. 25.
12. *Ibid.*
13. Rodríguez Expósito (1971), p. 128.

CHAPTER 21

1. Foner (1972), p. 262.
2. Kendrick (1955).
3. Foner (1972), p. 341.
4. *Ibid.,* p. 348.
5. *Ibid.,* p. 349.
6. Casasus (1962), p. 267.
7. *Ibid.,* p. 268.
8. Foner (1972), p. 355.
9. Portell Vilá (1949), p. 240.
10. Foner (1972), p. 357.
11. Post (1960), pp. 126-128.
12. Foner (1972), p. 370.
13. *Ibid.,* p. 365.

BIBLIOGRAPHY

CHAPTER 2

Biedma, Luis Hernández de. "Relation of the Conquest of Florida." In *Narratives of the Career of Hernando de Soto*, Vol. II, edited by Edward R. Bourne, pp. 1-40. New York: Allerton Book Co., 1922.

Bullen, Ripley P. "De Soto's Ucita and the Terra Ceia Site." *Florida Historical Quarterly* 30:317-323 (1952).

Castañeda, Paulino, Mariano Cuesta, and Pilar Hernández. *Transcripción, Estudio y Notas del "Espejo de Navegantes" de Alonso Chaves*. Madrid: Instituto de Historia y Cultura Naval, 1983.

DePratter, Chester, Charles Hudson, and Marvin Smith. "The Hernando de Soto Expedition: From Chiaha to Mabilia." In *Alabama and Its Borderlands from Prehistory to Statehood*, edited by Reid Badger and Lawrence A. Clayton, pp. 108-126. University: University of Alabama Press, 1985.

DeSoto, Hernando. (Letter). In *Narratives of the Career of Hernando de Soto in the Conquest of Florida*. Trans. by Buckingham Smith. New York: Bradford Club, 1866.

Elvas (Gentleman of Elvas). "True Relation. . ." in *Narratives of the Career of Hernando de Soto*, Vol. I, edited by Edward G. Bourne, pp. 1-222. New York: Allerton Book Co., 1922.

Garcilaso de la Vega. *The Florida of the Inca*. Trans. and ed. by John G. and Jeanette J. Varner. Austin: University of Texas Press, 1951.

Hudson, Charles. *The Southeastern Indians*. Knoxville: University of Tennessee Press, 1976.

Hudson, Charles, Chester DePratter, and Marvin Smith. "The Hernando de Soto Expedition: From Apalachee to Chiaha." *Southeastern Archaeology* 3:65-77 (1984).

Hudson, Charles, Marvin Smith, David Hally, Richard Polhemus, and Chester DePratter, "A Chiefdom in the Sixteenth Century Southeastern United States." *American Antiquity* 50:723-737 (1985).

Mitchem, Jeffrey, M., Martin T. Smith, Albert C. Goodyear, and Robert R. Allen. "Early Spanish Contact on the Florida Gulf Coast: The Weeki Wachee and Ruth Smith Mounds." In *Indians, Colonists, and Slaves; Essays in Memory of Charles H. Fairbanks*, pp. 179-219. *Florida Journal of Anthropology Special Publication 4*. Gainesville, 1985.

Robertson, James Alexander (Ed. and trans.). *True Relations of the Hardships Suffered by Governor Hernando de Soto and Certain Portuguese Gentlemen during the Discovery of the Province of Florida Now Newly Set Forth by a Gentleman of Elvas*. Vol. 2. Translation and Annotations. Publications of the Florida State Historical Society 11. Deland, 1933.

Ranjel, Rodrigo. "A Narrative of de Soto's Expedition" in *Narratives of the Career of Hernando de Soto*, Vol. II, ed. by Edward G. Bourne, pp. 41-158. New York: Allerton Book Co., 1922.

Southern Anthropological Society Proceedings 20. "An Unknown South: Spanish Explorers and Southeastern Chiefdoms," in *Visions and Revisions, Ethnohistoric Perspectives on Southern Cultures*, ed. by George Sabo III and William M. Schneider, pp. 6-24.

Swanton, John R., ed. *Final Report of the United States de Soto Expedition Commission*. 76th Congress, 1st Session, House Document 71. Washington: Government Printing Office, 1939.

"Tocobaga Indians and the Safety Harbor Culture," in *Tacachale: Essays on the Indians of Florida and Southeastern Georgia During the Historic Period*, pp. 50-58. Ed. by J.T. Milanich and S. Proctor. Gainesville: University Presses of Florida, 1978.

CHAPTER 3

Bleiberg, German. "Francisco de Garay." *Diccionario de Historia de España.* 1979 ed.

"El Descubrimiento Siglo XVI." *Gran Enciclopedia de España y América.* 1983 ed.

Heusinger, Edward W. *Early Explorations and Mission Establishments in Texas.* Naylor, Tx.: Naylor, 1936.

McDermott, John F. *The Spanish in the Mississippi Valley. 1762-1804.* Chicago: University of Illinois Press, 1974.

Magill, Frank M. *Great Events from History, American Series.* Englewood Cliffs, N.J.: Salem Press, 1975.

Mártir de Anglería, Pedro. *Décadas del Nuevo Mundo.* Buenos Aires: Editorial Bajel, 1944.

Morris, Allan. *The Florida Handbook, 1983-1984.* Tallahassee: Península Pub. Co., 1983.

"Panuco." *Diccionario Enciclopédico.* 1974 ed.

Wexler, Robert I. *Chronology and Documentary Handbook of the State of Texas.* Dobbs Ferry, N.Y.: Oceana, 1979.

CHAPTER 4

Battillon, Marcel. *Estudios Sobre Bartolomé de las Casas.* Barcelona: Ediciones Peninsula, 1976.

Galmes, Lorenzo. *Bartolomé de las Casas: Defensor de los Derechos Humanos.* Madrid: Biblioteca de Autores Cristianos de la Editorial Católica, 1982.

Hanke, Lewis. "The Great Debate Over Indian Policy" in *Historical Viewpoints: Notable Articles from American Heritage,* Vol. I. Edited by John A. Garraty. New York: Harper and Row, 1987.

Llorente, J.A. "Vida de Fray Bartolomé de Las Casas" in *Brevísima Relación de la Destrucción de las Indias.* Ed. by Bartolomé de las Casas. México: Distribuciones Fontamar, 1984.

Menéndez Pidal, Ramón. *El Padre Las Casas, Su Doble Personalidad.* Madrid: Espasa Calpe, 1963.

Simpson, Lesley Byrd. *The Encomienda in New Spain.* Berkeley: University of California Press, 1950.

Tebeau, Charlton W. *A History of Florida.* Coral Gables: University of Miami Press, 1971.

Zorita, Alonso de. *Life and Labor in Ancient Mexico.* New Brunswick, N.J.: Rutgers University Press, 1963.

CHAPTER 5

D'Anghiera, Pietro Martire. *Decades 1455-1526,* Vols. 7 and 8. Published in Latin by Richard Hakluyt's Collection of the Early Voyages. New edition, London, 1812, Vol. V. Modern English trans. by Francis Augustus MacNutt, *De Orbe Novo,* 1912.

Judge, Joseph, ed. "Exploring Our Forgotten Century." *National Geographic,* Vol. 173. No. 3, March 1988.

Johnson, Allen *et al.,* eds. *Dictionary of American Biography.* New York: Charles Scribner and Sons, 1964.

Lowery, Woodbury. *The Spanish Settlements — Within the Present Limits of the United States, 1513-1561.* New York: Russell and Russell, Inc. 1959.

Quattlebaum, Paul. *The Land Called Chicora: The Carolinas Under Spanish Rule with French Intrusions 1520-1670.* Gainesville, Fl.: University of Florida, 1956.

Sauer, Carl Ortwin. *Sixteenth Century North America.* Los Angeles: University of California Press, 1975.

CHAPTER 6

Adams, Eleanor B. and Fray Angélico Chávez, eds. *The Missions of New Mexico, 1776: A Description by Francisco Atanasio Domínguez, with Other Contemporary Documents.* Albuquerque: The University of New Mexico Press, 1956.

Bailey, Jessie Bromilow. *Diego de Vargas and the Reconquest of New Mexico.* Albuquerque: The University of New Mexico Press, 1940.

Bannon, John Francis. *The Spanish Borderlands Frontier, 1513-1821.* New York: Holt, Rinehart, and Winston, Inc., 1970.

Beck, Warren. *New Mexico: A History of Four Centuries.* Norman: Oklahoma University Press, 1962.

Cumming, W.P., and others. *The Exploration of North America, 1630-1776.* New York: G.P. Putnam's Sons, 1974.

Hackett, Charles Wilson and Charnion Clair Shelby, eds. *Revolt of the Pueblo Indians of New Mexico and Otermín's Attempted Reconquest, 1680-1682.* Coronado Historical Series, Vols. 8 and 9. Albuquerque: The University of New Mexico Press, 1953.

Hill, W.W. *An Ethnography of Santa Clara Pueblo New Mexico.* Albuquerque: The University of New Mexico Press, 1953.

Horgan, Paul. *Conquistadores in North American History.* New York: Farrar, Strauss, and Co., 1963.

Simmons, Marc. *Spanish Government in New Mexico.* Albuquerque: The University of New Mexico Press, 1968.

Workers of the Writers' Program of the Work Projects Administration in the State of New Mexico. *New Mexico: A Guide to the Colorful State.* American Guide Series. New York: Hastings House, 1940.

CHAPTER 7

Arnade, Charles. "The Failure of Spanish Florida." *The Americas* 16, No. 3 (January 1960), 271-281.

"Barcía" (Carballido y Zúñiga, Andrés González de). *Ensayo cronológico para la historia general de la Florida.* (First ed. 1723) Trans. by Anthony Kerrigan. Gainesville: University of Florida Press, 1951.

Barrientos, Bartolomé. *Pedro Menéndez de Avilés: su vida y hechos* (1567). In *Dos Antiguas Relaciones,* ed. by Genaro García. Mexico City: Tip. y Lit. de J. Aguilar y Vera y Compañía, 1902. Facsimile ed., Gainesville: University of Florida Press, 1965.

Bennett, Charles. *Laudonnière and Fort Caroline.* Gainesville: University of Florida Press, 1964.

Bushnell, Amy. "The Menéndez Marquéz Cattle Barony at La Chua and the Determinants of Economic Expansion in Seventeenth-Century Florida." *Florida Historical Quarterly* 56, No. 4 (April 1978), 407-431.

____. *The King's Coffer.* Gainesville: University Presses of Florida, 1982.

____. "The Noble and Loyal City, 1565-1668." In *The Oldest City,* 27-55. Ed. by Jean Parker Waterbury. St. Augustine: St. Augustine Historical Society, 1983.

____. "Rulers of the Republic of Indians In Seventeenth-Century Florida." Unpublished paper. St. Augustine, 1985.

____. "Background and Beginnings of the Deerskin Trade: Spanish Documentary Evidence." Unpublished paper. Johns Hopkins Univ., 1986.

Camín, Alfonso. *El Adelantado de la Florida.* Mexico City: Revista Norte, 1944.

Deagan, Kathleen. *Spanish St. Augustine.* New York: Academic Press, 1983.

DePratter, Chester B., Charles M. Hudson and Marvin T. Smith. "The Route of Juan Pardo's Explorations in the Interior Southeast, 1566-1568." *Florida Historical Quarterly* 62, No. 2 (October 1983): 125-158.

Fernández Duro, Cesaréo. *Armada Española.* Vol. 9. Madrid: Sucesores de Rivadeneyra, 1895-1903.

Gaffarel, Paul. *Histoire de la Floride Française.* Paris: Firmin-Didot et Cie., 1875.

Gannon, Michael V. *The Cross in the Sand.* Gainesville: University of Florida Press, 1965.

Hill, Roscoe. "The Office of Adelantado." *Political Science Quarterly* 28, No. 4 (December 1913): 646-668.

Hoffman, Paul E. "The Narrow Waters Strategy of Pedro Menéndez." *Florida Historical Quarterly* 45 (1966), 12-17.

____. "The Background and Development of Pedro Menéndez's Contributions to the Defense of the Spanish Indies." Master's thesis. Gainesville: University of Florida, 1965.

____. "Diplomacy and the Papal Donation." *The Americas* 30, No. 2 (October 1973) 151-183.

____. *The Spanish Crown and the Defense of the Caribbean, 1535-1585.* Baton Rouge: Louisiana State University Press, 1980.

____. "The Chicora Legend and Franco-Spanish Rivalry in *La Florida.*" *Florida Historical Quarterly* 62 (1984), 419-438.

____. "Menéndez de Avilés and His Contribution to the Defense of the Caribbean." Unpublished paper. Southern Historical Association, Houston, November 16, 1985.

Julien, Charles André. *Les voyages de découverte et les premiers établissements (xv-xvi siècles).* Paris: Presses universitaires de France, 1948.

Lussagnet, Suzanne. *Les Français en Amérique pendant la deuxième moitié du XVI siècle.* Vol. 2. Les Français en Floride. Paris: Presses universitaires de France, 1958.

Lyon, Eugene. "A Lost Son." Unpublished paper. P.K. Yonge Library of Florida History, University of Florida, 1968.

____. "The Enterprise of Florida," *Florida Historical Quarterly* 52, No. 4 (April 1974), 411-422.

____. *The Enterprise of Florida: Pedro Menéndez de Avilés and the Spanish Conquest of 1565-1568.* Gainesville: University Presses of Florida, 1976.

____. "The Control Structure of Spanish Florida, 1580." Unpublished paper. St. Augustine: St. Augustine Restoration Foundation, 1977.

____. "St. Augustine 1580: The Living Community." *El Escribano* (January 1978), 20-33.

____. "Spain's 16th-century Settlement Attempts: A Neglected Aspect." *Florida Historical Quarterly* 59, No. 3 (January 1981), 275-291.

____. "Forts Caroline and San Mateo — Vulnerable Outposts." Typescript. Fort Caroline National Memorial, National Parks Service, 1982.

____. *Santa Elena: A Brief History of the Colony.* Institute of Archaeology and Anthropology, University of South Carolina, 1984.

____. "The Spanish Mutineers." *Tequesta* 44 (1984), 44-61.

____. "Continuity in the Age of Conquest: The Establishment of Spanish Sovereignty in the Sixteenth Century." In *Alabama and the Borderlands.* Ed. by R. Reid Badger and Lawrence A. Clayton. University, Ala.: The University of Alabama Press, 1985.

____. "The Quirós Papers." Unpublished translation, from AGI *Santo Domingo* 231. St. Augustine Foundation, 1985.

____. "Aspects of Pedro Menéndez the Man." Annual address, St. Augustine Historical Society, January 1986. In press, *El Escribano.*

___. "Cultural Brokers in Sixteenth-Century Spanish Florida." Unpublished paper. Workshop in Atlantic History, Culture and Society. John Hopkins University, March 1987.

Manucy, Albert C. "The Man Who Was Pedro Menéndez de Avilés." *Florida Historical Quarterly* 44 (August 1965), 67-80.

___. *Florida's Menéndez.* St. Augustine: St. Augustine Historical Society, 1965.

McAlister, Lyle N. *Spain and Portugal in the New World 1492-1700.* Minneapolis: University of Minnesota Press, 1984.

Miguel Vigil, Ciriaco. *Noticias biográfico-genealógicas de Pedro Menéndez de Avilés.* Avilés: Imprenta La Unión, 1892.

Milanich, Jerald, and Charles Fairbanks. *Florida Archaeology.* New York: Academic Press, 1980.

Milanich, Jerald, and Samuel Proctor. *Tacachale.* Gainesville: University Presses of Florida, 1978.

Patac de las Traviesas, José María. *Guía del Archivo del Excmo. Señor Conde de Revillagigedo,* 4 Vol. See I, "Introducción."

Ribault, Jean. *The Whole and True Discoverye of Terra Florida.* London: R. Hall, 1563. Facsimile ed., Gainesville: University of Florida Press, 1964.

Ruidíaz y Caravía, Eugenio. *La Florida: sus conquista y colonización por Pedro Menéndez de Avilés.* 2 vol. Madrid: Imprenta de los hijos de J.A. García, 1893-94.

Solís de Merás, Gonzalo. *Pedro Menéndez de Avilés.* Trans. by Jeannette Thurber Connor. DeLand: Florida State Historical Society, 1922. Facsimile ed., Gainesville: University of Florida Press, 1964.

Zubillaga, Félix. *La Florida: La Misión Jesuítica (1566-1572) y la colonización española.* Rome: Institutum Historicum S.I., 1941.

Monumenta Antiquae Floridae. Rome: Monumenta Historica Societatis Iesu, 1946.

CHAPTER 8

Bowman, John S. *The Civil War Almanac.* New York: World Almanac Pubs., 1983.

Dewherst, William W. *The History of St. Augustine, Florida.* Rutland, Vt.: Academy Books, 1968.

Fairbanks, George R. *The History and Antiquities of the City of St. Augustine.* Gainesville: University Presses of Florida, 1975.

"Florida." *Encyclopedia Britannica.* 1968 ed.

"Florida." *Encyclopedia Britannica.* 1984 ed.

"Saint Augustine." *Encyclopedia Britannica.* 1968 ed.

"Saint Augustine." *Encyclopedia Britannica Micropaedia.* 1984 ed.

Sparke, John. "The Attractions of Florida." In *The Annals of America.* Chicago: Encyclopedia Britannica, 1976.

CHAPTER 9

TePaske, John J. *The Governorship of Spanish Florida, 1700-1763.* Chapel Hill, N.C.: Duke University Press, 1964.

Rout, Leslie B. *The African Experience in Spanish America.* Cambridge: Cambridge University Press, 1976.

Porter, Kenneth Wiggins. *The Negro on the American Frontier.* New York: Arno Press, 1971.

CHAPTER 10

Curley, Michael J. *Church and State in the Spanish Floridas (1783-1822).* Washington, D.C.: 1940.

Isern, José. *Pioneros Cubanos en U.S.A.* Miami: Cenit Printing, 1971.

Lockey, Joseph B. "Public Education in Spanish St. Augustine." *Florida Historical Society Quarterly* 15 (1937): 147-168.
Waterbury, Jean Parker, ed. *The Oldest City: St. Augustine Saga of Survival.* St. Augustine: 1983.

CHAPTER II

Aizenberg, Edna. "Sephardim and Neo-Sephardim in Latin American Literature." *The Sephardic Scholar* (1979-1982): 9-16.
Beton, Sol. "Was Christopher Columbus Really a Secret Spanish Jew?" In *Sephardim and a History of a Congregation Or VeShalom.* Atlanta, Ga.: Congregation Or VeShalom, 1981.
Birmingham, Stephen. The Grandees: *America's Sephardic Elite.* New York: Harper & Row, 1971.
Dobrinsky, Herbert C. *A Treasury of Sephardic Laws and Customs.* New Jersey: Ktav Publ. House, Inc. and New York: Yeshiva University Press, 1986.
Encyclopedia Judaica. Vol. 14. Jerusalem: Keter Publ. House Jerusalem Ltd., 1972.
Gaon, Solomon. "The Call for the Sephardim to Return to Spain." *The Sephardic Scholar* (1979-1982): 125-132.
Gross, David C. *The Jewish People's Almanac.* New York: Doubleday, 1981.
The New Encyclopedia Britannica. Vol. 3. 15th Ed. Chicago: Encyclopedia Britannica, Inc., 1987.

CHAPTER 12

Archivo Histórico Nacional. Legajo 4072. Sept. 7, 1776.
Archivo Histórico Nacional. Legajo 3898. Oct. 28, 1794.
Boeta, José Rodolfo. *Bernardo de Gálvez.* Madrid: Publicaciones Españoles, 1976.
Bonsal, Stephen. *When the French Were Here.* Garden City: Doubleday, 1945.
Caughey, John Walton. *Bernardo de Gálvez in Louisiana 1776-1787.* Berkeley: University of California Press, 1934.
Davis, O.L. Jr., Gerald Ponder, Lynn M. Burlbaw, María Garza-Lubeck, and Alfred Moss. *Looking at History: A Review of Major U.S. History Textbooks.* Washington, D.C.: People for the American Way, 1986.
Fernández y Fernández, Enrique. *Spain's Contribution to the Independence of the United States.* Washington, D.C.: Embassy of Spain in the United States of America, 1985.
Fernández-Flores, Darío. *La Herencia Española en Los Estados Unidos.* Barcelona: Gráficas Guarda, S.A., 1981.
Gálvez, Bernardo de. *Diario de las Operaciones de la Expedición Contra la Plaza de Panzacola Concluída por las Armas de S.M. Católica, baxo las órdenes del mariscal de Campo D. Bernardo de Gálvez.* Tallahassee: The Ashantilly Press, 1966.
Lasaga, José Ignacio. *Cuban Lives: Pages from Cuban History,* Vol. 1. Miami: Revista Ideal, 1984.
Martínez Figueras, Carlos. *Don Juan de Miralles: Spanish Royal Commissioner in the Thirteen Colonies.* (Unpublished article). 1987.
Parks, Virginia. *Siege! Spain and Britain: Battle of Pensacola March 9 - May 8, 1781.* Pensacola: Pensacola Historical Society, 1981.
Portell Vilá, Herminio. *Los Otros Extranjeros en la Revolución Norteamericana.* Miami: Ediciones Universal, 1978.
Reparaz, Carmen de. *Yo Solo: Bernardo de Gálvez y la Toma de Panzacola en 1781.* Miami: Ediciones del Serbal, 1986.
Rush, Orwin. Battle of Pensacola: *Spain's Final Triumph Over Great Britain in the Gulf of Mexico.* Tallahassee: Florida Classics Library, 1986.

Sariego del Castillo, José L. *Historia de la Marina Española en la América Septentrional y Pacífico.* Sevilla: Gráficas del Sur, 1975.

Thomson, Buchanan Parker. *Spain: Forgotten Ally of the American Revolution.* North Quincy, Mass.: The Christopher Publ. House, 1976.

Yela Utrilla, Juan F. *España ante la Independencia de Los Estados Unidos,* 2nd ed. Lerida: Gráficos Academia Mariana, 1925.

CHAPTER 13

Fernández, Enrique. "Spain's Contribution to the Independence of the United States." *Revista/Review Interamericana.* Vol. X, No. 3. (Fall 1980).

Isern, José. *Pioneros Cubanos en U.S.A. 1575-1898.* Miami: Cenit Printing, 1971.

Portell Vilá, Herminio. "Juan Miralles, un Habanero Amigo de Jorge Washington." La Habana: Sociedad Colombista Panamericana, Día de Washington, 1732-1947, 1947.

Reparaz, Carmen de. *Yo Solo.* Barcelona: Ediciones del Serbal, S.A., 1986.

Sparks, Jared. *The Writings of George Washington.* Boston: Ferdinand Andrews, 1838.

Van Doren, Carl. *Secret History of the American Revolution.* Garden City, N.Y.: Garden City Publ. Co., 1941.

CHAPTER 14

Anderson, R.C. *Naval Wars in the Levant.* Princeton: Princeton University Press, 1952.

Chopin, Frederick. *Chopin's Letters.* Collected by Henry Opiensky. New York: Vienna House, 1973.

Coletta, Paolo F. *American Secretaries of the Navy,* 2 Vols. Annapolis: Naval Institute Press, 1980.

Fernández-Flores, Darío. *La Herencia Española en los EE UU.* Barcelona: Plaza y Janez, S.A., 1981.

González López, Emilio. "Spanish Officers in the American Navy: George Ferragut." *New York Times Supplement,* May 30, 1976, pp. 16-17, 19.

Lewis, Charles. *David Glasgow Farragut: Admiral in the Making.* Annapolis: U.S. Naval Institute, 1941.

Long, David F. *Nothing Too Daring.* Annapolis: U.S. Naval Institute, 1970.

McCowen, Jr. George Smith. *The British Occupation of Charleston, 1870-1872.* Columbia, S.C.: University of South Carolina Press, 1972.

Mahan, Alfred Thayer. *Admiral Farragut.* New York: Appleton and Co., 1892. Reprinted. St. Clair Shores, Mich.: Scholarly Press, 1974.

Oltra, Joaquín. "Dos Menorquines de Origen, Crean la Marina Norte América." *Revista Historia y Vida.* April, 1972, pp. 25-29.

Paullin, Charles Oscar. *Paullin's History of Naval Administration.* Annapolis: U.S. Naval Institute, 1968.

Tunstall, Brian. *Admiral Byng and the Loss of Minorca.* London: Philip Allan and Co., 1928.

Ward, Christopher. *The War of the Revolution,* 2 Vols. New York: Macillan, 1952.

CHAPTER 15

Abislaiman, Rafael. "El Científico Félix Varela y Morales." *Ceola Newsletter* (Miami), December, 1987.

Foik, Paul J. *Pioneer Catholic Journalism.* U.S. Cath. Hist. Soc. Monograph Series, II (1930).

Griffin, Martin I.J. *The Children's Catholic Magazine of New York,* 1838-1839. American Cath. Hist. Soc. of Phila., Reviews, 15 (1904), 164-168.

Herbermann, Charles G. "The Right Reverend John Dubois, D.D., Third Bishop of New York." U.S. Cath. Soc., Hist. Resource and Stud., 1, Pt. II (Jan. 1900), 278-335.

Hernández Travieso, Antonio. *El Padre Varela: Biografía del Fundador de la Conciencia Cubana.* Havana: Montero, 1949.

Ilustración Americana de Franc Leslie (Spanish-Language Weekly). No. 56, Nov. 12, 1967, p. 59.

Lasaga, José I. "Vidas Cubanas/Cuban Lives." *Cuban History,* Vol. 1. Miami: Revista Ideal, 1984.

McCadden, Joseph and Helen M. *Félix Varela: Torch Bearer from Cuba.* San Juan, P.R.: Ramallo, 1984.

Presno, José A. "Homenaje a la Memoria del Doctor Tomás Romay." Universidad de la Habana, 15 (Nov.-Dec. 1937), 18-31.

Revista Ideal. (A publication of the Christian Commitment Foundation, Miami) August 1981, 56-64.

Rodríguez, José I. *Vida del Presbítero, Don Félix Varela.* New York: 1878.

Shea, John D. G. *The Catholic Churches of New York City with Sketches of Their History and Lives of the Present Pastors.* New York: Gouldin, 1878.

Smith, John Talbot. *The Catholic Church in New York, 2 vols.* New York: Hank Locke, 1905.

de la Torre, Monseñor Teodoro, *Félix Varela, Vida Ejemplar.* Miami: Padre Félix Varela Foundation.

Varela y Morales, Félix. *El Habanero, Papel Político, Científico y Literario.* Miami: Revista Ideal, 1974.

CHAPTER 16

Documents of the Naval Museum at Annapolis.

González, Isabel María Pérez. *Carolina Coronado. Biografías Extremeñas.* Madrid: Diputación de Badajoz, 1986.

Lewis, Charles Lee. *David Glasgow Farragut: Admiral in the Making.* Annapolis: U.S. Naval Institute, 1941.

Montgomery, James E. *Our Admiral's Flag Abroad: The Cruise of Admiral D. G. Farragut.* New York: 1869.

Pineda, Manuel Cencillo de. *David Glasgow Farragut.* Madrid: Editorial Naval, 1950.

Piedrabuena, Guillermo Florit. "El Primer Almirante de los Estados Unidos, David Farragut." *Panorama Balear,* n. 26. (1965).

"El Siglo Illustrado." *Diario.* December 10, 1867.

"Sunday News." *Diario.* Feb. 28, 1965.

U.S. Naval Institute. *David Glasgow Farragut: Our First Admiral.* Annapolis: U.S. Naval Institute, 1943.

Welles, Gideon. *Diary,* 3 Vols. Boston: 1911.

CHAPTER 17

Angle, Paul M. and Earl Schenck Mears. *Tragic Years, 1860 - 1865.* New York: Simon and Schuster, 1960.

Davis, O. Wilson. *Sketch of Frederick Fernández Cavada, a Native of Cuba.* Philadelphia: King and Baird, 1871.

Fernández Cavada, Federico. *Libby Life.* Philadelphia: King and Baird, 1864.

Gaceta de la Habana. *Periódico Oficial del Gobierno.* Number 157. July 4, 1871, p. 2.

Isern, José. *Pioneros Cubanos en U.S.A. — 1575 - 1898.* Miami: Cenit Printing, 1971.

CHAPTER 18

Batman, Richard. *The Outer Coast.* San Diego: Harcourt Brace Jovanovich, 1985.

Chapman, Charles E. *A History of California: The Spanish Period.* New York: MacMillan Co.: 1939.

Garrison, Myrtle. *Romance and History of California Ranchos.* San Francisco: Harr Wagner Pub. Co., 1935.

Hanna, Phil Townsend. *California Through Four Centuries.* New York: Farrar and Rinehart, Inc., 1935.

Hubbard, Harry D. *Vallejo.* Boston: Meador Pub. Co., 1941.

Hunt, Rockwell. *California in the Making: Essays and Papers in California History.* Westport, CT: Greenwood Press, 1935.

Lavender, David. *California: Land of New Beginnings.* New York: Harper and Row, 1972.

CHAPTER 19

Gray, Richard B. *José Martí: Cuban Patriot.* Gainesville: University of Florida Press, 1962.

Lizaso, Félix. *Martí: Martyr of Cuban Independence.* Albuquerque: The University of New Mexico Press, 1953.

Manach, Jorge. *Martí: Apostle of Freedom.* New York: David Adair, 1950.

Ripoll, Carlos. *José Martí: Thoughts/Pensamientos.* New York: Eliseo Torres and Sons — Las Américas Publ. Co., 1980.

Suchlicki, Jaime. *Cuba: From Columbus to Castro.* New York: Charles Scribner's Sons, 1974.

Thomas, Hugh. *Cuba: The Pursuit of Freedom.* New York: Harper and Row, 1971.

CHAPTER 20

Almendros, Herminio. *Pasteur y Finlay.* Cuba: Editora Juvenil, n.d.

Cepero, Gilberto E. "Apuntes Sobre la Evolución de la Medicina Tropical en Cuba Colonial." *The Journal of the Florida Medical Association, Inc.*, Vol. 64, No. 8, Aug. 1977.

Fabricant, Noah D. "Finlay, Carlos Juan." *World Book Encyclopedia,* 1974 ed.

Finlay, Carlos E. *Carlos Finlay and Yellow Fever.* New York: Oxford University Press, 1940.

Rivas Agüero, Miguel A. "Historia de un Grande de la Patria, Carlos Finlay." Miami: El Camagüeyano, Inc., 1983.

Rodríguez Expósito, César. *Finlay por Cuarta Vez ante el Congreso Internacional de Historia de la Medicina.* Havana: Ministerio de Salud Pública, 1971.

CHAPTER 21

Casasus, Juan J.E. *Calixto García* (El Estratega). La Habana: 1962.

Foner, Philip S. *The Spanish-Cuban-American War and the Birth of American Imperialism 1895 - 1902.* New York: Monthly Review Press, 1972.

Kendrick, John F. "The Cuban Army of Liberation." Speech of 1951. *William McKinley Camp Bulletin,* Vol. XXVIII, March-April 1955.

Post, Charles Johnson. *The Little War of Private Post.* Boston: 1960.

Portell Vilá, Herminio. *Historia de la Guerra de Cuba y los Estados Unidos Contra España.* La Habana: 1949.